PRAISE FOR

Savage Inequalities

"Easily the most passionate, and certain to be the most passionately debated, book about American education in several years . . . A classic American muckraker with an eloquent prose style, Kozol offers . . . an old-fashioned brand of moral outrage that will affect every reader whose heart has not yet turned to stone."

—*Entertainment Weekly*

"Moving . . . Shocking . . . Heartbreaking."

—Ruth Sidel, *The Nation*

"It is neither ironic nor paradoxical to call *Savage Inequalities* a wonderful book—for Kozol makes it clear that there are wonderful teachers and wonderful students in every American school, no matter what ugliness, violence, and horror surround the building."

—*Chicago Tribune*

"The great virtue of Jonathan Kozol's new book about inner-city schools is that it overcomes that 'everybody knows' problem by bringing an undulled capacity for shock and outrage to a tour of bad schools across the country. As soon as Kozol begins leading the way through a procession of overcrowded, underheated, textbookless, barely taught classrooms, the thought he surely intended to engender begins to take form: How can this be?"

—*Washington Post Book World*

Savage Inequalities

Savage Inequalities

CHILDREN IN AMERICA'S SCHOOLS

Jonathan Kozol

B\D\W\Y

BROADWAY BOOKS

NEW YORK

Copyright © 1991 by Jonathan Kozol

Published in the United States by Broadway Books,
an imprint of the Crown Publishing Group,
a division of Random House, Inc., New York.
www.crownpublishing.com

BROADWAY BOOKS and its logo, B \ D \ W \ Y, are trademarks of
Random House, Inc.

Originally published in hardcover in the United States
by Crown Publishers, Inc., a division of Random House, Inc.,
New York, in 1991.

Library of Congress Cataloging-in-Publication Data
is available upon request.

ISBN 978-0-7704-3568-4
eISBN 978-0-7704-3666-7

Printed in the United States of America

Cover design by Darren Haggar
Cover photograph: © Bettmann/CORBIS

10 9 8 7

First Broadway Paperbacks Edition

For Cassie

And for D.K. with love

CONTENTS

TO THE READER

A Clarification About Dates
and Data in This Book

The events in this book take place for the most part between 1988 and 1990, although a few events somewhat precede this period. Most events, however, are narrated in the present tense. This is important to keep in mind because statistics, such as money spent in a particular school district, or a description of the staff or student body in a given school, apply to the year of which I'm speaking, which is indicated in the text or notes.

The names of students in this book have sometimes been disguised at their request or that of school officials. The names of all adults are real, although in a few cases adults are not named at all at their request. Documentation for statistics and matters of record in this book is provided in the notes beginning on page 289.

Looking Backward:
1964–1991

It was a long time since I'd been with children in the public schools.

I had begun to teach in 1964 in Boston in a segregated school so crowded and so poor that it could not provide my fourth grade children with a classroom. We shared an auditorium with another fourth grade and the choir and a group that was rehearsing, starting in October, for a Christmas play that, somehow, never was produced. In the spring I was shifted to another fourth grade that had had a string of substitutes all year. The 35 children in the class hadn't had a permanent teacher since they entered kindergarten. That year, I was their thirteenth teacher.

The results were seen in the first tests I gave. In April, most were reading at the second grade level. Their math ability was at the first grade level.

In an effort to resuscitate their interest, I began to

read them poetry I liked. They were drawn especially to poems of Robert Frost and Langston Hughes. One of the most embittered children in the class began to cry when she first heard the words of Langston Hughes.

What happens to a dream deferred?
Does it dry up
like a raisin in the sun?

She went home and memorized the lines.

The next day, I was fired. There was, it turned out, a list of "fourth grade poems" that teachers were obliged to follow but which, like most first-year teachers, I had never seen. According to school officials, Robert Frost and Langston Hughes were "too advanced" for children of this age. Hughes, moreover, was regarded as "inflammatory."

I was soon recruited to teach in a suburban system west of Boston. The shock of going from one of the poorest schools to one of the wealthiest cannot be overstated. I now had 21 children in a cheerful building with a principal who welcomed innovation.

After teaching for several years, I became involved with other interests—the health and education of farmworkers in New Mexico and Arizona, the problems of adult illiterates in several states, the lives of homeless families in New York. It wasn't until 1988, when I returned to Massachusetts after a long stay in New York City, that I realized how far I'd been drawn away from my original concerns. I found that I missed being with schoolchildren, and I felt a longing to spend time in public schools again. So, in the fall of 1988, I set off on another journey.

During the next two years I visited schools and

spoke with children in approximately 30 neighborhoods from Illinois to Washington, D.C., and from New York to San Antonio. Wherever possible, I also met with children in their homes. There was no special logic in the choice of cities that I visited. I went where I was welcomed or knew teachers or school principals or ministers of churches.

What startled me most—although it puzzles me that I was not prepared for this—was the remarkable degree of racial segregation that persisted almost everywhere. Like most Americans, I knew that segregation was still common in the public schools, but I did not know how much it had intensified. The Supreme Court decision in *Brown* v. *Board of Education* 37 years ago, in which the court had found that segregated education was unconstitutional because it was "inherently unequal," did not seem to have changed very much for children in the schools I saw, not, at least, outside of the Deep South. Most of the urban schools I visited were 95 to 99 percent nonwhite. In no school that I saw anywhere in the United States were nonwhite children in large numbers truly intermingled with white children.

Moreover, in most cities, influential people that I met showed little inclination to address this matter and were sometimes even puzzled when I brought it up. Many people seemed to view the segregation issue as "a past injustice" that had been sufficiently addressed. Others took it as an unresolved injustice that no longer held sufficient national attention to be worth contesting. In all cases, I was given the distinct impression that my inquiries about this matter were not welcome.

None of the national reports I saw made even passing references to inequality or segregation. Low reading scores, high dropout rates, poor motivation—symptomatic

matters—seemed to dominate discussion. In three cities—
Baltimore, Milwaukee and Detroit—separate schools or
separate classes for black males had been proposed.
Other cities—Washington, D.C., New York and Philadelphia among them—were considering the same approach.
Black parents or black school officials sometimes seemed
to favor this idea. Booker T. Washington was cited with
increasing frequency, Du Bois never, and Martin Luther
King only with cautious selectivity. He was treated as
an icon, but his vision of a nation in which black and
white kids went to school together seemed to be effaced
almost entirely. Dutiful references to "The Dream" were
often seen in school brochures and on wall posters during
February, when "Black History" was celebrated in the
public schools, but the content of the dream was treated
as a closed box that could not be opened without ruining
the celebration.

For anyone who came of age during the years
from 1954 to 1968, these revelations could not fail to
be disheartening. What seems unmistakable, but, oddly
enough, is rarely said in public settings nowadays, is
that the nation, for all practice and intent, has turned
its back upon the moral implications, if not yet the legal
ramifications, of the *Brown* decision. The struggle being
waged today, where there is any struggle being waged
at all, is closer to the one that was addressed in 1896 in
Plessy v. *Ferguson,* in which the court accepted segregated
institutions for black people, stipulating only that they
must be equal to those open to white people. The dual
society, at least in public education, seems in general to
be unquestioned.

To the extent that school reforms such as "restructuring" are advocated for the inner cities, few of these
reforms have reached the schools that I have seen. In
each of the larger cities there is usually one school or

one subdistrict which is highly publicized as an example of "restructured" education; but the changes rarely reach beyond this one example. Even in those schools where some "restructuring" has taken place, the fact of racial segregation has been, and continues to be, largely uncontested. In many cities, what is termed "restructuring" struck me as very little more than moving around the same old furniture within the house of poverty. The perceived objective was a more "efficient" ghetto school or one with greater "input" from the ghetto parents or more "choices" for the ghetto children. The fact of ghetto education as a permanent American reality appeared to be accepted.

Liberal critics of the Reagan era sometimes note that social policy in the United States, to the extent that it concerns black children and poor children, has been turned back several decades. But this assertion, which is accurate as a description of some setbacks in the areas of housing, health and welfare, is not adequate to speak about the present-day reality in public education. In public schooling, social policy has been turned back almost one hundred years.

These, then, are a few of the impressions that remained with me after revisiting the public schools from which I had been absent for a quarter-century. My deepest impression, however, was less theoretical and more immediate. It was simply the impression that these urban schools were, by and large, extraordinarily unhappy places. With few exceptions, they reminded me of "garrisons" or "outposts" in a foreign nation. Housing projects, bleak and tall, surrounded by perimeter walls lined with barbed wire, often stood adjacent to the schools I visited. The schools were surrounded frequently by signs that indicated DRUG-FREE ZONE. Their doors were guarded. Police sometimes patrolled the halls. The windows of the schools were often covered with steel grates. Taxi drivers flatly refused to take me to some of these schools and would deposit me a dozen blocks away, in border areas beyond which they refused to go. I'd walk the last half-mile on my own. Once, in the Bronx, a woman stopped her car, told me I should not be walking there, insisted I get in, and drove me to the school. I was dismayed to walk or ride for blocks and blocks through neighborhoods where every face was black, where there were simply *no white people anywhere.*

In Boston, the press referred to areas like these as "death zones"—a specific reference to the rate of infant death in ghetto neighborhoods—but the feeling of the "death zone" often seemed to permeate the schools themselves. Looking around some of these inner-city schools, where filth and disrepair were worse than anything I'd seen in 1964, I often wondered why we would agree to let our children go to school in places where no politician, school board president, or business CEO would dream of working. Children seemed to wrestle with these kinds of questions too. Some of their observations were, indeed, so trenchant that a teacher sometimes would step back and raise her eyebrows and then nod to me across the children's heads, as if to say, "Well, there it is! They know what's going on around them, don't they?"

It occurred to me that we had not been listening much to children in these recent years of "summit conferences" on education, of severe reports and ominous prescriptions. The voices of children, frankly, had been missing from the whole discussion.

This seems especially unfortunate because the children often are more interesting and perceptive than the grownups are about the day-to-day realities of life in school. For this reason, I decided, early in my journey, to attempt to listen very carefully to children and, whenever possible, to let their voices and their judgments and their longings find a place within this book—and maybe, too, within the nation's dialogue about their destinies. I hope that, in this effort, I have done them justice.

CHAPTER 1

Life on the Mississippi:
East St. Louis, Illinois

"East of anywhere," writes a reporter for the *St. Louis Post-Dispatch,* "often evokes the other side of the tracks. But, for a first-time visitor suddenly deposited on its eerily empty streets, East St. Louis might suggest another world." The city, which is 98 percent black, has no obstetric services, no regular trash collection, and few jobs. Nearly a third of its families live on less than $7,500 a year; 75 percent of its population lives on welfare of some form. The U.S. Department of Housing and Urban Development describes it as "the most distressed small city in America."

Only three of the 13 buildings on Missouri Avenue, one of the city's major thoroughfares, are occupied. A 13-story office building, tallest in the city, has been boarded up. Outside, on the sidewalk, a pile of garbage fills a ten-foot crater.

The city, which by night and day is clouded by the

fumes that pour from vents and smokestacks at the Pfizer and Monsanto chemical plants, has one of the highest rates of child asthma in America.

It is, according to a teacher at the University of Southern Illinois, "a repository for a nonwhite population that is now regarded as expendable." The *Post-Dispatch* describes it as "America's Soweto."

Fiscal shortages have forced the layoff of 1,170 of the city's 1,400 employees in the past 12 years. The city, which is often unable to buy heating fuel or toilet paper for the city hall, recently announced that it might have to cashier all but 10 percent of the remaining work force of 230. In 1989 the mayor announced that he might need to sell the city hall and all six fire stations to raise needed cash. Last year the plan had to be scrapped after the city lost its city hall in a court judgment to a creditor. East St. Louis is mortgaged into the next century but has the highest property-tax rate in the state.

Since October 1987, when the city's garbage pickups ceased, the backyards of residents have been employed as dump sites. In the spring of 1988 a policeman tells a visitor that 40 plastic bags of trash are waiting for removal from the backyard of his mother's house. Public health officials are concerned the garbage will attract a plague of flies and rodents in the summer. The policeman speaks of "rats as big as puppies" in his mother's yard. They are known to the residents, he says, as "bull rats." Many people have no cars or funds to cart the trash and simply burn it in their yards. The odor of smoke from burning garbage, says the *Post-Dispatch,* "has become one of the scents of spring" in East St. Louis.

Railroad tracks still used to transport hazardous chemicals run through the city. "Always present," says the *Post-Dispatch,* "is the threat of chemical spills. . . . The wail of sirens warning residents to evacuate after a spill is common." The most recent spill, the paper says, "was at the Monsanto Company plant. . . . Nearly 300 gallons of phosphorous trichloride spilled when a railroad tank was overfilled. About 450 residents were taken to St. Mary's Hospital. . . . The frequency of the emergencies has caused Monsanto to have a 'standing account' at St. Mary's."

In March of 1989, a task force appointed by Governor James Thompson noted that the city was in debt by more than $40 million, and proposed emergency state loans to pay for garbage collection and to keep police and fire departments in continued operation. The governor, however, blamed the mayor and his administrators, almost all of whom were black, and refused to grant the loans unless the mayor resigned. Thompson's response, said a Republican state legislator, "made my heart feel good. . . . It's unfortunate, but the essence of the problem in East St. Louis is the people" who are running things.

Residents of Illinois do not need to breathe the garbage smoke and chemicals of East St. Louis. With the interstate highways, says a supervisor of the Illinois Power Company, "you can ride around the place and just keep going. . . ."

East St. Louis lies in the heart of the American Bottoms—the floodplain on the east side of the Mississippi River opposite St. Louis. To the east of the city lie the Illinois Bluffs, which surround the floodplain in a semicircle. Towns on the Bluffs are predominantly white and do not welcome visitors from East St. Louis.

"The two tiers—Bluffs and Bottoms—" writes James Nowlan, a professor of public policy at Knox College, "have long represented . . . different worlds." Their physical separation, he believes, "helps rationalize the psychological and cultural distance that those on the Bluffs have clearly tried to maintain." People on the Bluffs, says Nowlan, "overwhelmingly want this separation to continue."

Towns on the Bluffs, according to Nowlan, do not pay taxes to address flood problems in the Bottoms, "even though these problems are generated in large part by the water that drains from the Bluffs." East St. Louis lacks the funds to cope with flooding problems on its own, or to reconstruct its sewer system, which, according to local experts, is "irreparable." The problem is all the worse because the chemical plants in East St. Louis and adjacent towns have for decades been releasing toxins into the sewer system.

The pattern of concentrating black communities in easily flooded lowland areas is not unusual in the United States. Farther down the river, for example, in the Delta town of Tunica, Mississippi, people in the black community of Sugar Ditch live in shacks by open sewers that are commonly believed to be responsible for the high incidence of liver tumors and abscesses found in children there. Metaphors of caste like these are everywhere in the United States. Sadly, although dirt and water flow downhill, money and services do not.

The dangers of exposure to raw sewage, which backs up repeatedly into the homes of residents in East St. Louis, were first noticed, in the spring of 1989, at a public housing project, Villa Griffin. Raw sewage, says the *Post-Dispatch,* overflowed into a playground just behind the housing project, which is home to 187 children, "forming an oozing lake of . . . tainted water." Two schoolgirls, we are told, "experienced hair loss since raw sewage flowed into their homes."

While local physicians are not certain whether loss of hair is caused by the raw sewage, they have issued warnings that exposure to raw sewage can provoke a cholera or hepatitis outbreak. A St. Louis health official voices her dismay that children live with waste in their backyards. "The development of working sewage systems made cities livable a hundred years ago," she notes. "Sewage systems separate us from the Third World."

"It's a terrible way to live," says a mother at the Villa Griffin homes, as she bails raw sewage from her sink. Health officials warn again of cholera—and, this time, of typhoid also.

The sewage, which is flowing from collapsed pipes and dysfunctional pumping stations, has also flooded basements all over the city. The city's vacuum truck, which uses water and suction to unclog the city's sewers, cannot be used because it needs $5,000 in repairs. Even when it works, it sometimes can't be used because there isn't money to hire drivers. A single engineer now does the work that 14 others did before they were laid off. By April the pool of overflow behind the Villa Griffin project has expanded into a lagoon of sewage. Two million gallons of raw sewage lie outside the children's homes.

In May, another health emergency develops. Soil samples tested at residential sites in East St. Louis turn up disturbing quantities of arsenic, mercury and lead—as well as steroids dumped in previous years by stockyards in the area. Lead levels found in the soil around one family's home, according to lead-poison experts, measure "an astronomical 10,000 parts per million." Five of the children in the building have been poisoned. Although children rarely die of poisoning by lead, health experts note, its effects tend to be subtle and insidious. By the time the poisoning becomes apparent in a child's sleep disorders, stomach pains and hyperactive behavior, says a health official, "it is too late to undo the permanent brain damage." The poison, she says, "is chipping away at the learning potential of kids whose potential has already been chipped away by their environment."

The budget of the city's department of lead-poison control, however, has been slashed, and one person now does the work once done by six.

Lead poisoning in most cities comes from lead-based paint in housing, which has been illegal in most states for decades but which poisons children still because most cities, Boston and New York among them, rarely penalize offending landlords. In East St. Louis, however, there is a second source of lead. Health inspectors think it is another residue of manufacturing—including smelting—in the factories and mills whose plants surround the city. "Some of the factories are gone," a parent organizer says, "but they have left their poison in the soil where our children play." In one apartment complex where particularly high quantities of lead have been detected in the soil, 32 children with high levels in their blood have been identified.

"I anticipate finding the whole city contaminated," says a health examiner.

The Daughters of Charity, whose works of mercy are well known in the Third World, operate a mission at the Villa Griffin homes. On an afternoon in early spring of 1990, Sister Julia Huiskamp meets me on King Boulevard and drives me to the Griffin homes.

As we ride past blocks and blocks of skeletal structures, some of which are still inhabited, she slows the car repeatedly at railroad crossings. A seemingly endless railroad train rolls past us to the right. On the left: a blackened lot where garbage has been burning. Next to the burning garbage is a row of 12 white cabins, charred by fire. Next: a lot that holds a heap of auto tires and a mountain of tin cans. More burnt houses. More trash fires. The train moves almost imperceptibly across the flatness of the land.

Fifty years old, and wearing a blue suit, white blouse, and blue head-cover, Sister Julia points to the nicest house in sight. The sign on the front reads MOTEL. "It's a whorehouse," Sister Julia says.

When she slows the car beside a group of teen-age boys, one of them steps out toward the car, then backs away as she is recognized.

The 99 units of the Villa Griffin homes—two-story structures, brick on the first floor, yellow wood above—form one border of a recessed park and playground that were filled with fecal matter last year when the sewage mains exploded. The sewage is gone now and the grass is very green and looks inviting. When nine-year-old Serena and her seven-year-old brother take me for a walk, however, I discover that our shoes sink into what is still a sewage marsh. An inch-deep residue of fouled water still remains.

Serena's brother is a handsome, joyous little boy, but troublingly thin. Three other children join us as we walk along the marsh: Smokey, who is nine years old but cannot yet tell time; Mickey, who is seven; and a tiny child with a ponytail and big brown eyes who talks a constant stream of words that I can't always understand.

"Hush, Little Sister," says Serena. I ask for her name, but "Little Sister" is the only name the children seem to know.

"There go my cousins," Smokey says, pointing to two teen-age girls above us on the hill.

The day is warm, although we're only in the second week of March; several dogs and cats are playing by the edges of the marsh. "It's a lot of squirrels here," says Smokey. "There go one!"

"This here squirrel is a friend of mine," says Little Sister.

None of the children can tell me the approximate time that school begins. One says five o'clock. One says six. Another says that school begins at noon.

When I ask what song they sing after the flag pledge, one says "Jingle Bells."

Smokey cannot decide if he is in the second or third grade.

Seven-year-old Mickey sucks his thumb during the walk.

The children regale me with a chilling story as we stand beside the marsh. Smokey says his sister was raped and murdered and then dumped behind his school. Other children add more details: Smokey's sister was 11 years old. She was beaten with a brick until she died. The murder was committed by a man who knew her mother.

The narrative begins when, without warning, Smokey says, "My sister has got killed."

"She was my best friend," Serena says.

"They had beat her in the head and raped her," Smokey says.

"She was hollering out loud," says Little Sister.

I ask them when it happened. Smokey says, "Last year." Serena then corrects him and she says, "Last week."

"It scared me because I had to cry," says Little Sister.

"The police arrested one man but they didn't catch the other," Smokey says.

Serena says, "He was some kin to her."

But Smokey objects, "He weren't no kin to me. He was my momma's friend."

"Her face was busted," Little Sister says.

Serena describes this sequence of events: "They

told her go behind the school. They'll give her a quarter if she do. Then they knock her down and told her not to tell what they had did."

I ask, "Why did they kill her?"

"They was scared that she would tell," Serena says.

"One is in jail," says Smokey. "They cain't find the Other."

"Instead of raping little bitty children, they should find themselves a wife," says Little Sister.

"I hope," Serena says, "her spirit will come back and get that man."

"And *kill* that man," says Little Sister.

"Give her another chance to live," Serena says.

"My teacher came to the funeral," says Smokey.

"When a little child dies, my momma say a star go straight to Heaven," says Serena.

"My grandma was murdered," Mickey says out of the blue. "Somebody shot two bullets in her head."

I ask him, "Is she really dead?"

"She dead all right," says Mickey. "She was layin' there, just dead."

"I love my friends," Serena says. "I don't care if they no kin to me. I *care* for them. I hope his mother have another baby. Name her for my friend that's dead."

"I have a cat with three legs," Smokey says.

"Snakes hate rabbits," Mickey says, again for no apparent reason.

"Cats hate fishes," Little Sister says.

"It's a lot of hate," says Smokey.

Later, at the mission, Sister Julia tells me this: "The Jefferson School, which they attend, is a decrepit hulk. Next to it is a modern school, erected two years ago, which was to have replaced the one that they attend. But the construction was not done correctly. The roof is too heavy for the walls, and the entire structure has begun to sink. It can't be occupied. Smokey's sister was raped and murdered and dumped between the old school and the new one."

As the children drift back to their homes for supper, Sister Julia stands outside with me and talks about the health concerns that trouble people in the neighborhood. In the setting sun, the voices of the children fill the evening air. Nourished by the sewage marsh, a field of wild daffodils is blooming. Standing here, you wouldn't think that anything was wrong. The street is calm. The poison in the soil can't be seen. The sewage is invisible and only makes the grass a little greener. Bikes thrown down by children lie outside their kitchen doors. It could be an ordinary twilight in a small suburban town.

Night comes on and Sister Julia goes inside to telephone a cab. In another hour, the St. Louis taxis will not come into the neighborhood.

In the night, the sky above the East St. Louis area is brownish yellow. Illuminated by the glare from the Monsanto installation, the smoke is vented from four massive columns rising about 400 feet above the plant. The garish light and tubular structures lend the sky a strange, nightmarish look.

Safir Ahmed, a young reporter who has covered East St. Louis for the *Post-Dispatch* for several years, drives with me through the rutted streets close to the plant and points out blocks of wooden houses without plumbing. Straggling black children walk along a road that has no sidewalks. "The soil is all contaminated here," he says.

Almost directly over our heads the plant is puffing out a cloud of brownish smoke that rises above the girders of the plant within a glow of reddish-gold illumination.

Two auto bridges cross the Mississippi River to St. Louis. To the south is the Poplar Street Bridge. The bridge to the north is named for Martin Luther King. "It takes three minutes to cross the bridge," says Ahmed. "For white people in St. Louis, it could be a thousand miles long."

On the southern edge of East St. Louis, tiny shack-like houses stand along a lightless street. Immediately behind these houses are the giant buildings of Monsanto, Big River Zinc, Cerro Copper, the American Bottoms Sewage Plant and Trade Waste Incineration—one of the largest hazardous-waste-incineration companies in the United States.

"The entire city lies downwind of this. When the plant gives off emissions that are viewed as toxic, an alarm goes off. People who have breathed the smoke are given a cash payment of $400 in exchange for a release from liability. . . .

"The decimation of the men within the population is quite nearly total. Four of five births in East St. Louis are to single mothers. Where do the men go? Some to prison. Some to the military. Many to an early death. Dozens of men are living in the streets or sleeping in small, isolated camps behind the burnt-out buildings. There are several of these camps out in the muddy stretch there to the left.

"The nicest buildings in the city are the Federal Court House and the City Hall—which also holds the jail—the National Guard headquarters, and some funeral establishments. There are a few nice houses and a couple of high-rise homes for senior citizens. One of the nicest buildings is the whorehouse. There's also a branch of the University of Southern Illinois, but it no longer offers classes; it's a social welfare complex now.

"The chemical plants do not pay taxes here. They have created small incorporated towns which are self-

governed and exempt therefore from supervision by
health agencies in East St. Louis. Aluminum Ore created
a separate town called Alorton. Monsanto, Cerro Copper and Big River Zinc are all in Sauget. National Stock
Yards has its own incorporated town as well. Basically
there's no one living in some of these so-called towns.
Alorton is a sizable town. Sauget, on the other hand, isn't
much more than a legal fiction. It provides tax shelter
and immunity from jurisdiction of authorities in East
St. Louis."

The town of Sauget claims a population of about
200 people. Its major industries, other than Monsanto
and the other plants, are topless joints and an outlet for
the lottery. Two of the largest strip clubs face each other
on a side street that is perpendicular to the main highway.
One is named Oz and that is for white people. The other
strip club, which is known as Wiz, is for black people.
The lottery office, which is frequented primarily by black
people, is the largest in the state of Illinois.

"The lottery advertises mostly in black publica-
tions," Ahmed says. "So people who have nothing to
start with waste their money on a place that sells them
dreams. Lottery proceeds in Illinois allegedly go into
education; in reality they go into state revenues and they
add nothing to the education fund. So it is a total loss.
Affluent people do not play the lottery. The state is in the
business here of selling hopes to people who have none.
The city itself is full of bars and liquor stores and lots of
ads for cigarettes that feature pictures of black people.
Assemble all the worst things in America—gambling,
liquor, cigarettes and toxic fumes, sewage, waste disposal, prostitution—put it all together. Then you dump it
on black people."

East St. Louis begins at the Monsanto fence. Rain
starts falling as we cross the railroad tracks, and then

another set of tracks, and pass a series of dirt streets with houses that are mostly burnt-out shells, the lots between them piled with garbage bags and thousands of abandoned auto tires. The city is almost totally flat and lies below the Mississippi's floodline, protected by a levee. In 1986 a floodgate broke and filled part of the city. Houses on Bond Avenue filled up with sewage to their second floors.

The waste water emitted from the sewage plant, according to a recent Greenpeace study, "varies in color from yellow-orange to green." The toxic substances that it contains become embedded in the soil and the marshland in which children play. Dead Creek, for example, a creekbed that received discharges from the chemical and metal plants in previous years, is now a place where kids from East St. Louis ride their bikes. The creek, which smokes by day and glows on moonless nights, has gained some notoriety in recent years for instances of spontaneous combustion. The Illinois EPA believes that the combustion starts when children ride their bikes across the creek bed, "creating friction which begins the smoldering process."

"Nobody in East St. Louis," Ahmed says, "has ever had the clout to raise a protest. Why Americans permit this is so hard for somebody like me, who grew up in the real Third World, to understand. . . . .

"I'm from India. In Calcutta this would be explicable, perhaps. I keep thinking to myself, 'My God! This is the United States!' "

By midnight, hardly anyone is out on foot. In block after block, there is no sense of life. Only the bars and liquor stores are open—but the windows of the liquor stores are barred. There is a Woolworth's store that has no windows. Silently in the persistent rain a dark shape looms before us and cuts off the street: a freight train loaded with chemicals or copper, moving slowly to the north. There is no right or wrong side of the tracks in East St. Louis. The tracks are everywhere. Behind us still: the eerie specter of the lights and girders of Monsanto. In front of us, perhaps two miles away: the beautiful St. Louis Arch and, under it, the brightly lighted skyline of St. Louis.

"The ultimate terror for white people," Ahmed says, "is to leave the highway by mistake and find themselves in East St. Louis. People speak of getting lost in East St. Louis as a nightmare. The nightmare to me is that they never leave that highway so they never know what life is like for all the children here. They *ought* to get off that highway. The nightmare isn't in their heads. It's a real place. There are children living here.

"Jesse Jackson came to speak at East St. Louis High. There were three thousand people packed into the gym. He was nearly two hours late. When he came in, the feeling was electric. There was pin-drop silence while he spoke. An old man sat beside me, leaning forward on his cane. He never said a word but he was crying.

"You would think, with all the chemical and metals plants, that there would be unlimited employment. It doesn't work that way. Most of these are specialized jobs. East St. Louis men don't have the education. I go into the Monsanto plant and almost every face I see is white.

"The biggest employer in the town is public education. Next, perhaps, the Pfizer plant, which is situated just behind one of the high schools. After that, the biggest businesses may be the drug trade, funerals and bars and prostitution. The mayor's family owns the largest funeral home in East St. Louis. The Catholic high school was shut down last year. There's talk of turning it into a prison."

There is a pornography theater in the center of the

town but no theater showing movies suitable for children. East St. Louis is the largest city south of Springfield in the state of Illinois but was left off the Illinois map four years ago. The telephone directory that serves the region does not list phone numbers of the residents or businesses of East St. Louis, even though the city lies right at the center of the service area that the directory is supposed to cover. Two years ago, the one pedestrian bridge across the Mississippi River to St. Louis was closed off to East St. Louis residents.

"It's a third bridge, smaller than the others," Ahmed says, "very old—the only one that's open to pedestrians. It puts you right into downtown St. Louis, quite close to the Arch. The closing of the bridge was ordered on the day before a street fair that takes place each summer during the July Fourth celebration. Three or four million people flood into the city. There are booths for food, and rides and music. For people in East St. Louis, it's an opportunity to bring their children to the city and relax. Mothers walk their kids across the bridge. . . .

"The police announced that they were shutting down the bridge. The reason they gave was that there had been some muggings in the past. They were concerned, they said, that teen-age blacks would mug the people at the fair, then run across the bridge and disappear into the streets of East St. Louis. Regardless of the reason, it was a decision that denied the folks in East St. Louis access to the fair."

According to a story published later in *Life* magazine, black leaders in East St. Louis said "it looked suspiciously like a racist action." The fact that it was pegged to Independence Day intensified the sense of injury. The president of the NAACP in East St. Louis said, "We seem to have been isolated. . . ."

The bridge was later opened by court order.

"In recent years," says Ahmed, "letters have been going out to people who have homes in a half-mile zone next to Monsanto. The letters offer to buy your home, no questions asked, for cash: $4,000 flat for any house. The speculation is that Monsanto wants a buffer zone to fend off further suits for damages from chemical emissions. These offers are appealing to poor people who have nothing and who have no faith the courts would ever honor their concerns. . . .

"The land between the two main bridges and along the river is regarded as prime real estate by white developers. Given the fantastic view of the St. Louis skyline and the Gateway Arch, the land would be immensely valuable if its black residents could be removed. When people ask, 'What should we do with East St. Louis?' they don't speak about the people. They are speaking of the land."

Emerging from another rutted street of houses that do not appear to be inhabited, but from the interior of which some lights are seen, we pass the segregated topless joints again and stop the car along Monsanto Avenue to scrutinize Big River Zinc, Cerro Copper ("America's Largest Recycler of Copper," according to its sign) and the Monsanto plant. Then, making a U-turn, we head west onto the access road that climbs back to the bridge across the Mississippi.

"Every time I cross that bridge I feel that I am getting off a plane within a different country," Ahmed says.

From the St. Louis side, one sees the dark breadth of the river, another wider strip of blackness where the dwellings of East St. Louis lie, and the glowing cluster of industrial illumination slightly to the south. Off to the east lie the Illinois Bluffs, far above the chemical pollutants.

East St. Louis—which the local press refers to as "an inner city without an outer city"—has some of the sickest children in America. Of 66 cities in Illinois, East St. Louis ranks first in fetal death, first in premature birth, and third in infant death. Among the negative factors listed by the city's health director are the sewage running in the streets, air that has been fouled by the local plants, the high lead levels noted in the soil, poverty, lack of education, crime, dilapidated housing, insufficient health care, unemployment. Hospital care is deficient too. There is no place to have a baby in East St. Louis. The maternity ward at the city's Catholic hospital, a 100-year-old structure, was shut down some years ago. The only other hospital in town was forced by lack of funds to close in 1990. The closest obstetrics service open to the women here is seven miles away. The infant death rate is still rising.

As in New York City's poorest neighborhoods, dental problems also plague the children here. Although dental problems don't command the instant fears associated with low birth weight, fetal death or cholera, they do have the consequence of wearing down the stamina of children and defeating their ambitions. Bleeding gums, impacted teeth and rotting teeth are routine matters for the children I have interviewed in the South Bronx. Children get used to feeling constant pain. They go to sleep with it. They go to school with it. Sometimes their teachers are alarmed and try to get them to a clinic. But it's all so slow and heavily encumbered with red tape and waiting lists and missing, lost or canceled welfare cards, that dental care is often long delayed. Children live for months with pain that grown-ups would find unendurable. The gradual attrition of accepted pain erodes their energy and aspiration. I have seen children in New York with teeth that look like brownish, broken sticks. I have also seen teen-agers who were missing half their teeth. But, to me, most shocking is to see a child with an abscess that has been inflamed for weeks and that he has simply lived with and accepts as part of the routine of life. Many teachers in the urban schools have seen this. It is almost commonplace.

Compounding these problems is the poor nutrition of the children here—average daily food expenditure in East St. Louis is $2.40 for one child—and the under-immunization of young children. Of every 100 children recently surveyed in East St. Louis, 55 were incompletely immunized for polio, diphtheria, measles and whooping cough. In this context, health officials look with all the more uneasiness at those lagoons of sewage outside public housing.

On top of all else is the very high risk of death by homicide in East St. Louis. In a recent year in which three cities in the state of roughly the same size as East St. Louis had an average of four homicides apiece, there were 54 homicides in East St. Louis. But it is the heat of summer that officials here particularly dread. The heat that breeds the insects bearing polio or hepatitis in raw sewage also heightens asthma and frustration and reduces patience. "The heat," says a man in public housing, "can bring out the beast. . . ."

The fear of violence is very real in East St. Louis. The CEO of one of the large companies out on the edge of town has developed an "evacuation plan" for his employees. State troopers are routinely sent to East St. Louis to put down disturbances that the police cannot control. If the misery of this community explodes some-day in a real riot (it has happened in the past), residents believe that state and federal law-enforcement agencies will have no hesitation in applying massive force to keep the violence contained.

As we have seen, it is believed by people here that white developers regard the land beside the river and adjacent sections of the city as particularly attractive sites for condominiums and luxury hotels. It is the fear of violence, people believe, and the proximity of the black population that have, up to now, prevented plans like these from taking shape. Some residents are convinced, therefore, that they will someday be displaced. "It's happened in other cities," says a social worker who has lived here for ten years, "East St. Louis is a good location, after all."

This eventuality, however, is not viewed as very likely—or not for a long, long time. The soil would have to be de-leaded first. The mercury and arsenic would have to be dealt with. The chemical plants would have to be shut down or modified before the area could be regarded as attractive to developers. For now, the people of East St. Louis probably can rest assured that nobody much covets what is theirs.

"The history of East St. Louis," says the *Post-Dispatch,* is "rife with greed and lust and bigotry." At the turn of the century, the city was the second largest railroad center in the nation. It led the nation in sale of horses, mules and hogs, and in the manufacture of aluminum. Meat-packing, steel, and paint manufacture were important here as well. Virtually all these industries were owned, however, by outsiders.

Blacks were drawn to East St. Louis from the South by promises of jobs. When they arrived, the corporations used them as strikebreakers. In 1917 a mounting white resentment of strikebreaking blacks, combined

with racial bigotry, ignited one of the most bloody riots
in the nation's history. White mobs tore into black neighborhoods. Beatings and hangings took place in the
streets. The mob, whose rage was indiscriminate, killed
a 14-year-old boy and scalped his mother. Before it was
over, 244 buildings were destroyed.

It may be said that the unregulated private market did not serve the city well. By the 1930s, industries
that had enticed black people here with promises of
jobs began to leave for areas where even cheaper labor
could be found. Proximity to coal, which had attracted
industry into the area, also ceased to be important as
electric power came to be commercially available in
other regions. The Aluminum Ore Company, which had
brought 10,000 blacks to East St. Louis to destroy the
unions, now shut down and moved to the Deep South.
During the Depression, other factories—their operations
obsolete—shut down as well.

The city underwent a renaissance of sorts in World
War II, when deserted factory space was used for military
manufacturing. Cheap black labor was again required.
Prostitution also flourished as a market answer to the
presence of so many military men at nearby bases. Orga-
nized crime set up headquarters in the city. For subsequent decades, East St. Louis was the place where young
white men would go for sexual adventures.

Population peaked in 1945 at 80,000, one third
being black. By 1971, with the population down to
50,000, less than one-third white, a black mayor was
elected. A second black mayor, elected in 1979, remained
in office until 1991.

The problems of the streets in urban areas, as teachers often note, frequently spill over into public schools.

In the public schools of East St. Louis this is literally the case.

"Martin Luther King Junior High School," notes the *Post-Dispatch* in a story published in the early spring of 1989, "was evacuated Friday afternoon after sewage flowed into the kitchen. . . . The kitchen was closed and students were sent home." On Monday, the paper continues, "East St. Louis Senior High School was awash in sewage for the second time this year." The school had to be shut because of "fumes and backed-up toilets." Sewage flowed into the basement, through the floor, then up into the kitchen and the students' bathrooms. The backup, we read, "occurred in the food preparation areas."

School is resumed the following morning at the high school, but a few days later the overflow recurs. This time the entire system is affected, since the meals distributed to every student in the city are prepared in the two schools that have been flooded. School is called off for all 16,500 students in the district. The sewage backup, caused by the failure of two pumping stations, forces officials at the high school to shut down the furnaces.

At Martin Luther King, the parking lot and gym are also flooded. "It's a disaster," says a legislator. "The streets are underwater; gaseous fumes are being emitted from the pipes under the schools," she says, "making people ill."

In the same week, the schools announce the layoff of 280 teachers, 166 cooks and cafeteria workers, 25 teacher aides, 16 custodians and 18 painters, electricians, engineers and plumbers. The president of the teachers' union says the cuts, which will bring the size of kindergarten and primary classes up to 30 students, and the size of fourth to twelfth grade classes up to 35, will have "an unimaginable impact" on the students. "If you have a high school teacher with five classes each day and between 150 and 175 students . . . , it's going to have a devastating effect." The school system, it is also noted, has been using more than 70 "permanent substitute teachers," who are paid only $10,000 yearly, as a way of saving money.

Governor Thompson, however, tells the press that he will not pour money into East St. Louis to solve long-term problems. East St. Louis residents, he says, must help themselves. "There is money in the community," the governor insists. "It's just not being spent for what it should be spent for."

The governor, while acknowledging that East St. Louis faces economic problems, nonetheless refers dismissively to those who live in East St. Louis. "What in the community," he asks, "is being done right?" He takes the opportunity of a visit to the area to announce a fiscal grant for sewer improvement to a relatively wealthy town nearby.

In East St. Louis, meanwhile, teachers are running out of chalk and paper, and their paychecks are arriving two weeks late. The city warns its teachers to expect a cut of half their pay until the fiscal crisis has been eased.

The threatened teacher layoffs are mandated by the Illinois Board of Education, which, because of the city's fiscal crisis, has been given supervisory control of the school budget. Two weeks later the state superintendent partially relents. In a tone very different from that of the governor, he notes that East St. Louis does not have the means to solve its education problems on its own. "There is no natural way," he says, that "East St. Louis can bring itself out of this situation." Several cuts will be required in any case—one quarter of the system's teachers, 75 teacher aides, and several dozen others will be given notice—but, the state board notes, sports and music programs will not be affected.

East St. Louis, says the chairman of the state board, "is simply the worst possible place I can imagine to have a child brought up. . . . The community is in desperate circumstances." Sports and music, he observes, are, for many children here, "the only avenues of success." Sadly enough, no matter how it ratifies the stereotype, this is the truth; and there is a poignant aspect to the fact that, even with class size soaring and one quarter of the system's teachers being given their dismissal, the state board of education demonstrates its genuine but skewed compassion by attempting to leave sports and music untouched by the overall austerity.

Even sports facilities, however, are degrading by comparison with those found and expected at most high schools in America. The football field at East St. Louis High is missing almost everything—including goalposts. There are a couple of metal pipes—no crossbar, just the pipes. Bob Shannon, the football coach, who has to use his personal funds to purchase footballs and has had to cut and rake the football field himself, has dreams of having goalposts someday. He'd also like to let his students have new uniforms. The ones they wear are nine years old and held together somehow by a patchwork of repairs. Keeping them clean is a problem, too. The school cannot afford a washing machine. The uniforms are carted to a corner laundromat with fifteen dollars' worth of quarters.

Other football teams that come to play, according to the coach, are shocked to see the field and locker rooms. They want to play without a halftime break and get away. The coach reports that he's been missing paychecks, but he's trying nonetheless to raise some money to help out a member of the team whose mother has just died of cancer.

"The days of the tight money have arrived," he says. "It don't look like Moses will be coming to this school."

He tells me he has been in East St. Louis 19 years and has been the football coach for 14 years. "I was born," he says, "in Natchez, Mississippi. I stood on the courthouse steps of Natchez with Charles Evers. I was a teen-age boy when Michael Schwerner and the other boys were murdered. I've been in the struggle all along. In Mississippi, it was the fight for legal rights. This time, it's a struggle for survival.

"In certain ways," he says, "it's harder now because in those days it was a clear enemy you had to face, a man in a hood and not a statistician. No one could persuade you that you were to blame. Now the choices seem like they are left to you and, if you make the wrong choice, you are made to understand you are to blame. . . .

"Night-time in this city, hot and smoky in the summer, there are dealers standin' out on every street. Of the kids I see here, maybe 55 percent will graduate from school. Of that number, maybe one in four will go to college. How many will stay? That is a bigger question.

"The basic essentials are simply missing here. When we go to wealthier schools I look at the faces of my boys. They don't say a lot. They have their faces to the windows, lookin' out. I can't tell what they are thinking. I am hopin' they are saying, 'This is something I will give my kids someday.'"

Tall and trim, his black hair graying slightly, he is 45 years old.

"No, my wife and I don't live here. We live in a town called Ferguson, Missouri. I was born in poverty and raised in poverty. I feel that I owe it to myself to live where they pick up the garbage."

In the visitors' locker room, he shows me lockers with no locks. The weight room stinks of sweat and water-rot. "See, this ceiling is in danger of collapsing. See, this room don't have no heat in winter. But we got to come here anyway. We wear our coats while working out. I tell the boys, 'We got to get it done. Our fans don't know that we do not have heat.'"

He tells me he arrives at school at 7:45 A.M. and leaves at 6:00 P.M.—except in football season, when he leaves at 8:00 P.M. "This is my life. It isn't all I dreamed of and I tell myself sometimes that I might have accomplished more. But growing up in poverty rules out some avenues. You do the best you can."

In the wing of the school that holds vocational classes, a damp, unpleasant odor fills the halls. The school has a machine shop, which cannot be used for lack of staff, and a woodworking shop. The only shop that's occupied this morning is the auto-body class. A man with long blond hair and wearing a white sweat suit swings a paddle to get children in their chairs. "What we need the most is new equipment," he reports. "I have equipment for alignment, for example, but we don't have money to install it. We also need a better form of egress. We bring the cars in through two other classes." Computerized equipment used in most repair shops, he reports, is far beyond the high school's budget. It looks like a very old gas station in an isolated rural town.

Stopping in the doorway of a room with seven stoves and three refrigerators, I am told by a white teacher that this is a class called "Introductory Home Ec." The 15 children in the room, however, are not occupied with work. They are scattered at some antiquated tables, chatting with each other. The teacher explains that students do no work on Friday, which, she says, is "clean-up day." I ask her whether she regards this class as preparation for employment. "Not this class," she says. "The ones who move on to Advanced Home Ec. are given job instruction." When I ask her what jobs they are trained for, she says: "Fast food places—Burger King, McDonald's."

The science labs at East St. Louis High are 30 to 50 years outdated. John McMillan, a soft-spoken man, teaches physics at the school. He shows me his lab. The six lab stations in the room have empty holes where pipes were once attached. "It would be great if we had water," says McMillan.

Wiping his hand over his throat, he tells me that he cannot wear a tie or jacket in the lab. "I want you to notice the temperature," he says. "The heating system's never worked correctly. Days when it's zero outside it will be 100 Fahrenheit within this room. I will be here 25 years starting September—in the same room, teaching physics. I have no storage space. Those balance scales are trash. There are a few small windows you can open. We are on the side that gets the sun."

Stepping outside the lab, he tells me that he lives in East St. Louis, one block from the school. Balding and damp-looking in his open collar, he is a bachelor 58 years old.

The biology lab, which I visit next, has no laboratory tables. Students work at regular desks. "I need dissecting kits," the teacher says. "The few we have are incomplete." Chemical supplies, she tells me, in a city poisoned by two chemical plants, are scarce. "I need more microscopes," she adds.

The chemistry lab is the only one that's properly equipped. There are eight lab tables with gas jets and water. But the chemistry teacher says he rarely brings his students to the lab. "I have 30 children in a class and cannot supervise them safely. Chemical lab work is unsafe with more than 20 children to a teacher. If I had some lab assistants, we could make use of the lab. As it is, we have to study mainly from a text."

Even texts are scarce, however. "We were short of books for four months last semester. When we got replacement copies, they were different from the texts that we already had. So that presented a new problem. . . .

"Despite these failings, I have had two students graduate from MIT."

"In how many years?" I ask.

He tells me, "Twenty-three."

Leaving the chemistry labs, I pass a double-sized classroom in which roughly 60 kids are sitting fairly still but doing nothing. "This is supervised study hall," a teacher tells me in the corridor. But when we step inside, he finds there is no teacher. "The teacher must be out today," he says.

Irl Solomon's history classes, which I visit next, have been described by journalists who cover East St. Louis as the highlight of the school. Solomon, a man of 54 whose reddish hair is turning white, has taught in urban schools for almost 30 years. A graduate of Brandeis University in 1961, he entered law school but was drawn away by a concern with civil rights. "After one semester, I decided that the law was not for me. I said, 'Go and find the toughest place there is to teach. See if you like it.' I'm still here. . . .

"This is not by any means the worst school in the city," he reports, as we are sitting in his classroom on the first floor of the school. "But our problems are severe. I don't even know where to begin. I have no materials with the exception of a single textbook given to each child. If I bring in anything else—books or tapes or magazines—I pay for it myself. The high school has no VCRs. They are such a crucial tool. So many good things run on public television. I can't make use of anything I see unless I can unhook my VCR and bring it into school. The AV equipment in the building is so old that we are pressured not to use it."

Teachers like Mr. Solomon, working in low-income districts such as East St. Louis, often tell me that they feel cut off from educational developments in modern public schools. "Well, it's amazing," Solomon says. "I have done without so much so long that, if I were assigned to a suburban school, I'm not sure I'd recognize what they are doing. We are utterly cut off."

Of 33 children who begin the history classes in the standard track, he says, more than a quarter have dropped out by spring semester. "Maybe 24 are left by June. Mind you, this is in the junior year. We're speaking of the children who survived. Ninth and tenth grades are the more horrendous years for leaving school.

"I have four girls right now in my senior home room who are pregnant or have just had babies. When I ask them why this happens, I am told, 'Well, there's no reason not to have a baby. There's not much for me in public school.' The truth is, that's a pretty honest answer. A diploma from a ghetto high school doesn't count for much in the United States today. So, if this is really the last education that a person's going to get, she's probably perceptive in that statement. Ah, there's so much bitterness—unfairness—there, you know. Most of these pregnant girls are not the ones who have much self-esteem. . . .

"Very little education in the school would be considered academic in the suburbs. Maybe 10 to 15 percent of students are in truly academic programs. Of the 55 percent who graduate, 20 percent may go to four-year colleges: something like 10 percent of any entering class. Another 10 to 20 percent may get some other kind of higher education. An equal number join the military. . . .

"I get $38,000 after nearly 30 years of teaching. If I went across the river to one of the suburbs of St. Louis, I'd be earning $47,000, maybe more. If I taught in the Chicago suburbs, at a wealthy high school like New Trier, for example, I'd be getting close to $60,000. Money's not an issue for me, since I wouldn't want to leave; but, for new, incoming teachers, this much differential is a great deterrent. When you consider that many teachers are afraid to come here in the first place, or, if they are not afraid, are nonetheless offended by the setting or intimidated by the challenge of the job, there should be a premium and not a punishment for teaching here.

"Sometimes I get worried that I'm starting to burn out. Still, I hate to miss a day. The department frequently can't find a substitute to come here, and my kids don't like me to be absent."

Solomon's advanced class, which soon comes into the room, includes some lively students with strong views.

"I don't go to physics class, because my lab has no equipment," says one student. "The typewriters in my typing class don't work. The women's toilets . . ." She makes a sour face. "I'll be honest," she says. "I just don't use the toilets. If I do, I come back into class and I feel dirty."

"I wanted to study Latin," says another student. "But we don't have Latin in this school."

"We lost our only Latin teacher," Solomon says.

A girl in a white jersey with the message DO THE RIGHT THING on the front raises her hand. "You visit other schools," she says. "Do you think the children in this school are getting what we'd get in a nice section of St. Louis?"

I note that we are in a different state and city.

"Are we citizens of East St. Louis or America?" she asks.

A tall girl named Samantha interrupts. "I have a comment that I want to make." She then relates the following incident: "Fairview Heights is a mainly white community. A friend of mine and I went up there once to buy some books. We walked into the store. Everybody lookin' at us, you know, and somebody says, 'What do you want?' And lookin' at each other like, 'What are these black girls doin' here in Fairview Heights?' I just said, 'I want to buy a book!' It's like they're scared we're goin' to rob them. Take away a privilege that's theirs by rights. Well, that goes for school as well.

"My mother wanted me to go to school there and she tried to have me transferred. It didn't work. The reason, she was told, is that we're in a different 'jurisdiction.' If you don't live up there in the hills, or further back, you can't attend their schools. That, at least, is what they told my mother."

"Is that a matter of race?" I ask. "Or money?"

"Well," she says, choosing her words with care, "the two things, race and money, go so close together—what's the difference? I live here, they live there, and they don't want me in their school."

A boy named Luther speaks about the chemical pollution. "It's like this," he says. "On one side of us you have two chemical corporations. One is Pfizer—that's out there. They make paint and pigments. The other is Monsanto. On the other side are companies incinerating toxic waste. So the trash is comin' at us this direction. The chemicals is comin' from the other. We right in the middle."

Despite these feelings, many of the children voice a curiously resilient faith in racial integration. "If the government would put a huge amount of money into East St. Louis, so that this could be a modern, well-equipped and top-rate school," I ask, "with everything that you could ever want for education, would you say that racial segregation was no longer of importance?"

Without exception, the children answer, "No."

"Going to a school with all the races," Luther says, "is more important than a modern school."

"They still believe in that dream," their teacher

says. "They have no reason to do so. That is what I find so wonderful and . . . ah, so moving. . . . These kids are the only reason I get up each day."

I ask the students, "What would happen if the government decided that the students in a nearby town like Fairview Heights and the students here in East St. Louis had to go to school together next September?"

Samantha: "The buses going to Fairview Heights would all be full. The buses coming to East St. Louis would be empty."

"What if East St. Louis had the very best computer classes in the state—and if there were no computer classes in the school of Fairview Heights?"

"The buses coming here," she says, "would still be empty."

When I ask her why, she answers in these quiet words: "I don't know why."

Sam Morgan, principal of East St. Louis High, was born and raised in East St. Louis. He tells me he didn't go to East St. Louis High, however. "This was the white high school in those days," he says.

His office was ruined in a recent fire, so he meets me in a tiny room with space for three chairs and a desk. Impeccably dressed in a monogrammed shirt with gold links in his cuffs, a purple tie and matching purple handkerchief in his suit pocket, he is tall, distinguished-looking and concerned that I will write a critical report on East St. Louis High. When I ask, however, what he'd do if he were granted adequate funds, he comes up with a severe assessment of the status quo.

"First, we're losing thousands of dollars in our heating bills because of faulty windows and because the heating system cannot be controlled. So I'd renovate the building and install a whole new heating system and replace the windows. We've had fire damage but I see that as a low priority. I need computers—that's a low priority as well. I'd settle for a renovation of the typing rooms and new typewriters. The highest priorities are to subdivide the school and add a modern wing, then bring the science laboratories up to date. Enlarge the library. Buy more books. The books I've got, a lot of them are secondhand. I got them from the Catholic high school when it closed. Most of all, we need a building renovation. This is what I'd do to start with, if I had an extra $20 million."

After he's enumerated all the changes he would like to make, he laughs and looks down at his hands. "This, of course, is pie in the sky. You asked me what I need so I have told you. If I'm dreaming, why not dream the big dreams for our children?"

His concerns are down-to-earth. He's not pretentious and does not appropriate the cloudy jargon that some educators use to fill a vacuum of specifics—no talk of "restructuring," of "teacher competency" or any of the other buzzwords of the decade. His focus is on the bare necessities: typewriters, windows, books, a renovated building.

While we are speaking in his temporary office, a telephone call from the police informs him that his house has just been robbed—or that the theft alarm, at least, has just gone off. He interrupts the interview to try to reach his wife. His poise and his serene self-discipline do not desert him. I gain the impression this has happened before. He's a likable man and he smiles a lot, but there is tremendous tension in his body and his fingers grip the edges of his desk as if he's trying very hard to hold his world together.

Before I leave the school, I take a final stroll along

the halls. In a number of classrooms, groups of children seem to be involved in doing nothing. Sometimes there's a teacher present, doing something at his desk. Sometimes there's no adult in the room. I pass the cooking class again, in which there is no cooking and no teaching taking place. The "supervised" study hall is still unsupervised.

In one of the unattended classrooms on the second floor, seven students stand around a piano. When I stick my head into the room, they smile and invite me to come in. They are rehearsing for a concert: two young women, five young men. Another young man is seated at the piano. One of the students, a heavyset young woman, steps out just before the others. When she sings, her pure soprano voice transforms the room. "Sometimes I feel like a motherless child," she begins. The pianist gazes up at her with an attentive look of admiration.

The loveliness and the aesthetic isolation of the singer in the squalor of the school and city bring to my mind the words of Dr. Lillian Parks, the superintendent of the East St. Louis schools. "Gifted children," says Dr. Parks, "are everywhere in East St. Louis, but their gifts are lost to poverty and turmoil and the damage done by knowing they are written off by their society. Many of these children have no sense of something they belong to. They have no feeling of belonging to America. Gangs provide the boys, perhaps, with something to belong to. . . .

"There is a terrible beauty in some of these girls—terrible, I mean, because it is ephemeral, foredoomed. The language that our children speak may not be standard English but there still is wisdom here. Our children have become wise by necessity."

* * *

Clark Junior High School is regarded as the top school in the city. I visit, in part, at the request of school officials, who would like me to see education in the city at its very best. Even here, however, there is a disturbing sense that one has entered a backwater of America.

"We spend the entire eighth grade year preparing for the state exams," a teacher tells me in a top-ranked English class. The teacher seems devoted to the children, but three students sitting near me sleep through the entire period. The teacher rouses one of them, a girl in the seat next to me, but the student promptly lays her head back on her crossed arms and is soon asleep again. Four of the 14 ceiling lights are broken. The corridor outside the room is filled with voices. Outside the window, where I see no schoolyard, is an empty lot.

In a mathematics class of 30 children packed into a space that might be adequate for 15 kids, there is one white student. The first white student I have seen in East St. Louis, she is polishing her nails with bright red polish. A tiny black girl next to her is writing with a one-inch pencil stub.

In a seventh grade social studies class, the only book that bears some relevance to black concerns—its title is *The American Negro*—bears a publication date of 1967. The teacher invites me to ask the class some questions. Uncertain where to start, I ask the students what they've learned about the civil rights campaigns of recent decades.

A 14-year-old girl with short black curly hair says this: "Every year in February we are told to read the same old speech of Martin Luther King. We read it every year. 'I have a dream. . . .' It does begin to seem—what is the word?" She hesitates and then she finds the word: "perfunctory."

I ask her what she means.

"We have a school in East St. Louis named for Dr. King," she says. "The school is full of sewer water and the doors are locked with chains. Every student in that school is black. It's like a terrible joke on history."

It startles me to hear her words, but I am startled even more to think how seldom any press reporter has observed the irony of naming segregated schools for Martin Luther King. Children reach the heart of these hypocrisies much quicker than the grown-ups and the experts do.

"I would like to comment on that," says another 14-year-old student, named Shalika. "I have had to deal with this all of my life. I started school in Fairview Heights. My mother pushes me and she had wanted me to get a chance at better education. Only one other student in my class was black. I was in the fifth grade, and at that age you don't understand the ugliness in people's hearts. They wouldn't play with me. I couldn't understand it. During recess I would stand there by myself beside the fence. Then one day I got a note: 'Go back to Africa.'

"To tell the truth, it left a sadness in my heart. Now you hear them sayin' on TV, 'What's the matter with these colored people? Don't they care about their children's education?' But my mother did the best for me she knew. It was not my mother's fault that I was not accepted by those people."

"It does not take long," says Christopher, a light-skinned boy with a faint mustache and a somewhat heated and perspiring look, "for little kids to learn they are not wanted."

Shalika is small and looks quite young for junior high. In each ear she wears a small enameled pin of Mickey Mouse. "To some degree I do believe," she says, "that this is caused by press reports. You see a lot about the crimes committed here in East St. Louis when you turn on the TV. Do they show the crimes committed by the government that *puts* black people here? Why are all the dirty businesses like chemicals and waste disposal here? This is a big country. Couldn't they find another place to put their poison?"

"Shalika," the teacher tells me afterward, "will go to college."

"Why is it this way?" asks Shalika in a softer voice again. But she doesn't ask the question as if she is waiting for an answer.

"Is it 'separate but equal,' then?" I ask. "Have we gone back a hundred years?"

"It is separate. That's for sure," the teacher says. She is a short and stocky middle-aged black woman. "Would you want to tell the children it is equal?"

Christopher approaches me at the end of class. The room is too hot. His skin looks warm and his black hair is damp. "Write this down. You asked a question about Martin Luther King. I'm going to say something. All that stuff about 'the dream' means nothing to the kids I know in East St. Louis. So far as they're concerned, he died in vain. He was famous and he lived and gave his speeches and he died and now he's gone. But we're still here. Don't tell students in this school about 'the dream.' Go and look into a toilet here if you would like to know what life is like for students in this city."

Before I leave, I do as Christopher asked and enter a boy's bathroom. Four of the six toilets do not work. The toilets stalls, which are eaten away by red and brown corrosion, have no doors. The toilets have no seats. One has a rotted wooden stump. There are no paper towels and no soap. Near the door there is a loop of wire with an empty toilet-paper roll.

"This," says Sister Julia, "is the best school that we have in East St. Louis."

In East St. Louis, as in every city that I visit, I am forced to ask myself if what I've seen may be atypical. One would like to think that this might be the case in East St. Louis, but it would not be the truth.

At Landsdowne Junior High School, the *St. Louis Sun* reports, "there are scores of window frames without glass, like sockets without eyes." Hallways in many schools are dark, with light bulbs missing or burnt out. One walks into a school, a member of the city's board of education notes, "and you can smell the urinals a hundred feet away. . . ."

A teacher at an elementary school in East St. Louis has only one full-color workbook for her class. She photocopies workbook pages for her children, but the copies can't be made in color and the lessons call for color recognition by the children.

A history teacher at the Martin Luther King School has 110 students in four classes—but only 26 books. Some of the books are missing the first hundred pages.

Each year, Solomon observes of East St. Louis High, "there's one more toilet that doesn't flush, one more drinking fountain that doesn't work, one more classroom without texts. . . . Certain classrooms are so cold in winter that the students have to wear their coats to class, while children in other classrooms swelter in a suffocating heat that cannot be turned down."

Critics in the press routinely note that education spending in the district is a trifle more than in surrounding districts. They also note that public schools in East St. Louis represent the largest source of paid employment in the city, and this point is often used to argue that the schools are overstaffed. The implication of both statements is that East St. Louis spends excessively on education. One could as easily conclude, however, that the conditions of existence here call for even larger school expenditures to draw and to retain more gifted staff and to offer all those extra services so desperately needed in a poor community. What such critics also fail to note, as Solomon and principal Sam Morgan have observed, is that the crumbling infrastructure uses up a great deal more of the per-pupil budget than would be the case in districts with updated buildings that cost less to operate. Critics also willfully ignore the health conditions and the psychological disarray of children growing up in burnt-out housing, playing on contaminated land, and walking past acres of smoldering garbage on their way to school. They also ignore the vast expense entailed in trying to make up for the debilitated skills of many parents who were prior victims of these segregated schools or those of Mississippi, in which many of the older residents of East St. Louis led their early lives. In view of the extraordinary miseries of life for children in the district, East St. Louis should be spending far more than is spent in wealthy suburbs. As things stand, the city spends approximately half as much each year on every pupil as the state's top-spending districts.

It is also forgotten that dramatic cuts in personnel within the East St. Louis schools—for example, of 250 teachers and 250 nonprofessional employees, as demanded recently by state officials—would propel 500 families with perhaps 2,000 children and dependents to the welfare lists and deny the city the stability afforded by a good chunk of its rapidly diminished lower middle class. Nothing, in short, that the East St. Louis school board does within the context of its penury can benefit one interest in the city without damaging another.

It is accurate to note that certain of the choices and priorities established by the East St. Louis school board do at times strike an observer as misguided, and state politicians are not hesitant to emphasize this point. The mayor of the city for many years, a controversial young man named Carl Officer, was frequently attacked by the same critics for what sometimes was alleged to be his lack of probity and of far-sighted planning. There may have been some real truth to these charges. But the diligence of critics in observing the supposed irregularities of his behavior stands in stunning contrast to their virtual refusal to address the governing realities of destitution and near-total segregation and the willingness of private industry to flee a population it once courted and enticed to East St. Louis but now finds expendable.

In very few cases, in discussing the immiseration of this city, do Illinois officials openly address the central fact, the basic evil, of its racial isolation. With more efficient local governance, East St. Louis might become a better-managed ghetto, a less ravaged racial settlement, but the soil would remain contaminated and the schools would still resemble relics of the South post-Reconstruction. They might be a trifle cleaner and they might perhaps provide their children with a dozen more computers or typewriters, better stoves for cooking classes, or a better shop for training future gas-station mechanics; but the children would still be poisoned in their bodies and disfigured in their spirits.

Now and then the possibility is raised by somebody in East St. Louis that the state may someday try to end the isolation of the city as an all-black entity. This is something, however, that no one with power in the state has ever contemplated. Certainly, no one in government proposes busing 16,000 children from this city to the nearby schools of Bellevue, Fairview Heights or Collinsville; and no one intends to force these towns to open up their neighborhoods to racially desegregated and low-income housing. So there is, in fact, no exit for these children. East St. Louis will likely be left just as it is for a good many years to come: a scar of sorts, an ugly metaphor of filth and overspill and chemical effusions, a place for blacks to live and die within, a place for other people to avoid when they are heading for St. Louis.

CHAPTER 2

Other People's Children:
North Lawndale and the
South Side of Chicago

Almost anyone who visits in the schools of East St. Louis, even for a short time, comes away profoundly shaken. These are innocent children, after all. They have done nothing wrong. They have committed no crime. They are too young to have offended us in any way at all. One searches for some way to understand why a society as rich and, frequently, as generous as ours would leave these children in their penury and squalor for so long—and with so little public indignation. Is this just a strange mistake of history? Is it unusual? Is it an American anomaly? Even if the destitution and the racial segregation and the toxic dangers of the air and soil cannot be immediately addressed, why is it that we can't at least pour vast amounts of money, ingenuity and talent into public education for these children?

Admittedly, the soil cannot be de-leaded overnight, and the ruined spirits of the men who camp out in the

mud and shacks close to the wire fencing of Monsanto
can't be instantly restored to life, nor can the many illnesses these children suffer suddenly be cured, nor can
their asthma be immediately relieved. Why not, at least,
give children in this city something so spectacular, so
wonderful and special in their public schools that hundreds of them, maybe thousands, might be able somehow
to soar up above the hopelessness, the clouds of smoke
and sense of degradation all around them?

Every child, every mother, in this city is, to a
degree, in the position of a supplicant for someone else's
help. The city turns repeatedly to outside agencies—the
federal Department of Housing and Urban Development, the federal and Illinois EPA, the U.S. Congress,
the Illinois State Board of Education, religious charities,
health organizations, medical schools and educational
foundations—soliciting help in much the way that African
and Latin American nations beg for grants from agencies like AID. And yet we stop to tell ourselves: *These are
Americans.* Why do we reduce them to this beggary—and
why, particularly, in public education? Why not spend
on children here at least what we would be investing in
their education if they lived within a wealthy district
like Winnetka, Illinois, or Cherry Hill, New Jersey, or
Manhasset, Rye, or Great Neck in New York? Wouldn't
this be natural behavior in an affluent society that seems
to value fairness in so many other areas of life? Is fairness
less important to Americans today than in some earlier
times? Is it viewed as slightly tiresome and incompatible
with hard-nosed values? What do Americans believe
about equality?

"Drive west on the Eisenhower Expressway," writes
the *Chicago Tribune,* "out past the hospital complex, and

look south." Before your eyes are block after block of old, abandoned, gaping factories. "The overwhelming sensation is emptiness. . . . What's left is, literally, nothing."

This emptiness—"an industrial slum without the industry," a local resident calls it—is North Lawndale. The neighborhood, according to the *Tribune,* "has one bank, one supermarket, 48 state lottery agents . . . and 99 licensed bars and liquor stores." With only a single supermarket, food is of poor quality and overpriced. Martin Luther King, who lived in this neighborhood in 1966, said there was a 10-to-20-percent "color tax" on produce, an estimate that still holds true today. With only a single bank, there are few loans available for home repair; private housing therefore has deteriorated quickly.

According to the 1980 census, 58 percent of men and women 17 and older in North Lawndale had no jobs. The 1990 census is expected to show no improvement. Between 1960 and 1970, as the last white families left the neighborhood, North Lawndale lost three quarters of its businesses, one quarter of its jobs. In the next ten years, 80 percent of the remaining jobs in manufacturing were lost.

"People carry a lot of crosses here," says Reverend Jim Wolff, who directs a mission church not far from one of the deserted factories. "God's beautiful people live here in the midst of hell."

As the factories have moved out, he says, the street gangs have moved in. Driving with me past a sprawling redbrick complex that was once the world headquarters of Sears, Roebuck, he speaks of the increasing economic isolation of the neighborhood: "Sears is gone. International Harvester is gone, Sunbeam is gone. Western Electric has moved out. The Vice Lords, the Disciples and the Latin Kings have, in a sense, replaced them.

"With the arrival of the gangs there is, of course,

more violence and death. I buried a young man 21 years old a week ago. Most of the people that I bury are between the ages of 18 and 30."

He stops the car next to a weed-choked lot close to the corner of Sixteenth and Hamlin. "Dr. King," he says, "lived on this corner." There is no memorial. The city, I later learn, flattened the building after Dr. King moved out. A broken truck now occupies the place where Dr. King resided. From an open side door of the truck, a very old man is selling pizza slices. Next door is a store called Jumbo Liquors. A menacing group of teen-age boys is standing on the corner of the lot where Dr. King lived with his family. "Kids like these will kill each other over nothing—for a warm-up jacket," says the pastor.

"There are good people in this neighborhood," he says, "determined and persistent and strong-minded people who have character and virtues you do not see everywhere. You say to yourself, 'There's something here that's being purified by pain.' All the veneers, all the façades, are burnt away and you see something genuine and beautiful that isn't often found among the affluent. I see it in children—in the youngest children sometimes. Beautiful sweet natures. It's as if they are refined by their adversity. But you cannot sentimentalize. The odds they face are hellish and, for many, many people that I know, life here is simply unendurable.

"Dr. King once said that he had met his match here in Chicago. He said that he faced more bigotry and hatred here than anywhere he'd been in the Deep South. Now he's gone. The weeds have overgrown his memory. I sometimes wonder if the kids who spend their lives out on that corner would be shocked, or even interested, to know that he had lived there once. If you told them, I suspect you'd get a shrug at most. . . ."

On a clear October day in 1990, the voices of children in the first-floor hallway of the Mary McLeod Bethune School in North Lawndale are as bright and optimistic as the voices of small children anywhere. The school, whose students are among the poorest in the city, serves one of the neighborhoods in which the infant death rate is particularly high. Nearly 1,000 infants die within these very poor Chicago neighborhoods each year. An additional 3,000 infants are delivered with brain damage or with other forms of neurological impairment But, entering a kindergarten classroom on this autumn morning, one would have no sense that anything was wrong. Kindergarten classes almost anywhere are cheerful places, and whatever damage may already have been done to children here is not initially apparent to a visitor.

When the children lie down on the floor to have their naps, I sit and watch their movements and their breathing. A few of them fall asleep at once, but others are restless and three little boys keep poking one another when the teacher looks away. Many tiny coughs and whispers interrupt the silence for a while.

The teacher is not particularly gentle. She snaps at the ones who squirm around—"Relax!" and "Sleep!"—and forces down their arms and knees.

A little boy lying with his head close to my feet looks up, with his eyes wide open, at the ceiling. Another, lying on his stomach, squints at me with one eye while the other remains closed. Two little girls, one in blue jeans, one in purple tights, are sound asleep.

The room is sparse: a large and clean but rather cheerless space. There are very few of those manipulable objects and bright-colored shelves and boxes that adorn suburban kindergarten classrooms. The only decorations on the walls are posters supplied by companies that market school materials: "Winter," "Spring," "Summer," "Autumn," "Zoo Animals," "Community Helpers." Nothing the children or teacher made themselves.

As the minutes pass, most of the children seem to sleep, some of them with their arms flung out above their heads, others with their hands beneath their cheeks, though four or five are wide awake and stare with boredom at the ceiling.

On the door is a classroom chart ("Watch us grow!" it says) that measures every child's size and weight. Nakisha, according to the chart, is 38 inches tall and weighs 40 pounds. Lashonda, is 42 inches and weighs 45. Seneca is only 36 inches tall. He weighs only 38.

After 30 minutes pass, the teacher tells the children to sit up. Five of the boys who were most restless suddenly are sound asleep. The others sit up. The teacher tells them, "Folded hands!" They fold their hands. "Wiggle your toes!" They wiggle their toes. "Touch your nose!" They touch their noses.

The teacher questions them about a trip they made the week before. "Where did we go?" The children answer, "Farm!" "What did we see?" The children answer, "Sheep!" "What did we feed them?" A child yells out, "Soup!" The teacher reproves him: "You weren't there! What is the right answer?" The other children answer, "Corn!"

In a somewhat mechanical way, the teacher lifts a picture book of Mother Goose and flips the pages as the children sit before her on the rug.

"Mary had a little lamb, its fleece was white as snow. . . . Old Mother Hubbard went to the cupboard to fetch her poor dog a bone. . . . Jack and Jill went up the hill. . . . This little piggy went to market. . . ."

The children recite the verses with her as she turns

the pages of the book. She's not very warm or animated as she does it, but the children are obedient and seem to like the fun of showing that they know the words. The book looks worn and old, as if the teacher's used it many, many years, and it shows no signs of adaptation to the race of the black children in the school. Mary is white. Old Mother Hubbard is white. Jack is white. Jill is white. Little Jack Horner is white. Mother Goose is white. Only Mother Hubbard's dog is black.

"Baa, baa, black sheep," the teacher reads, "have you any wool?" The children answer: "Yessir, yessir, three bags full. One for my master. . . ." The master is white. The sheep are black.

Four little boys are still asleep on the green rug an hour later when I leave the room. I stand at the door and look at the children, most of whom are sitting at a table now to have their milk. Nine years from now, most of these children will go on to Manley High School, an enormous, ugly building just a block away that has a graduation rate of only 38 percent. Twelve years from now, by junior year of high school, if the neighborhood statistics hold true for these children, 14 of these 23 boys and girls will have dropped out of school. Fourteen years from now, four of these kids, at most, will go to college. Eighteen years from now, one of those four may graduate from college, but three of the 12 boys in this kindergarten will already have spent time in prison.

If one stands here in this kindergarten room and does not know these things, the moment seems auspicious. But if one knows the future that awaits them, it is terrible to see their eyes look up at you with friendliness and trust—to see this and to know what is in store for them.

* * *

In a fifth grade classroom on the third floor of the school, the American flag is coated with chalk and bunched around a pole above a blackboard with no writing on it. There are a couple of pictures of leaves against the windowpanes but nothing like the richness and the novelty and fullness of expression of the children's creativity that one would see in better schools where principals insist that teachers fill their rooms with art and writing by the children. The teacher is an elderly white woman with a solid bun of sensible gray hair and a depleted grayish mood about her. Among the 30 children in the room, the teacher says that several, all of whom are black, are classified "learning disabled."

The children are doing a handwriting lesson when I enter. On a board at the back of the room the teacher has written a line of letters in the standard cursive script. The children sit at their desks and fill entire pages with these letters. It is the kind of lesson that is generally done in second grade in a suburban school. The teacher seems bored by the lesson, and the children seem to feel this and compound her boredom with their own. Next she does a social studies lesson on the Bering Strait and spends some time in getting the class to give a definition of a "strait." About half of the children pay attention. The others don't talk or interrupt or fidget. They are well enough behaved but seem sedated by the teacher's voice.

Another fifth grade teacher stops me in the corridor to ask me what I'm doing in the building. He's 50 years old, he tells me, and grew up here in North Lawndale when it was a middle-class white neighborhood but now lives in the suburbs. "I have a low fifth grade," he says without enthusiasm, then—although he scarcely knows me—launches into an attack upon the principal, the neighborhood and the school.

"It's all a game," he says. "Keep them in class for seven years and give them a diploma if they make it to eighth grade. They can't read, but give them the diploma. The parents don't know what's going on. They're satisfied."

When I ask him if the lack of money and resources is a problem in the school, he looks amused by this. "Money would be helpful but it's not the major factor," he replies. "The parents are the problem."

The principal, Warren Franczyk, later tells me this: "Teachers are being dumped from high school jobs because of low enrollment. But if they've got tenure they cannot be fired so we get them here. I've got two of them as subs right now and one as a permanent teacher. He's not used to children of this age and can't control them. But I have no choice."

The city runs a parallel system of selective schools— some of which are known as "magnet" schools—and these schools, the principal tells me, do not have the staffing problems that he faces. "They can select their teachers and their pupils, So it represents a drain on us. They attract the more sophisticated families, and it leaves us with less motivated children."

Chicago, he tells me, does not have a junior high school system. Students begin Bethune in kindergarten and remain here through eighth grade. Eighth grade graduation, here as elsewhere in Chicago, is regarded as a time for celebration, much as twelfth grade graduation would be celebrated in the suburbs. So there are parties, ball gowns and tuxedos, everything that other kids would have at high school graduation. "For more than half our children," says the principal, "this is the last thing they will have to celebrate."

* * *

Even in the most unhappy schools there are certain classes that stand out like little islands of excitement, energy and hope. One of these classes is a combination fifth and sixth grade at Bethune, taught by a woman, maybe 40 years of age, named Corla Hawkins.

The classroom is full of lively voices when I enter. The children are at work, surrounded by a clutter of big dictionaries, picture books and gadgets, science games and plants and colorful milk cartons, which the teacher purchased out of her own salary. An oversized Van Gogh collection, open to a print of a sunflower, is balanced on a table-ledge next to a fish tank and a turtle tank. Next to the table is a rocking chair. Handwritten signs are on all sides: "Getting to know you," "Keeping you safe," and, over a wall that holds some artwork by the children, "Mrs. Hawkins's Academy of Fine Arts." Near the windows, the oversized leaves of several wild-looking plants partially cover rows of novels, math books, and a new World Book Encyclopedia. In the opposite corner is a "Science Learning Board" that holds small packets which contain bulb sockets, bulbs and wires, lenses, magnets, balance scales and pliers. In front of the learning board is a microscope. Several rugs are thrown around the floor. On another table are a dozen soda bottles sealed with glue and lying sideways, filled with colored water.

The room looks like a cheerful circus tent. In the center of it all, within the rocking chair, and cradling a newborn in her arms, is Mrs. Hawkins.

The 30 children in the class are seated in groups of six at five of what she calls "departments." Each department is composed of six desks pushed together to create a table. One of the groups is doing math, another something that they call "math strategy." A third is doing reading. Of the other two groups, one is doing something they describe as "mathematics art"—painting composites of geometric shapes—and the other is studying "careers," which on this morning is a writing exercise about successful business leaders who began their lives in poverty. Near the science learning board a young-looking woman is preparing a new lesson that involves a lot of gadgets she has taken from a closet.

"This woman," Mrs. Hawkins tells me, "is a parent. She wanted to help me. So I told her, 'If you don't have somebody to keep your baby, bring the baby here. I'll be the mother. I can do it.' "

As we talk, a boy who wears big glasses brings his book to her and asks her what the word *salvation* means. She shows him how to sound it out, then tells him, "Use your dictionary if you don't know what it means." When a boy at the reading table argues with the boy beside him, she yells out, "You ought to be ashamed. You woke my baby."

After 15 minutes she calls out that it is time to change their tables. The children get up and move to new departments. As each group gets up to move to the next table, one child stays behind to introduce the next group to the lesson.

"This is the point of it," she says. "I'm teaching them three things. Number one: self-motivation. Number two: self-esteem. Number three: you help your sister and your brother. I tell them they're responsible for one another. I give no grades in the first marking period because I do not want them to be too competitive. Second marking period, you get your grade on what you've taught your neighbors at your table. Third marking period, I team them two-and-two. You get the same grade as your partner. Fourth marking period, I tell them, 'Every fish swims on its own.' But I wait a while for that. The most important thing for me is that they teach each other. . . .

"All this stuff"—she gestures at the clutter in the

room—"I bought myself because it never works to order things through the school system. I bought the VCR. I bought the rocking chair at a flea market. I got these books here for ten cents apiece at a flea market. I bought that encyclopedia"—she points at the row of World Books—"so that they can do their research right here in this room."

I ask her if the class reads well enough to handle these materials. "Most of them can read some of these books. What they cannot read, another child can read to them," she says.

"I tell the parents, 'Any time your child says, "I don't have no homework," call me up. Call me at home.' Because I give them homework every night and weekends too. Holidays I give them extra. Every child in this classroom has my phone."

Cradling the infant in her lap, she says, "I got to buy a playpen."

The bottles of colored water, she explains, are called "wave bottles." The children make them out of plastic soda bottles which they clean and fill with water and food coloring and seal with glue. She takes one in her hand and rolls it slowly to and fro. "It shows them how waves form," she says. "I let them keep them at their desks. Some of them hold them in their hands while they're at work. It seems to calm them: seeing the water cloud up like a storm and then grow clear. . . .

"I take them outside every day during my teacher-break. On Saturdays we go to places like the art museum. Tuesdays, after school, I coach the drill team. Friday afternoons I tutor parents for their GED [high school equivalency exam]. If you're here this afternoon, I do the gospel choir."

When I ask about her own upbringing, she replies,

"I went to school here in Chicago. My mother believed I was a 'gifted' child, but the system did not challenge me and I was bored at school. Fortunately one of my mother's neighbors was a teacher and she used to talk to me and help me after school. If it were not for her I doubt that I'd have thought that I could go to college. I promised myself I would return that favor."

At the end of class I go downstairs to see the principal, and then return to a second-floor room to see the gospel choir in rehearsal. When I arrive, they've already begun. Thirty-five children, ten of whom are boys, are standing in rows before a piano player. Next to the piano, Mrs. Hawkins stands and leads them through the words. The children range in age from sixth and seventh graders to three second graders and three tiny children, one of whom is Mrs. Hawkins's daughter, who are kindergarten pupils in the school.

They sing a number of gospel songs with Mrs. Hawkins pointing to each group—soprano, alto, bass— when it is their turn to join in. When they sing, "I love you, Lord," their voices lack the energy she wants. She interrupts and shouts at them, "Do you love Him? Do you?" They sing louder. The children look as if they're riveted to her directions.

"This next song," she says, "I dreamed about this. This song is my favorite."

The piano begins. The children start to clap their hands. When she gives the signal they begin to sing:

> Clap your hands!
> Stamp your feet!
> Get on up
> Out of your seats!
> Help me

Lift 'em up, Lord!
Help me
Lift 'em up!

When a child she calls "Reverend Joe" does not come in at the right note, Mrs. Hawkins stops and says to him: "I thought you told me you were saved!"

The children smile. The boy called "Reverend Joe" stands up a little straighter. Then the piano starts again. The sound of children clapping and then stamping with the music fills the room. Mrs. Hawkins waves her arms. Then, as the children start, she also starts to sing.

Help me lift 'em up, Lord!
Help me lift 'em up!

There are wonderful teachers such as Corla Hawkins almost everywhere in urban schools, and sometimes a number of such teachers in a single school. It is tempting to focus on these teachers and, by doing this, to paint a hopeful portrait of the good things that go on under adverse conditions. There is, indeed, a growing body of such writing; and these books are sometimes very popular, because they are consoling.

The rationale behind much of this writing is that pedagogic problems in our cities are not chiefly matters of injustice, inequality or segregation, but of insufficient information about teaching strategies: If we could simply learn "what works" in Corla Hawkins's room, we'd then be in a position to repeat this all over Chicago and in every other system.

But what is unique in Mrs. Hawkins's classroom is not what she does but who she is. Warmth and humor and contagious energy cannot be replicated and cannot be written into any standardized curriculum. If they could, it would have happened long ago; for wonderful teachers have been heroized in books and movies for at least three decades. And the problems of Chicago are, in any case, not those of insufficient information. If Mrs. Hawkins's fellow fifth grade teachers simply needed information, they could get it easily by walking 20 steps across the hall and visiting her room. The problems are systemic: The number of teachers over 60 years of age in the Chicago system is twice that of the teachers under 30. The salary scale, too low to keep exciting, youthful teachers in the system, leads the city to rely on low-paid subs, who represent more than a quarter of Chicago's teaching force. "We have teachers," Mrs. Hawkins says, "who only bother to come in three days a week. One of these teachers comes in usually around nine-thirty. You ask her how she can expect the kids to care about their education if the teacher doesn't even come until nine-thirty. She answers you, 'It makes no difference. Kids like these aren't going anywhere.' The school board thinks it's saving money on the subs. I tell them, 'Pay now or pay later.'"

But even substitute teachers in Chicago are quite frequently in short supply. On an average morning in Chicago, 5,700 children in 190 classrooms come to school to find they have no teacher. The number of children who have no teachers on a given morning in Chicago's public schools is nearly twice the student population of New Trier High School in nearby Winnetka.

"We have been in this class a whole semester," says a 15-year-old at Du Sable High, one of Chicago's poorest secondary schools, "and they still can't find us a teacher."

A student in auto mechanics at Du Sable says he'd been in class for 16 weeks before he learned to change a tire. His first teacher quit at the beginning of the year. Another teacher slept through most of the semester. He would come in, the student says, and tell the students, "You can talk. Just keep it down." Soon he would be asleep.

"Let's be real," the student says. "Most of us ain't going to college.... We could have used a class like this."

The shortage of teachers finds its parallel in a shortage of supplies. A chemistry teacher at the school reports that he does not have beakers, water, bunsen burners. He uses a popcorn popper as a substitute for a bunsen burner, and he cuts down plastic soda bottles to make laboratory dishes.

Many of these schools make little effort to instruct their failing students. "If a kid comes in not reading," says an English teacher at Chicago's South Shore High, "he goes out not reading."

Another teacher at the school, where only 170 of 800 freshmen graduate with their class, indicates that the dropout rate makes teaching easier. "We lose all the dregs by the second year," he says.

"We're a general high school," says the head of counseling at Chicago's Calumet High School. "We have second and third grade readers.... We hope to do better, but we won't die if we don't."

At Bowen High School, on the South Side of Chicago, students have two or three "study halls" a day, in part to save the cost of teachers. "Not much studying goes on in study hall," a supervising teacher says. "I let the students play cards.... I figure they might get some math skills out of it."

At the Lathrop Elementary School, a short walk from the corner lot where Dr. King resided in North Lawndale, there are no hoops on the basketball court and no swings in the playground. For 21 years, according to the *Chicago Tribune,* the school has been without a library. Library books, which have been piled and abandoned in the lunch room of the school, have "sprouted mold," the paper says. Some years ago the school received the standard reading textbooks out of sequence: The second workbook in the reading program came to the school before the first. The principal, uncertain what to do with the wrong workbook, was told by school officials it was "all right to work backwards. . . ."

This degree of equanimity in failure, critics note, has led most affluent parents in Chicago to avoid the public system altogether. The school board president in 1989, although a teacher and administrator in the system for three decades, did not send his children to the public schools. Nor does Mayor Richard Daley, Jr., nor did any of the previous four mayors who had school-age children.

"Nobody in his right mind," says one of the city's aldermen "would send [his] kids to public school."

Many suburban legislators representing afflu- ent school districts use terms such as "sinkhole" when opposing funding for Chicago's children. "We can't keep throwing money," said Governor Thompson in 1988, "into a black hole."

The *Chicago Tribune* notes that, when this phrase is used, people hasten to explain that it is not intended as a slur against the race of many of Chicago's children. "But race," says the *Tribune*, "never is far from the surface. . . ."

As spring comes to Chicago, the scarcity of sub- stitutes grows more acute. On Mondays and Fridays in early May, nearly 18,000 children—the equivalent of all the elementary students in suburban Glencoe, Wilmette, Glenview, Kenilworth, Winnetka, Deerfield, Highland Park and Evanston—are assigned to classes with no teacher.

In this respect, the city's dropout rate of nearly 50

percent is regarded by some people as a blessing. If over 200,000 of Chicago's total student population of 440,000 did not disappear during their secondary years, it is not clear who would teach them.

In 1989, Chicago spent some $5,500 for each student in its secondary schools. This may be compared to an investment of some $8,500 to $9,000 in each high school student in the highest-spending suburbs to the north. Stated in the simplest terms, this means that any high school class of 30 children in Chicago received approximately $90,000 less each year than would have been spent on them if they were pupils of a school such as New Trier High.

The difference in spending between very wealthy suburbs and poor cities is not always as extreme as this in Illinois. When relative student needs, however, have been factored into the discussion, the disparities in funding are enormous. Equity, after all, does not mean simply equal funding. Equal funding for unequal needs is not equality. The need is greater in Chicago, and its children, if they are to have approximately equal opportunities, need more than the children who attend New Trier. Seen in this light, the $90,000 annual difference is quite startling.

Lack of money is not the only problem in Chicago, but the gulf in funding we have seen is so remarkable and seems so blatantly unfair that it strikes many thoughtful citizens at first as inexplicable. How can it be that inequalities as great as these exist in neighboring school districts?

The answer is found, at least in part, in the arcane machinery by which we finance public education. Most public schools in the United States depend for their initial funding on a tax on local property. There are also state and federal funding sources, and we will discuss them later, but the property tax is the decisive force in shaping inequality. The property tax depends, of course, upon the taxable value of one's home and that of local industries. A typical wealthy suburb in which homes are often worth more than $400,000 draws upon a larger tax base in proportion to its student population than a city occupied by thousands of poor people. Typically, in the United States, very poor communities place high priority on education, and they often tax themselves at higher rates than do the very affluent communities. But, even if they tax themselves at several times the rate of an extremely wealthy district, they are likely to end up with far less money for each child in their schools.

Because the property tax is counted as a tax deduction by the federal government, home-owners in a wealthy suburb get back a substantial portion of the money that they spend to fund their children's schools— effectively, a federal subsidy for an unequal education. Home-owners in poor districts get this subsidy as well, but, because their total tax is less, the subsidy is less. The mortgage interest that homeowners pay is also treated as a tax deduction—in effect, a second federal subsidy. These subsidies, as I have termed them, are considerably larger than most people understand. In 1984, for instance, property-tax deductions granted by the federal government were $9 billion. An additional $23 billion in mortgage-interest deductions were provided to home-owners: a total of some $32 billion. Federal grants to local schools, in contrast, totaled only $7 billion, and only part of this was earmarked for low-income districts. Federal policy, in this respect, increases the existing gulf between the richest and the poorest schools.

All of these disparities are also heightened, in the case of larger cities like Chicago, by the disproportionate number of entirely tax-free institutions—colleges and hospitals and art museums, for instance—that are sited in such cities. In some cities, according to Jonathan Wilson, former chairman of the Council of Urban Boards of Education, 30 percent or more of the potential tax base is exempt from taxes, compared to as little as 3 percent in the adjacent suburbs. Suburbanites, of course, enjoy the use of these nonprofit, tax-free institutions; and, in the case of private colleges and universities, they are far *more* likely to enjoy their use than are the residents of inner cities.

Cities like Chicago face the added problem that an overly large portion of their limited tax revenues must be diverted to meet nonschool costs that wealthy suburbs do not face, or only on a far more modest scale. Police expenditures are higher in crime-ridden cities than in most suburban towns. Fire department costs are also higher where dilapidated housing, often with substandard wiring, and arson-for-profit are familiar problems. Public health expenditures are also higher where poor people cannot pay for private hospitals. All of these expenditures compete with those for public schools. So the districts that face the toughest challenges are also likely to be those that have the fewest funds to meet their children's needs.

Many people, even those who view themselves as liberals on other issues, tend to grow indignant, even rather agitated, if invited to look closely at these inequalities. "Life isn't fair," one parent in Winnetka answered flatly when I pressed the matter. "Wealthy children also go to summer camp. All summer. Poor kids maybe not at all. Or maybe, if they're lucky, for two weeks. Wealthy children have the chance to go to Europe and they have the access to good libraries, encyclopedias, computers, better doctors, nicer homes. Some of my neighbors send their kids to schools like Exeter and Groton. Is government supposed to equalize these things as well?"

But government, of course, does not assign us to our homes, our summer camps, our doctors—or to Exeter. It does assign us to our public schools. Indeed, it forces us to go to them. Unless we have the wealth to pay for private education, we are compelled by law to go to public school—and to the public school in our district. Thus the state, by requiring attendance but refusing to require equity, effectively requires inequality. Compulsory inequity, perpetuated by state law, too frequently condemns our children to unequal lives.

In Illinois, as elsewhere in America, local funds for education raised from property taxes are supplemented by state contributions and by federal funds, although the federal contribution is extremely small, constituting only 6 percent of total school expenditures. State contributions represent approximately half of local school expenditures in the United States; although intended to make up for local wealth disparities, they have seldom been sufficient to achieve this goal. Total yearly spending—local funds combined with state assistance and the small amount that comes from Washington—ranges today in Illinois from $2,100 on a child in the poorest district to above $10,000 in the richest. The system, writes John Coons, a professor of law at Berkeley University, "bears the appearance of calculated unfairness."

There is a belief advanced today, and in some cases by conservative black authors, that poor children and particularly black children should not be allowed to hear too much about these matters. If they learn how much less they are getting than rich children, we are told, this knowledge may induce them to regard themselves as "victims," and such "victim-thinking," it is argued, may then undermine their capability to profit from whatever opportunities may actually exist. But this is a matter of psychology—or strategy—and not reality. The matter, in any case, is academic since most adolescents in the poorest neighborhoods learn very soon that they are getting less than children in the wealthier school districts. They see suburban schools on television and they see them when they travel for athletic competitions. It is a waste of time to worry whether we should tell them something they could tell to us. About injustice, most poor children in America cannot be fooled.

Children, of course, don't understand at first that they are being cheated. They come to school with a degree of faith and optimism, and they often seem to thrive during the first few years. It is sometimes not until the third grade that their teachers start to see the warning signs of failure. By the fourth grade many children see it too.

"These kids are aware of their failures," says a fourth grade teacher in Chicago. "Some of them act like the game's already over."

By fifth or sixth grade, many children demonstrate their loss of faith by staying out of school. The director of a social service agency in Chicago's Humboldt Park estimates that 10 percent of the 12- and 13-year-old children that he sees are out of school for all but one or two days every two weeks. The route from truancy to full-fledged dropout status is direct and swift. Reverend Charles Kyle, a professor at Loyola University, believes that 10 percent of students in Chicago drop out prior to their high school years, usually after seventh or eighth grade—an estimate that I have also heard from several teachers. This would put the city's actual dropout rate, the *Chicago Tribune* estimates, at "close to 60 percent."

Even without consideration of these early dropouts or of the *de facto* dropouts who show up at school a couple of times a month but still are listed as enrolled—excluding all of this and simply going by official school board numbers—the attrition rates in certain of the poorest neighborhoods are quite remarkable. For children who begin their school career at Andersen Elementary School, for instance, the high school dropout rate is 76 percent. For those who begin at the McKinley School, it is 81 percent. For those who start at Woodson Elementary School, the high school dropout rate is 86 percent. These schools—which Fred Hess of the Chicago Panel on School Policy and Finance, a respected watchdog group, calls "dumping grounds" for kids with special problems—are among the city's worst; but, even for children who begin their schooling at Bethune and then go on to nearby Manley High, the dropout rate, as we have seen, is 62 percent.

Not all of the kids who get to senior year and finish it and graduate, however, will have reading skills at high school level. Citywide, 27 percent of high school graduates read at the eighth grade level or below; and a large proportion of these students read at less than sixth grade level. Adding these children to the many dropouts who have never learned to read beyond the grade-school level, we may estimate that nearly half the kindergarten children in Chicago's public schools will exit school as marginal illiterates.

Reading levels are the lowest in the poorest schools. In a survey of the 18 high schools with the highest rates of poverty within their student populations, Designs for Change, a research center in Chicago, notes that only 3.5 percent of students graduate and also read up to the national norm. Some 6,700 children enter ninth grade in these 18 schools each year. Only 300 of these students, says Don Moore, director of Designs for Change, "both graduate and read at or above the national average." Those very few who graduate and go to college rarely read well enough to handle college-level courses. At the city's community colleges, which receive most of their students from Chicago's public schools, the noncompletion rate is 97 percent. Of 35,000 students working toward degrees in the community colleges that serve Chicago, only 1,000 annually complete the program and receive degrees.

Looking at these failure rates again—and particularly at the reading scores of high school graduates—it is difficult to know what argument a counselor can make to tell a failing student that she ought to stay in school, except perhaps to note that a credential will, statistically, improve her likelihood of finding work. In strictly pedagogic terms, the odds of failure for a student who starts out at Woodson Elementary School, and then continues at a nonselective high school, are approximately ten to one. The odds of learning math and reading on the street are probably as good or even better. The odds of finding a few moments of delight, or maybe even happiness, outside these dreary schools are better still. For many, many students at Chicago's nonselective high schools, it is hard to know if a decision to drop out of school, no matter how much we discourage it, is not, in fact, a logical decision.

The one great exception in Chicago is the situation that exists for children who can win admission to the magnet or selective schools: The *Chicago Tribune* has called the magnet system, in effect, "a private school system . . . operated in the public schools." Very poor children, excluded from this system, says the *Tribune,* are "even more isolated" as a consequence of the removal of the more successful students from their midst.

The magnet system is, not surprisingly, highly attractive to the more sophisticated parents, disproportionately white and middle class, who have the ingenuity and, now and then, political connections to obtain admission for their children. It is also viewed by some of its defenders as an ideal way to hold white people in the public schools by offering them "choices" that resemble what they'd find in private education. "Those the system chooses to save," says the *Tribune,* "are the brightest youngsters, selected by race, income and achievement" for "magnet schools where teachers are hand-picked" and which "operate much like private institutions."

Children who have had the benefits of preschool and one of the better elementary schools are at a great advantage in achieving entrance to selective high schools; but an even more important factor seems to be the social class and education level of their parents. This is the case because the system rests on the initiative of parents. The poorest parents, often the products of inferior education, lack the information access and the skills of navigation in an often hostile and intimidating situation to channel their children to the better schools, obtain the applications, and (perhaps a little more important) help them to get ready for the necessary tests and then persuade their elementary schools to recommend them. So, even in poor black neighborhoods, it tends to be children of the less poor and the better educated who are likely to break through the obstacles and win admission.

The system has the surface aspects of a meritocracy, but merit in this case is predetermined by conditions that are closely tied to class and race. While some defend it as, in theory, "the survival of the fittest," it is more accurate to call it the survival of the children of the fittest—or

of the most favored. Similar systems exist in every major
city. They are defended stoutly by those who succeed in
getting into the selective schools.

The parallel system extends to elementary schools
as well. A recent conflict around one such school illus-
trates the way the system pits the middle class against the
poor. A mostly middle-income condominium development was built close to a public housing project known as
Hilliard Homes. The new development, called Dearborn
Park, attracted a number of young professionals, many
of whom were fairly affluent white people, who asked
the school board to erect a new school for their children.
This request was honored and the South Loop Elementary School was soon constructed. At this point a bitter
struggle ensued. The question: Who would get to go to
the new school?

The parents from Dearborn Park insist that, if the
school is attended by the children from the projects—
these are the children who have lived there all along—the
standards of the school will fall. The school, moreover,
has a special "fine arts" magnet program; middle-class
children, drawn to the school from other sections of Chicago, are admitted. So the effort to keep out the kids who
live right in the neighborhood points up the class and
racial factors. The city, it is noted, had refused to build
a new school for the project children when they were
the only children in the neighborhood. Now that a new
school has been built, they find themselves excluded.

The Dearborn parents have the political power to
obtain agreement from the Board of Education to enter
their children beginning in kindergarten but to keep the
Hilliard children out until third grade—by which time,
of course, the larger numbers of these poorer children
will be at a disadvantage and will find it hard to keep up
with the children who were there since kindergarten. In

the interim, according to the *New York Times,* the younger children from the project are obliged to go to class within "a temporary branch school" in "a small, prefabricated metal building surrounded on three sides by junkyards."

The Chicago Panel on Public School Policy and Finance tells the press that it "is only fair" to let the kids from Hilliard Homes share in the resources "that the middle-class kids enjoy." The panel also notes that poorer children do not tend to bring the top kids down. "It is more likely that the high-achieving kids will bring the others up." But the truth is that few middle-class parents in Chicago, or in any other city, honestly believe this. They see the poorer children as a tide of mediocrity that threatens to engulf them. They are prepared to see those children get their schooling in a metal prefab in a junkyard rather than admit them to the beautiful new school erected for their own kids.

The conflict around South Loop Elementary in Chicago helps to illustrate some of the reasons for the reservations that black leaders sometimes voice about the prospect of a fully implemented plan for "schools of choice"—a notion strongly favored by the White House and, particularly, by Mr. Bush: If the children of the Hilliard project are successfully excluded from the magnet school across the street, how much harder will it be to get those children into magnet schools in other sections of the city? And will those children "choose" to go to "schools of choice" if it is made clear they are not wanted? This is an example of the ways that people may be taught to modify and to restrict their choices. The parents, of course, conditioned already by a lifetime of such lessons, may not even need to have their dreams further restricted. The energy to break out of their isolation may have atrophied already.

School boards think that, if they offer the same

printed information to all parents, they have made choice equally accessible. That is not true, of course, because the printed information won't be read, or certainly will not be scrutinized aggressively, by parents who can't read or who read very poorly. But, even if a city could contrive a way to get the basic facts disseminated widely, can it disseminate audacity as well? Can it disseminate the limitless horizons of the middle class to those who have been trained to keep their eyes close to ground?

People can only choose among the things they've heard of. That is one problem that a "choice" plan must confront. But it is no less true that they can only choose the things they think they have a right to and the things they have some reason to believe they will receive. People who have forever been turned down by neighborhoods where they have looked for housing and by hospitals where they have looked for care when they were ill are not likely to have hopeful expectations when it comes to public schools.

The White House, in advancing the agenda for a "choice" plan, rests its faith on market mechanisms. What reason have the black and very poor to lend their credence to a market system that has proved so obdurate and so resistant to their pleas at every turn? Placing the burden on the individual to break down doors in finding better education for a child is attractive to conservatives because it reaffirms their faith in individual ambition and autonomy. But to ask an individual to break down doors that we have chained and bolted in advance of his arrival is unfair.

There are conscientious people who believe that certain types of "choice" within the public schools can help to stimulate variety and foster deeper feelings of empowerment in parents. There are also certain models—in East Harlem in New York, for instance—which suggest that this is sometimes possible; but these models are the ones that also place a high priority on not excluding children of the less successful and less knowledgeable parents and, in the East Harlem situation, they are also models that grew out of social activism, and their faculty and principals continue to address the overarching inequalities that render their experiment almost unique. Without these countervailing forces—and they are not often present—"choice" plans of the kind the White House has proposed threaten to compound the present fact of racial segregation with the added injury of caste discrimination, further isolating those who, like the kids at Hilliard Homes, have been forever, as it seems, consigned to places *nobody* would choose if he had any choice at all.

In a system where the better teachers and the more successful students are attracted to the magnet and selective schools, neighborhood schools must settle for the rest. "I take anything that walks in," says the principal of Goudy Elementary School.

Far from the worst school in Chicago, Goudy's building is nonetheless depressing. According to Bonita Brodt, a writer for the *Chicago Tribune* who spent several months at Goudy during 1988, teachers use materials in class long since thrown out in most suburban schools. Slow readers in an eighth grade history class are taught from 15-year-old textbooks in which Richard Nixon is still president. There are no science labs, no art or music teachers. There is no playground. There are no swings. There is no jungle gym. Soap, paper towels and toilet paper are in short supply. There are two working bathrooms for some 700 children.

These children "cry out for something more. . . .

They do not get it," says Ms. Brodt, whose *Tribune* article I have relied upon for this description of a school in
trouble.

"Keisha, look at me," an adult shouts at a slow reader
in a sixth grade class. "Look me in the eye." Keisha has
been fighting with her classmate. Over what? As it turns
out, over a crayon. The child is terrified and starts to cry.
Tears spill out of her eyes and drop onto the pages of her
math book. In January the school begins to ration crayons, pencils, writing paper.

Keisha's teacher is a permanent sub who, according
to the *Tribune,* doesn't want to teach this class but has
no choice. "It was my turn," the teacher says. "I have
a room of 39 overage, unmotivated sixth and seventh
graders. . . . I am not prepared for this. I have absolutely
no idea of what to do."

"All right, we must read," another teacher at Goudy
announces to a third grade class. She stands in the middle of the room, her glasses askew, holding a teacher's
manual that tells her what to do. The room is in chaos.
A child is passing out red construction paper to her
friends. Another is busy at the pencil sharpener.

The teacher looks around and blinks and eyes the
child at the pencil sharpener. The child at the pencil
sharpener says, "I got to sharpen my pencil."

"Your pencil is sharp," the teacher says.

The child makes a face and breaks her pencil point
to spite the teacher.

Three years ago, the *Tribune* explains, this teacher
received "official warning" at another elementary school.
Transferred here, but finding herself unable to control
the class, she was removed in March. Instead of firing
her, however, the principal returned her to the children
for their morning reading class. It is a class of "academi-

cally deficient children." But the teacher does not know how to teach reading.

On the third floor, in a barren-looking room, a teacher observed by the *Tribune*'s reporter gives a sharp tongue-lashing to his 33 sixth graders. "If you're stupid, sit there like a dummy," he says to a boy who cannot estimate a quotient.

To punish the children for their poor behavior, he makes them climb and then descend three flights of stairs for half an hour.

"I'm the SOB of the third floor," he says.

The bleakness of the children's lives is underlined by one of Goudy's third grade teachers: "I passed out dictionaries once. . . . One of my students started ripping out the pages when he found a word. I said, 'What are you doing? You leave the pages there for the next person.' And he told me, 'That's their problem. This is my word.' "

Children who go to school in towns like Glencoe and Winnetka do not need to steal words from a dictionary. Most of them learn to read by second or third grade. By the time they get to sixth or seventh grade, many are reading at the level of the seniors in the best Chicago high schools. By the time they enter ninth grade at New Trier High, they are in a world of academic possibilities that far exceed the hopes and dreams of most schoolchildren in Chicago.

"Our goal is for students to be successful," says the New Trier principal. With 93 percent of seniors going on to four-year colleges—many to schools like Harvard, Princeton, Berkeley, Brown and Yale—this goal is largely realized.

New Trier's physical setting might well make the

students of Du Sable High School envious. The *Washington Post* describes a neighborhood of "circular driveways, chirping birds and white-columned homes." It is, says a student, "a maple land of beauty and civility." While Du Sable is sited on one crowded city block, New Trier students have the use of 27 acres. While Du Sable's science students have to settle for makeshift equipment, New Trier's students have superior labs and up-to-date technology. One wing of the school, a physical education center that includes three separate gyms, also contains a fencing room, a wrestling room and studios for dance instruction. In all, the school has seven gyms as well as an Olympic pool.

The youngsters, according to a profile of the school in *Town and Country* magazine, "make good use of the huge, well-equipped building, which is immaculately maintained by a custodial staff of 48."

It is impossible to read this without thinking of a school like Goudy, where there are no science labs, no music or art classes and no playground—and where the two bathrooms, lacking toilet paper, fill the building with their stench.

"This is a school with a lot of choices," says one student at New Trier; and this hardly seems an overstatement if one studies the curriculum. Courses in music, art and drama are so varied and abundant that students can virtually major in these subjects in addition to their academic programs. The modern and classical language department offers Latin (four years) and six other foreign languages. Elective courses include the literature of Nobel winners, aeronautics, criminal justice, and computer languages. In a senior literature class, students are reading Nietzsche, Darwin, Plato, Freud and Goethe. The school also operates a television station with a broadcast license from the FCC, which broadcasts on four channels to three counties.

Average class size is 24 children; classes for slower learners hold 15. This may be compared to Goudy—where a remedial class holds 39 children and a "gifted" class has 36.

Every freshman at New Trier is assigned a faculty adviser who remains assigned to him or her through graduation. Each of the faculty advisers—they are given a reduced class schedule to allow them time for this—gives counseling to about two dozen children. At Du Sable, where the lack of staff prohibits such reduction in class schedules, each of the guidance counselors advises 420 children.

The ambience among the students at New Trier, of whom only 1.3 percent are black, says *Town and Country,* is "wholesome and refreshing, a sort of throwback to the Fifties." It is, we are told, "a preppy kind of place." In a cheerful photo of the faculty and students, one cannot discern a single nonwhite face.

New Trier's "temperate climate" is "aided by the homogeneity of its students," *Town and Country* notes. ". . . . Almost all are of European extraction and harbor similar values."

"Eighty to 90 percent of the kids here," says a counselor, "are good, healthy, red-blooded Americans."

The wealth of New Trier's geographical district provides $340,000 worth of taxable property for each child; Chicago's property wealth affords only one-fifth this much. Nonetheless, *Town and Country* gives New Trier's parents credit for a "willingness to pay enough . . . in taxes" to make this one of the state's best-funded schools. New Trier, according to the magazine, is "a striking example of what is possible when citizens want to achieve the best for their children." Families move here "seeking the best," and their children "make good use" of what they're given. Both statements may be true, but giving people lavish praise for spending what they have strikes one as disingenuous. "A supportive attitude on the part of families in the district translates into a willingness to pay . . . ," the writer says. By this logic, one would be obliged to say that "unsupportive attitudes" on the part of Keisha's mother and the parents of Du Sable's children translate into fiscal selfishness, when, in fact, the economic options open to the parents in these districts are not even faintly comparable. *Town and Country* flatters the privileged for having privilege but terms it aspiration.

"Competition is the lifeblood of New Trier," *Town and Country* writes. But there is one kind of competition that these children will not need to face. They will not compete against the children who attended Goudy and Du Sable. They will compete against each other and against the graduates of other schools attended by rich children. They will not compete against the poor.

It is part of our faith, as Americans, that there is potential in all children. Even among the 700 children who must settle for rationed paper and pencils at Goudy Elementary School, there are surely several dozen, maybe several hundred, who, if given the chance, would thrive and overcome most of the obstacles of poverty if they attended schools like those of Glencoe and Winnetka. We know that very few of them will have that opportunity. Few, as a result, will graduate from high school; fewer still will go to college; scarcely any will attend good colleges. There will be more space for children of New Trier as a consequence.

The denial of opportunity to Keisha and the superfluity of opportunity for children at New Trier High School are not unconnected. The parents of New Trier's feeder districts vote consistently against redistribution of school funding. By a nine-to-one ratio, according to a recent survey, suburban residents resist all efforts to provide more money for Chicago's schools.

Efforts at reform of the Chicago schools have been begun with a new wave of optimism every ten or 15 years. The newest wave, a highly publicized restructuring of governing arrangements that increases the participation of the parents in their children's schools, was launched in 1989. There are those who are convinced that this will someday have a payoff for the children in the poorest schools. Others regard it as a purely mechanistic alteration that cannot address the basic problems of a segregated system isolated by surrounding suburbs which, no matter what the governing arrangements in Chicago, will retain the edge provided by far higher spending and incomparable advantages in physical facilities and teacher salaries. It is, in any case, too soon to draw conclusions. A visitor in 1991, certainly, will see few comprehensive changes for the better.

Certain schools are obviously improved. Goudy, for example, is more cheerful and much better managed than it was three years ago. There is a new principal who seems to be far more demanding of his teachers than his predecessor was, and there are a number of new teachers, and there have been major structural improvements.

Goudy, however, has received so much adverse publicity that it was expected, and predictable, that it would get some extra funds to ward off any further condemnation. School boards, threatened by disturbing reportage, frequently make rapid changes in the schools that are spotlighted by the press. Limited resources guarantee, however, that such changes have to be selective. Extra funds for Goudy's children mean a little less for children somewhere else.

Conditions at Du Sable High School, which I visited in 1990, seem in certain ways to be improved. Improvement, however, is a relative term. Du Sable is better than it was three or four years ago. It is still a school that would be shunned—or, probably, shut down—if it were serving a white middle-class community. The building, a three-story Tudor structure, is in fairly good repair and, in this respect, contrasts with its immediate surroundings, which are almost indescribably despairing. The school, whose student population is 100 percent black, has no campus and no schoolyard, but there is at least a full-sized playing field and track. Overcrowding is not a problem at the school. Much to the reverse, it is uncomfortably empty. Built in 1935 and holding some 4,500 students in past years, its student population is now less than 1,600. Of these students, according to data provided by the school, 646 are "chronic truants."

The graduation rate is 25 percent. Of those who get to senior year, only 17 percent are in a college-preparation program. Twenty percent are in the general curriculum, while a stunning 63 percent are in vocational classes, which most often rule out college education.

A vivid sense of loss is felt by standing in the cafeteria in early spring when students file in to choose their courses for the following year. "These are the ninth graders," says a supervising teacher; but, of the official freshman class of some 600 children, only 350 fill the room. An hour later the eleventh graders come to choose their classes: I count at most 170 students.

The faculty includes some excellent teachers, but there are others, says the principal, who don't belong in education. "I can't do anything with them but I'm not allowed to fire them," he says, as we head up the stairs to visit classes on a day in early June. Entering a biology class, we find a teacher doing absolutely nothing. She tells us that "some of the students have a meeting," but this doesn't satisfy the principal, who leaves the room irate. In a room he calls "the math headquarters," we come upon two teachers watching a soap opera on TV. In a mathematics learning center, seven kids are gazing out the window while the teacher is preoccupied with something at her desk. The principal again appears disheartened.

Top salary in the school, he says, is $40,000. "My faculty is aging. Average age is 47. Competing against the suburbs, where the salaries go up to $60,000, it is very, very hard to keep young teachers. That, you probably know, is an old story. . . . I do insist," he says, "that every student has a book." He says this with some pride and, in the context of Chicago, he has reason to be proud of this; but, in a wealthy nation like America, it is a sad thing to be proud of.

In a twelfth grade English class, the students are learning to pronounce a list of words. The words are not derived from any context; they are simply written on a list. A tall boy struggles hard to read "fastidious," "gregarious," "auspicious," "fatuous." Another reads "dour," "demise," "salubrious," "egregious" and "consommé." Still another reads "aesthetic," "schism," "heinous," "fetish," and "concerto." There is something poignant, and embarrassing, about the effort that these barely literate kids put into handling these odd, pretentious words. When the tall boy struggles to pronounce "egregious," I ask him if he knows its meaning. It turns out that he has no idea. The teacher never asks the children to define the words or use them in a sentence. The lesson baffles me. It may be that these are words that will appear on one of those required tests that states impose now in the name of "raising standards," but it all seems dreamlike and surreal.

After lunch I talk with a group of students who are hoping to go on to college but do not seem sure of what they'll need to do to make this possible. Only one out of five seniors in the group has filed an application, and it is already April. Pamela, the one who did apply, however, tells me she neglected to submit her grades and college-entrance test results and therefore has to start again. The courses she is taking seem to rule out application to a four-year college. She tells me she is taking Spanish, literature, physical education, Afro-American history and a class she terms "job strategy." When I ask her what this is, she says, "It teaches how to dress and be on time and figure your deductions." She's a bright, articulate student, and it seems quite sad that she has not had any of the richness of curriculum that would have been given to her at a high school like New Trier.

The children in the group seem not just lacking in important, useful information that would help them to achieve their dreams, but, in a far more drastic sense, cut off and disconnected from the outside world. In talking of some recent news events, they speak of Moscow and Berlin, but all but Pamela are unaware that Moscow is the capital of the Soviet Union or that Berlin is in Germany. Several believe that Jesse Jackson is the mayor of New York City. Listening to their guesses and observing their confusion, I am thinking of the students at New Trier High. These children live in truly separate worlds. What do they have in common? And yet the kids before me seem so innocent and spiritually clean and also—most of all—so vulnerable. It's as if they have been stripped of all the armament—the words, the reference points, the facts, the reasoning, the elemental weapons—that suburban children take for granted.

At the end of school the principal, Charles Mingo, a heavyset man of 49, stands beside me at a top-floor window and looks out across a line of uniform and ugly 16-story buildings, the Robert Taylor Homes, which constitute, he says, the city's second-poorest neighborhood.

Strutting about beneath us, in the central courtyard of the school, are several peacocks. Most of them are white. A few are black. And two or three are orange-red. The trees and foliage in the courtyard are attractively arranged to give it the appearance of an atrium within an elegant hotel.

"There's so little beauty in my students' lives. I want these kids to come to school and find a little space of something pastoral and lovely. If I had a lot of money I would empty out three of those high-rise buildings, put up a fence and build a residential school. I'd run me a pastoral prep school in the middle of Chicago. Tear another building down. Plant some trees, some grass, some flowers. Build me a patio around a pool. Grow some ivy on those walls. I'd call it Hyde Park West. . . .

"I spent a summer once at Phillips Academy in Massachusetts. Beautiful brick buildings. Trees and lawns. Students walking by those buildings, so at home there, utterly relaxed. I thought to myself: My students need this more than people like George Bush."

He tells me that there is a horticulture teacher in the school. "He's the one that tends the patio. He and the children in his class. That's the kind of thing the back-to-basics folks do not find to their liking. Making flowers grow, I'm told, is not 'essential' and will not improve their chances of employment. 'Get these kids to pass their tests! Forget about the flowers!' We need jobs, of course we do; but we need flowers."

On the wall of his office is a photograph of Martin Luther King surrounded by police within a crowd of angry-looking people. Next to Dr. King there is a heavy-set black man who has been clubbed or pushed down to the street. "That was right here in Chicago. That big man there next to Dr. King—"

"That's you?" I ask.

"No. That's my daddy."

He tells me that the photograph was taken in North Lawndale. "It was an open-housing march. My daddy was his bodyguard. It was a march to Cicero. He got turned back. One of his few defeats. . . .

"What he managed in the South he could not pull off in Chicago. He couldn't march to Cicero. Police would not permit it. They were sure he would be killed. In certain ways that picture says it all. This is where the struggle stopped. You see the consequence around you in this school."

"It took an extraordinary combination of greed, racism, political cowardice and public apathy," writes James D. Squires, the former editor of the *Chicago Tribune,* "to let the public schools in Chicago get so bad." He speaks of the schools as a costly result of "the political orphaning of the urban poor . . . daytime warehouses for inferior students . . . a bottomless pit."

The results of these conditions are observed in thousands of low-income children in Chicago who are virtually disjoined from the entire worldview, even from the basic reference points, of the American experience. A 16-year-old girl who has dropped out of school discusses her economic prospects with a TV interviewer.

"How much money would you like to make in a year?" asks the reporter.

"About $2,000," she replies.

The reporter looks bewildered by this answer. This

teen-age girl, he says, "has no clue that $2,000 a year isn't enough to survive anywhere in America, not even in her world."

This sad young woman, who already has a baby and is pregnant once again, lives in a truly separate universe of clouded hopes and incomplete cognition. "We are creating an entire generation of incompetents," a black sociologist observes. "Her kids will fail. There is a good chance that she'll end up living with a man who is addicted or an alcoholic. She'll be shot or killed, or else her children will be shot or killed, or else her boyfriend will be shot or killed. Drugs will be overwhelmingly attractive to a person living in a world so bare of richness or amenities. No one will remember what we did to her when she was eight years old in elementary school or 15 years old at Du Sable High. No one will remember that her mother might have tried and failed to get her into Head Start when she was a baby. Who knows if her mother even got prenatal care? She may be brain-damaged—or lead-poisoned. Who will ask these questions later on? They will see her as a kind of horrible deformity. Useless too. Maybe a maid. Maybe not. Maybe just another drain upon society."

The students of Du Sable High School are, of course, among the poorest in America. New Trier's children are among the richest. But New Trier is not the only high school in Chicago's suburbs that spends vast amounts of money to assure superb results; nor are Chicago's schools the only ones where poor results and grossly insufficient funding coincide. In 1987, for example, Proviso High School, serving children in the black suburban town of Maywood, spent only about $5,000 for each pupil: virtually the same as what was spent on high school students in Chicago, but $3,000 less than what was spent on children in the highest-spending suburb.

But even Maywood's underfunded schools are not the poorest in the area around Chicago. In East Aurora, Illinois, in 1987, a little girl in the fourth grade received an education costing $2,900. Meanwhile, a little boy the same age in the town of Niles could expect some $7,800 to be spent on each year of his elementary education—a figure that would rise to $8,950 in his secondary years.

Over the course of 13 years, from kindergarten to twelfth grade, $38,000 would be spent on the first child's education, and over $100,000 on the second child's education. If the former child should become one of the casualties of the high dropout rate at East Aurora High, she would receive significantly less—as little as $30,000 worth of education. There was a good chance, moreover, that this child would not finish school. The dropout rate at East Aurora High was 35 percent. In Niles, it was less than 2 percent.

The focus in this book is on the inner-city schools; inevitably, therefore, I am describing classrooms in which almost all the children are black or Latino. But there are also poor and mainly white suburban districts and, of course, some desperately poor and very isolated rural districts. Children in the rural districts of Kentucky, northern Maine, and Arkansas, for instance, face a number of the problems we have seen in East St. Louis and Chicago, though the nature of the poverty in rural schools is often somewhat different. The most important difference in the urban systems, I believe, is that they are often just adjacent to the nation's richest districts, and this ever-present contrast adds a heightened bitterness to the experience of children. The ugliness of racial segregation adds its special injuries as well. It is this killing combination, I believe, that renders life within these urban schools not merely grim but also desperate and often pathological. The fact of destitution is compounded by the sense of being viewed as, somehow, morally infected. The poorest rural schools I've visited feel, simply, bleak. The segregated urban schools feel more like lazarettos.

A recent emphasis of certain business-minded authors writing about children in the kinds of schools we have examined in Chicago urges us to settle for "realistic" goals, by which these authors mean the kinds of limited career objectives that seem logical or fitting for low-income children. Many corporate leaders have resisted this idea, and there are some who hold out high ideals and truly democratic hopes for these low-income children; but other business leaders speak quite openly of "training" kids like these for nothing better than the entry-level jobs their corporations have available. Urban schools, they argue, should dispense with "frills" and focus on "the basics" needed for employment. Emphasis in the suburban schools, they add, should necessarily be more expansive, with a focus upon college preparation.

Investment strategies, according to this logic, should be matched to the potential economic value of each person. Future service workers need a different and, presumably, a lower order of investment than the children destined to be corporate executives, physicians, lawyers, engineers. Future plumbers and future scientists require different schooling—maybe different schools. Segregated education is not necessarily so unattractive by this reasoning.

Early testing to assign each child to a "realistic" course of study, the tracking of children by ability determined by the tests, and the expansion of a parallel system for the children who appear to show the greatest promise (gifted classes and selective schools) are also favored from this vantage point. In terms of sheer efficiency and of cost-benefit considerations, it is a sensible approach to education. If children are seen primarily as raw material for industry, a greater investment in the better raw material makes sense. Market values do not favor much investment in the poorest children.

One cannot dispute the fact that giving poor black adolescents job skills, if it is self-evident that they do not possess the academic skills to go to college, is a good thing in itself. But the business leaders who put emphasis on filling entry-level job slots are too frequently the people who, by prior lobbying and voting patterns and their impact upon social policy, have made it all but certain that few of these urban kids would get the education in their early years that would have made them *look* like college prospects by their secondary years. First we circumscribe their destinies and then we look at the diminished product and we say, "Let's be pragmatic and do with them what we can."

The evolution of two parallel curricula, one for urban and one for suburban schools, has also underlined the differences in what is felt to be appropriate to different kinds of children and to socially distinct communities. "This school is right for this community," says a former director of student services at New Trier High. But, he goes on, "it certainly wouldn't be right for every community." What is considered right for children at Du Sable and their counterparts in other inner-city schools becomes self-evident to anyone who sees the course of study in such schools. Many urban high school students do not study math but "business math"—essentially, a very elemental level of bookkeeping. Job-specific courses such as "cosmetology" (hairdressing, manicures), which would be viewed as insults by suburban parents, are a common item in the segregated high schools and are seen as realistic preparation for the adult roles that 16-year-old black girls may expect to fill.

Inevitably this thinking must diminish the horizons and the aspirations of poor children, locking them at a very early age into the slots that are regarded as appropriate to their societal position. On its darkest side, it also leads to greater willingness to write off certain children. "It doesn't make sense to offer something that most of these urban kids will never use," a businessman said to me flatly in Chicago. "No one expects these ghetto kids to go to college. Most of them are lucky if they're even literate. If we can teach some useful skills, get them to stay in school and graduate, and maybe into jobs, we're giving them the most that they can hope for."

"Besides," a common line of reasoning continues, "these bottom-level jobs exist. They need to be done. Somebody's got to do them." It is evident, however, who that somebody will be. There is no sentimentalizing here. No corporate CEO is likely to confess a secret wish to see his children trained as cosmetologists or clerical assistants. So the prerogatives of class and caste are clear.

Some years ago, New Trier High School inaugurated an "office education" course that offered instruction in shorthand, filing and typing. "It was an acknowledged flop," the *Washington Post* reports. Not enough students were enrolled. The course was discontinued. "I guess," a teacher said, kids at New Trier "just don't think of themselves as future secretaries."

What does money buy for children in Chicago's suburbs?

At the wealthiest suburban schools it buys them truly scholarly instruction from remarkable and well-rewarded teachers, and it also buys them a great deal of thoughtful counseling from well-prepared advisers. In the suburbs, says the *Chicago Sun-Times,* "it is not uncommon for the ratio between students and counselors to be 250 to one," and, at its lowest, at New Trier, where, as we have seen, faculty members are released from teaching to give counseling, it is only 25 to one. "In the city the ratio is 400 to one." While a suburban school library is likely to have 60,000 volumes, a Chicago school library "is lucky to have 13,000 volumes," says the *Sun-Times.* "In the suburbs, extracurricular activities are supported as an integral part of education, and summer school tends to be standard. In the city, both were sliced thin years ago as money became tight."

Is money the main difference?

It is obviously the difference in provision of school libraries: 60,000 books cost four and a half times as much as 13,000 books.

It is, at least in part, the difference in attracting gifted and experienced teachers: Teachers earning nearly $60,000 cost a system half again as much as teachers earning $40,000. The differences, by any standard, are enormous.

"Of course one might assert," John Coons observes, "that, though money may be a good measure of quality, this could hold true for rich districts only." From this point of view, "these children of poor districts" can absorb "only the most rudimentary" and "inexpensive" instruction. "Rich children," on the other hand, "are capable of soaking up the most esoteric offering. Hence it is proper to prefer them in spending."

The "gross condescension of this argument," he says, "should be enough to condemn it" but "it is regrettably persistent in important private circles."

Even accepting, he continues, "that you 'get less

for your money' with poor children, this doesn't mean such children haven't the right to equal schools." True, he says, "equal opportunity across the board" will not automatically "produce equality" in school performance. Still, "one doesn't force a losing baseball team to play with seven men."

Not surprisingly, when parents of poor children or their advocates raise their voices to protest the rigging of the game, they ask initially for things that seem like fairly obvious improvements: larger library collections, a reduction in the size of classes, or a better ratio of children to school counselors. What seems obvious to them, however, is by no means obvious to those who have control over their children's destinies, and the arguments these parents make are often met with flat rebuttals.

In 1988 a number of Chicago's more responsive leaders told the press that cutting class size ought to be a top priority and indicated it would cost about $100 million to begin to do this. The rebuttal started almost instantly. Efforts to improve a school by lowering its class size, said Assistant U.S. Secretary of Education Chester Finn, would be a "costly waste of money." Reducing class size is "not a very prudent investment strategy," said Mr. Finn, who sent his daughter to Exeter, where class size is 13. "There are a lot of better and less costly things you can do and get results."

Around the same time, Education Secretary William Bennett came to Illinois and told taxpayers, "If the citizens of Chicago [want to] put more money in, then they are free to do so. But you will not buy your way to better performance."

The *New York Times* responded to the views of Mr. Bennett with this observation: "Parents who have scrimped to send their children to private school" or voted for higher taxes to improve their local public schools "may be confused by the Education Department's recent statements. . . . According to the department's fourth annual statistical picture of the nation's public schools, the amount spent per pupil, on higher teacher salaries or on improving the teacher-student ratio has almost no correlation with performance." This, said the *Times,* bolsters "the message [Mr. Bennett] has been preaching: Money is not primarily 'what works' in education."

In Chicago, where the issue had been posed, the question was now asked: If money and class size did not matter, then what other changes might be helpful to the city's poorest children? The *Chicago Tribune,* after doing a superb job of describing the inequities that faced Chicago's children, seemed to be dissuaded by the words of Mr. Finn and Mr. Bennett. Instead of proposing answers to the problems stemming from short funding that it had so candidly described, the paper now backed off and made a recommendation that did not apply directly to the public schools at all.

"What would make measurable improvement . . . ," said the *Tribune,* "would be a major expansion of early childhood programs." Unlike costlier proposals, said the paper, preschool education "pays off in measurable ways—not only in improved achievement but also in tax savings." What the *Tribune* failed to say was that this "better" solution—preschool guarantees for all poor children, which, of course, would be too late for 12-year-olds like Keisha—had been turned down by the president who had appointed Mr. Finn and Mr. Bennett, and that a similar statewide plan for Illinois had recently been vetoed by the governor.

Thus it is that what poor people, in a plain and simple way, had felt impelled to ask for was declared the "wrong" solution. What they did not ask for at that moment (but had asked for, only to be turned down, many times before) was now declared the "right" solution. But neither solution, in any case, was going to be funded. A balancing act of equally unlikely options was the only answer that the city and the nation gave to the requests of these poor people. This juggling of options—in this instance, countering school-funding efforts with the need for preschool—does no good if neither of these options is to be enacted anyway and if the act of balancing only serves to guarantee our permanent inaction in both areas.

It is also fair to ask what rule it is that says poor children in Chicago have to choose between a glass of milk when they are three years old or a glass of milk when they are seven. The children of Winnetka do not have to make this choice. They get the best of preschool and the smallest class size in their elementary schools (and they also get superior health care, and they also get a lot of milk). This is like exhorting Keisha, "You can have more crayons; or you can be given a real teacher; or you can have a bunsen burner someday in a high school science laboratory. But you cannot have all three. You'll have to choose."

One would not have thought that children in America would ever have to choose between a teacher or a playground or sufficient toilet paper. Like grain in a time of famine, the immense resources which the nation does in fact possess go not to the child in the greatest need but to the child of the highest bidder—the child of parents who, more frequently than not, have also enjoyed the same abundance when they were schoolchildren.

"A caste society," wrote U.S. Commissioner of Education Francis Keppel 25 years ago, "violates the style of American democracy. . . . The nation in effect does not have a truly public school system in a large part of its communities; it has permitted what is in effect a private school system to develop under public auspices. . . . Equality of educational opportunity throughout the nation continues today for many to be more a myth than a reality." This statement is as true today as it was at the time when it was written. For all the rhetoric of school reform that we have heard in recent years, there are no indications that this is about to change.

City and state business associations, in Chicago as in many other cities, have lobbied for years against tax increments to finance education of low-income children. "You don't dump a lot of money into guys who haven't done well with the money they've got in the past," says the chief executive officer of Citicorps Savings of Illinois. "You don't rearrange deck chairs on the *Titanic*."

In recent years, however, some of the corporate leaders in Chicago who opposed additional school funding and historically resisted efforts at desegregation have nonetheless attempted to portray themselves as allies to poor children—or, as they sometimes call themselves, "school partners"—and they even offer certain kinds of help. Some of the help they give is certainly of use, although it is effectively the substitution of a form of charity, which can be withheld at any time, for the more permanent assurances of justice; but much of what the corporations do is simply superficial and its worth absurdly overstated by the press.

Celebrities are sometimes hired, for example, by the corporations to come into the Chicago schools and organize a rally to sell children on the wisdom of not dropping out of school. A local counterpart to Jesse Jackson often gives a motivational address. He tells the kids, "You are somebody." They are asked to chant it in response. But the fact that they are in this school, and doomed to be here for no reason other than their race and class, gives them a different message: "In the eyes of this society, you are not much at all." This is the message they get every day when no celebrities are there and when their business partners have departed for their homes in the white suburbs.

Business leaders seem to have great faith in exhortation of this kind—a faith that comes perhaps from marketing traditions. Exhortation has its role. But hope cannot be marketed as easily as blue jeans. Human liberation doesn't often come this way—from mass hypnosis. Certain realities—race and class and caste—are there, and they remain.

Not surprisingly, the notion that such private-sector boosterism offers a solution to the miseries of education for poor children is not readily accepted by some parents in Chicago who have seen what private-sector forces have achieved in housing, in employment and in medical provision for their children. "The same bank presidents who offer gifts to help our segregated schools," a mother in Chicago said, "are the ones who have assured their segregation by redlining neighborhoods like these for 30 years, and they are the ones who send their kids to good schools in Winnetka and who vote against the equalizing plans to give our public schools more money. Why should we trust their motives? They may like to train our children to be good employees. That would make their businesses more profitable. Do they want to see our children taking corporate positions from their children? If they gave our kids what their kids have, we might earn enough to move into their neighborhoods."

The phrasing "private-sector partner" is employed somewhat disarmingly in corporate pronouncements, but the language does not always strike responsive chords among sophisticated leaders of the poor. "These people aren't my children's friends," said the woman I have quoted in Chicago. "What have things come to in America when I am told they are the people that I have to trust? If they want to be my 'partner,' let them open up their public schools and bring my children out into their neighborhoods to go to school beside their children. Let them use their money to buy buses, not to hold expensive conferences in big hotels. If they think that busing is too tiring for poor black children—I do find it interesting that they show so much concern for poor black children—I don't mind if they would like to go for limousines. But do not lock us in a place where you don't need to live beside us and then say you want to be my 'partner.' I don't accept that kind of 'partner.' No one would—unless he was a fool or had no choice."

But that is the bitter part of it. The same political figures who extol the role of business have made certain that these poor black people would have no real choice. Cutting back the role of government and then suggesting that the poor can turn to businessmen who lobbied for such cuts is cynical indeed. But many black principals in urban schools know very well that they have no alternative; so they learn to swallow their pride, subdue their recognitions and their dignity, and frame their language carefully to win the backing of potential "business partners." At length they are even willing to adjust their schools and their curricula to serve the corporate will: as the woman in Chicago said, to train the ghetto children to be good employees. This is an accomplished fact today. A new generation of black urban school officials has been groomed to settle for a better version of unequal segregated education.

CHAPTER 3

The Savage Inequalities of Public Education in New York

"In a country where there is no distinction of class," Lord Acton wrote of the United States 130 years ago, "a child is not born to the station of its parents, but with an indefinite claim to all the prizes that can be won by thought and labor. It is in conformity with the theory of equality . . . to give as near as possible to every youth an equal state in life." Americans, he said, "are unwilling that any should be deprived in childhood of the means of competition."

It is hard to read these words today without a sense of irony and sadness. Denial of "the means of competition" is perhaps the single most consistent outcome of the education offered to poor children in the schools of our large cities; and nowhere is this pattern of denial more explicit or more absolute than in the public schools of New York City.

Average expenditures per pupil in the city of New

York in 1987 were some $5,500. In the highest spend-
ing suburbs of New York (Great Neck or Manhasset,
for example, on Long Island) funding levels rose above
$11,000, with the highest districts in the state at $15,000.
"Why . . . ," asks the city's Board of Education, "should
our students receive less" than do "similar students" who
live elsewhere? "The inequity is clear."

But the inequality to which these words refer goes
even further than the school board may be eager to
reveal. "It is perhaps the supreme irony," says the nonprofit Community Service Society of New York, that
"the same Board of Education which perceives so clearly
the inequities" of funding between separate towns and
cities "is perpetuating similar inequities" right in New
York. And, in comment on the Board of Education's final
statement—"the inequity is clear"—the CSS observes,
"New York City's poorest . . . districts could adopt that
eloquent statement with few changes."

New York City's public schools are subdivided into
32 school districts. District 10 encompasses a large part of
the Bronx but is, effectively, two separate districts. One
of these districts, Riverdale, is in the northwest section of
the Bronx. Home to many of the city's most sophisticated
and well-educated families, its elementary schools have
relatively few low-income students. The other section, to
the south and east, is poor and heavily nonwhite.

The contrast between public schools in each of these
two neighborhoods is obvious to any visitor. At Public
School 24 in Riverdale, the principal speaks enthusiasti-
cally of his teaching staff. At Public School 79, serving
poorer children to the south, the principal says that he
is forced to take the "tenth-best" teachers. "I thank God
they're still breathing," he remarks of those from whom
he must select his teachers.

Some years ago, District 10 received an allocation

for computers. The local board decided to give each elementary school an equal number of computers, even though the schools in Riverdale had smaller classes and far fewer students. When it was pointed out that schools in Riverdale, as a result, had twice the number of computers in proportion to their student populations as the schools in the poor neighborhoods, the chairman of the local board replied, "What is fair is what is determined . . . to be fair."

The superintendent of District 10, Fred Goldberg, tells the *New York Times* that "every effort" is made "to distribute resources equitably." He speculates that some gap might exist because some of the poorer schools need to use funds earmarked for computers to buy basic supplies like pens and paper. Asked about the differences in teachers noted by the principals, he says there are no differences, then adds that next year he'll begin a program to improve the quality of teachers in the poorer schools. Questioned about differences in physical appearances between the richer and the poorer schools, he says, "I think it's demographics."

Sometimes a school principal, whatever his background or his politics, looks into the faces of the children in his school and offers a disarming statement that cuts through official ambiguity. "These are the kids most in need," says Edward Flanery, the principal of one of the low-income schools, "and they get the worst teachers." For children of diverse needs in his overcrowded rooms, he says, "you need an outstanding teacher. And what do you get? You get the worst."

In order to find Public School 261 in District 10, a visitor is told to look for a mortician's office. The funeral home, which faces Jerome Avenue in the North Bronx, is easy to identify by its green awning. The school is next door, in a former roller-skating rink. No sign identifies the building as a school. A metal awning frame without an awning supports a flagpole, but there is no flag.

In the street in front of the school there is an elevated public transit line. Heavy traffic fills the street. The existence of the school is virtually concealed within this crowded city block.

In a vestibule between the outer and inner glass doors of the school there is a sign with these words: "All children are capable of learning."

Beyond the inner doors a guard is seated. The lobby is long and narrow. The ceiling is low. There are no windows. All the teachers that I see at first are middle-aged white women. The principal, who is also a white woman, tells me that the school's "capacity" is 900 but that there are 1,300 children here. The size of classes for fifth and sixth grade children in New York, she says, is "capped" at 32, but she says that class size in the school goes "up to 34." (I later see classes, however, as large as 37.) Classes for younger children, she goes on, are "capped at 25," but a school can go above this limit if it puts an extra adult in the room. Lack of space, she says, prevents the school from operating a pre-kindergarten program.

I ask the principal where her children go to school. They are enrolled in private school, she says.

"Lunchtime is a challenge for us," she explains. "Limited space obliges us to do it in three shifts, 450 children at a time."

Textbooks are scarce and children have to share their social studies books. The principal says there is one full-time pupil counselor and another who is here two days a week: a ratio of 930 children to one counselor. The carpets are patched and sometimes taped together to conceal an open space. "I could use some new rugs," she observes.

To make up for the building's lack of windows and the crowded feeling that results, the staff puts plants and fish tanks in the corridors. Some of the plants are flourishing. Two boys, released from class, are in a corridor beside a tank, their noses pressed against the glass. A school of pinkish fish inside the tank are darting back and forth. Farther down the corridor a small Hispanic girl is watering the plants.

Two first grade classes share a single room without a window, divided only by a blackboard. Four kindergartens and a sixth grade class of Spanish-speaking children have been packed into a single room in which, again, there is no window. A second grade bilingual class of 37 children has its own room but again there is no window.

By eleven o'clock, the lunchroom is already packed with appetite and life. The kids line up to get their meals, then eat them in ten minutes. After that, with no place they can go to play, they sit and wait until it's time to line up and go back to class.

On the second floor I visit four classes taking place within another undivided space. The room has a low ceiling. File cabinets and movable blackboards give a small degree of isolation to each class. Again, there are no windows.

The library is a tiny, windowless and claustrophobic room. I count approximately 700 books. Seeing no reference books, I ask a teacher if encyclopedias and other reference books are kept in classrooms.

"We don't have encyclopedias in classrooms," she replies. "That is for the suburbs."

The school, I am told, has 26 computers for its 1,300 children. There is one small gym and children get one period, and sometimes two, each week. Recess, however, is not possible because there is no playground. "Head Start," the principal says, "scarcely exists in District 10. We have no space."

The school, I am told, is 90 percent black and Hispanic; the other 10 percent are Asian, white or Middle Eastern.

In a sixth grade social studies class the walls are bare of words or decorations. There seems to be no ventilation system, or, if one exists, it isn't working.

The class discusses the Nile River and the Fertile Crescent.

The teacher, in a droning voice: "How is it useful that these civilizations developed close to rivers?"

A child, in a good loud voice: "What kind of question is that?"

In my notes I find these words: "An uncomfortable feeling—being in a building with no windows. There are metal ducts across the room. Do they give air? I feel asphyxiated. . . ."

On the top floor of the school, a sixth grade of 30 children shares a room with 29 bilingual second graders. Because of the high class size there is an assistant with each teacher. This means that 59 children and four grown-ups—63 in all—must share a room that, in a suburban school, would hold no more than 20 children and one teacher. There are, at least, some outside windows in this room—it is the only room with windows in the school—and the room has a high ceiling. It is a relief to see some daylight.

I return to see the kindergarten classes on the ground floor and feel stifled once again by lack of air and the low ceiling. Nearly 120 children and adults are doing what they can to make the best of things: 80 children in four kindergarten classes, 30 children in the sixth grade class, and about eight grown-ups who are aides and teachers. The kindergarten children sitting on the worn rug, which is patched with tape, look up at me and turn their heads to follow me as I walk past them.

As I leave the school, a sixth grade teacher stops to talk. I ask her, "Is there air conditioning in warmer weather?"

Teachers, while inside the building, are reluctant to give answers to this kind of question. Outside, on the sidewalk, she is less constrained: "I had an awful room last year. In the winter it was 56 degrees. In the summer it was up to 90. It was sweltering."

I ask her, "Do the children ever comment on the building?"

"They don't say," she answers, "but they know."

I ask her if they see it as a racial message.

"All these children see TV," she says. "They know what suburban schools are like. Then they look around them at their school. This was a roller-rink, you know. . . . They don't comment on it but you see it in their eyes. They understand."

On the following morning I visit P.S. 79, another elementary school in the same district. "We work under difficult circumstances," says the principal, James Carter, who is black. "The school was built to hold one thousand students. We have 1,550. We are badly overcrowded. We need smaller classes but, to do this, we would need more space. I can't add five teachers. I would have no place to put them."

Some experts, I observe, believe that class size isn't a real issue. He dismisses this abruptly. "It doesn't take a genius to discover that you learn more in a smaller class. I have to bus some 60 kindergarten children elsewhere, since I have no space for them. When they return next year, where do I put them?

"I can't set up a computer lab. I have no room. I had to put a class into the library. I have no librarian. There are two gymnasiums upstairs but they cannot be used for sports. We hold more classes there. It's unfair to measure us against the suburbs. They have 17 to 20 children in a class. Average class size in this school is 30.

"The school is 29 percent black, 70 percent Hispanic. Few of these kids get Head Start. There is no space in the district. Of 200 kindergarten children, 50 maybe get some kind of preschool."

I ask him how much difference preschool makes.

"Those who get it do appreciably better. I can't overestimate its impact but, as I have said, we have no space."

The school tracks children by ability, he says. "There are five to seven levels in each grade. The highest level is equivalent to 'gifted' but it's not a full-scale gifted program. We don't have the funds. We have no science room. The science teachers carry their equipment with them."

We sit and talk within the nurse's room. The window is broken. There are two holes in the ceiling. About a quarter of the ceiling has been patched and covered with a plastic garbage bag.

"Ideal class size for these kids would be 15 to 20. Will these children ever get what white kids in the suburbs take for granted? I don't think so. If you ask me why, I'd have to speak of race and social class. I don't think the powers that be in New York City understand, or want to understand, that if they do not give these children a sufficient education to lead healthy and productive lives, we will be their victims later on. We'll pay the price someday—in violence, in economic costs. I despair of making this appeal in any terms but these. You cannot issue an appeal to conscience in New York today. The fair-play argument won't be accepted. So you speak of violence and hope that it will scare the city into action."

While we talk, three children who look six or seven years old come to the door and ask to see the nurse, who isn't in the school today. One of the children, a Puerto Rican girl, looks haggard. "I have a pain in my tooth," she says. The principal says, "The nurse is out. Why don't you call your mother?" The child says, "My mother doesn't have a phone." The principal sighs. "Then go back to your class." When she leaves, the principal is angry. "It's amazing to me that these children ever make it with the obstacles they face. Many *do* care and they *do* try, but there's a feeling of despair. The parents of these children want the same things for their children that the parents in the suburbs want. Drugs are not the cause of this. They are the symptom. Nonetheless, they're used by people in the suburbs and rich people in Manhattan as another reason to keep children of poor people at a distance."

I ask him, "Will white children and black children ever go to school together in New York?"

"I don't see it," he replies. "I just don't think it's going to happen. It's a dream. I simply do not see white folks in Riverdale agreeing to cross-bus with kids like these. A few, maybe. Very few. I don't think I'll live to see it happen."

I ask him whether race is the decisive factor. Many experts, I observe, believe that wealth is more important in determining these inequalities.

"This," he says—and sweeps his hand around him at the room, the garbage bag, the ceiling—"would not happen to white children."

In a kindergarten class the children sit cross-legged on a carpet in a space between two walls of books. Their 26 faces are turned up to watch their teacher, an elderly black woman. A little boy who sits beside me is involved in trying to tie bows in his shoelaces. The children sing a song: "Lift Every Voice." On the wall are these handwritten words: "Beautiful, also, are the souls of my people."

In a very small room on the fourth floor, 52 people in two classes do their best to teach and learn. Both are first grade classes. One, I am informed, is "low ability." The other is bilingual.

"The room is barely large enough for one class," says the principal.

The room is 25 by 50 feet. There are 26 first graders and two adults on the left, 22 others and two adults on the right. On the wall there is the picture of a small white child, circled by a Valentine, and a Gainsborough painting of a child in a formal dress.

"We are handicapped by scarcity," one of the teachers says. "One fifth of these children may be at grade level by the year's end."

A boy who may be seven years old climbs on my lap without an invitation and removes my glasses. He studies my face and runs his fingers through my hair. "You have nice hair," he says. I ask him where he lives and he replies, "Times Square Hotel," which is a homeless shelter in Manhattan.

I ask him how he gets here.

"With my father. On the train," he says.

"How long does it take?"

"It takes an hour and a half."

I ask him when he leaves his home.

"My mother wakes me up at five o'clock."

"When do you leave?"

"Six-thirty."

I ask him how he gets back to Times Square.

"My father comes to get me after school."

From my notes: "He rides the train three hours

every day in order to attend this segregated school. It would be a shorter ride to Riverdale. There are rapid shuttle-vans that make that trip in only 20 minutes. Why not let him go to school right in Manhattan, for that matter?"

At three o'clock the nurse arrives to do her record-keeping. She tells me she is here three days a week. "The public hospital we use for an emergency is called North Central. It's not a hospital that I will use if I am given any choice. Clinics in the private hospitals are far more likely to be staffed by an experienced physician."

She hesitates a bit as I take out my pen, but then goes on: "I'll give you an example. A little girl I saw last week in school was trembling and shaking and could not control the motions of her arms. I was concerned and called her home. Her mother came right up to school and took her to North Central. The intern concluded that the child was upset by 'family matters'—nothing more— that there was nothing wrong with her. The mother was offended by the diagnosis. She did not appreciate his words or his assumptions. The truth is, there was nothing wrong at home. She brought the child back to school. I thought that she was ill. I told her mother, 'Go to Monte-fiore.' It's a private hospital, and well respected. She took my advice, thank God. It turned out that the child had a neurological disorder. She is now in treatment.

"This is the kind of thing our children face. Am I saying that the city underserves this population? You can draw your own conclusions."

Out on the street, it takes a full half hour to flag down a cab. Taxi drivers in New York are sometimes disconcertingly direct in what they say. When they are contemptuous of poor black people, their contempt is unadorned. When they're sympathetic and compassionate, their observations often go right to the heart of things.

"Oh . . . they neglect these children," says the driver. "They leave them in the streets and slums to live and die." We stop at a light. Outside the window of the taxi, aimless men are standing in a semicircle while another man is working on his car. Old four-story buildings with their windows boarded, cracked or missing are on every side.

I ask the driver where he's from. He says Afghanistan. Turning in his seat, he gestures at the street and shrugs. "If you don't, as an American, begin to give these kids the kind of education that you give the kids of Donald Trump, you're asking for disaster."

Two months later, on a day in May, I visit an elementary school in Riverdale. The dogwoods and magnolias on the lawn in front of P.S. 24 are in full blossom on the day I visit. There is a well-tended park across the street, another larger park three blocks away. To the left of the school is a playground for small children, with an innovative jungle gym, a slide and several climbing toys. Behind the school there are two playing fields for older kids. The grass around the school is neatly trimmed.

The neighborhood around the school, by no means the richest part of Riverdale, is nonetheless expensive and quite beautiful. Residences in the area—some of which are large, free-standing houses, others condominiums in solid redbrick buildings—sell for prices in the region of $400,000; but some of the larger Tudor houses on the winding and tree-shaded streets close to the school can cost up to $1 million. The excellence of P.S. 24, according to the principal, adds to the value of these homes. Advertisements in the *New York Times* will frequently inform prospective buyers that a house is "in the neighborhood of P.S. 24."

The school serves 825 children in the kindergarten through sixth grade. This is approximately half the student population crowded into P.S. 79, where 1,550 children fill a space intended for 1,000, and a great deal smaller than the 1,300 children packed into the former skating rink; but the principal of P.S. 24, a capable and energetic man named David Rothstein, still regards it as excessive for an elementary school.

The school is integrated in the strict sense that the middle- and upper-middle-class white children here do occupy a building that contains some Asian and Hispanic and black children; but there is little integration in the classrooms since the vast majority of the Hispanic and black children are assigned to "special" classes on the basis of evaluations that have classified them "EMR"—"educable mentally retarded"—or else, in the worst of cases, "TMR"—"trainable mentally retarded."

I ask the principal if any of his students qualify for free-lunch programs. "About 130 do," he says. "Perhaps another 35 receive their lunches at reduced price. Most of these kids are in the special classes. They do not come from this neighborhood."

The very few nonwhite children that one sees in mainstream classes tend to be Japanese or else of other Asian origins. Riverdale, I learn, has been the residence of choice for many years to members of the diplomatic corps.

The school therefore contains effectively two separate schools: one of about 130 children, most of whom are poor, Hispanic, black, assigned to one of the 12 special classes; the other of some 700 mainstream students, almost all of whom are white or Asian.

There is a third track also—this one for the students who are labeled "talented" or "gifted." This is termed a "pull-out" program since the children who are so identified remain in mainstream classrooms but are taken out for certain periods each week to be provided with intensive and, in my opinion, excellent instruction in some areas of reasoning and logic often known as "higher-order skills" in the contemporary jargon of the public schools. Children identified as "gifted" are admitted to this program in first grade and, in most cases, will remain there for six years. Even here, however, there are two tracks of the gifted. The regular gifted classes are provided with only one semester of this specialized instruction yearly. Those very few children, on the other hand, who are identified as showing the most promise are assigned, beginning in the third grade, to a program that receives a full-year regimen.

In one such class, containing ten intensely verbal and impressive fourth grade children, nine are white and one is Asian. The "special" class I enter first, by way of contrast, has twelve children of whom only one is white and none is Asian. These racial breakdowns prove to be predictive of the schoolwide pattern.

In a classroom for the gifted on the first floor of the school, I ask a child what the class is doing. "Logic and syllogisms," she replies. The room is fitted with a planetarium. The principal says that all the elementary schools in District 10 were given the same planetariums ten years ago but that certain schools, because of overcrowding, have been forced to give them up. At P.S. 261, according to my notes, there was a domelike space that had been built to hold a planetarium, but the planetarium had been removed to free up space for the small library collection. P.S. 24, in contrast, has a spacious library that holds almost 8,000 books. The windows are decorated with attractive, brightly colored curtains and look out on flowering trees. The principal says that it's inadequate, but it appears spectacular to me after the cubicle that holds a meager 700 books within the former skating rink.

The district can't afford librarians, the principal says, but P.S. 24, unlike the poorer schools of District 10, can draw on educated parent volunteers who staff the room in shifts three days a week. A parent organization also raises independent funds to buy materials, including books, and will soon be running a fund-raiser to enhance the library's collection.

In a large and sunny first grade classroom that I enter next, I see 23 children, all of whom are white or Asian. In another first grade, there are 22 white children and two others who are Japanese. There is a computer in each class. Every classroom also has a modern fitted sink.

In a second grade class of 22 children, there are two black children and three Asian children. Again, there is a sink and a computer. A sixth grade social studies class has only one black child. The children have an in-class research area that holds some up-to-date resources. A set of encyclopedias (World Book, 1985) is in a rack beside a window. The children are doing a Spanish language lesson when I enter. Foreign languages begin in sixth grade at the school, but Spanish is offered also to the kindergarten children. As in every room at P.S. 24, the window shades are clean and new, the floor is neatly tiled in gray and green, and there is not a single light bulb missing.

Walking next into a special class, I see twelve children. One is white. Eleven are black. There are no Asian children. The room is half the size of mainstream classrooms. "Because of overcrowding," says the principal, "we have had to split these rooms in half." There is no computer and no sink.

I enter another special class. Of seven children, five are black, one is Hispanic, one is white. A little black boy with a large head sits in the far corner and is gazing at the ceiling.

"Placement of these kids," the principal explains, "can usually be traced to neurological damage."

In my notes: "How could so many of these children be brain-damaged?"

Next door to the special class is a woodworking shop. "This shop is only for the special classes," says the principal. The children learn to punch in time cards at the door, he says, in order to prepare them for employment.

The fourth grade gifted class, in which I spend the last part of the day, is humming with excitement. "I start with these children in the first grade," says the teacher. "We pull them out of mainstream classes on the basis of their test results and other factors such as the opinion of their teachers. Out of this group, beginning in third grade, I pull out the ones who show the most potential, and they enter classes such as this one."

The curriculum they follow, she explains, "emphasizes critical thinking, reasoning and logic." The planetarium, for instance, is employed not simply for the study of the universe as it exists. "Children also are designing their own galaxies," the teacher says.

A little girl sitting around a table with her classmates speaks with perfect poise: "My name is Susan. We are in the fourth grade gifted program."

I ask them what they're doing and a child says, "My name is Laurie and we're doing problem-solving."

A rather tall, good-natured boy who is half-standing at the table tells me that his name is David. "One thing that we do," he says, "is logical thinking. Some problems, we find, have more than one good answer. We need to learn not simply to be logical in our own thinking but to show respect for someone else's logic even when an answer may be technically incorrect."

When I ask him to explain this, he goes on, "A person who gives an answer that is not 'correct' may none-theless have done some interesting thinking that we should examine. 'Wrong' answers may be more useful to examine than correct ones."

I ask the children if reasoning and logic are innate or if they're things that you can learn.

"You know some things to start with when you enter school," Susan says. "But we also learn some things that other children don't."

I ask her to explain this.

"We know certain things that other kids don't know because we're *taught* them."

She has braces on her teeth. Her long brown hair falls almost to her waist. Her loose white T-shirt has the word TRI-LOGIC on the front. She tells me that Tri-Logic is her father's firm.

Laurie elaborates on the same point: "Some things you know. Some kinds of logic are inside of you to start with. There are other things that someone needs to teach you."

David expands on what the other two have said: "Everyone can think and speak in logical ways unless they have a mental problem. What this program does is bring us to a higher form of logic."

The class is writing a new "Bill of Rights." The children already know the U.S. Bill of Rights and they explain its first four items to me with precision. What they are examining today, they tell me, is the very *concept* of a "right." Then they will create their own compendium of rights according to their own analysis and definition. Along one wall of the classroom, opposite the planetarium, are seven Apple II computers on which children have developed rather subtle color animations that express the themes—of greed and domination, for example—that they also have described in writing.

"This is an upwardly mobile group," the teacher later says. "They have exposure to whatever New York City has available. Their parents may take them to the theater, to museums. . . ."

In my notes: "Six girls, four boys. Nine white, one Chinese. I am glad they have this class. But what about the others? Aren't there ten black children in the school who could enjoy this also?"

The teacher gives me a newspaper written, edited and computer-printed by her sixth grade gifted class. The children, she tells me, are provided with a link to kids in Europe for transmission of news stories.

A science story by one student asks if scientists have ever falsified their research. "Gregor Mendel," the sixth grader writes, "the Austrian monk who founded the science of genetics, published papers on his work with peas that some experts say were statistically too good to be true. Isaac Newton, who formulated the law of gravitation, relied on unseemly mathematical sleight of hand in his calculations. . . . Galileo Galilei, founder of modern scientific method, wrote about experiments that were so difficult to duplicate that colleagues doubted he had done them."

Another item in the paper, also by a sixth grade student, is less esoteric: "The Don Cossacks dance company, from Russia, is visiting the United States. The last time it toured America was 1976. . . . The Don Cossacks will be in New York City for two weeks at the Neil Simon Theater. Don't miss it!"

The tone is breezy—and so confident! That phrase— "Don't miss it!"—speaks a volume about life in Riverdale.

"What makes a good school?" asks the principal when we are talking later on. "The building and teachers are part of it, of course. But it isn't just the building and the teachers. Our kids come from good families and the neighborhood is good. In a three-block area we have a public library, a park, a junior high. . . . Our typical sixth grader reads at eighth grade level." In a quieter voice he says, "I see how hard my colleagues work in schools like P.S. 79. You have children in those neighborhoods who live in virtual hell. They enter school five years behind. What do they get?" Then, as he spreads his hands out on his desk, he says: "I have to ask myself why there should be an elementary school in District 10 with fifteen hundred children. Why should there be an elementary school within a skating rink? Why should the Board of Ed allow this? This is not the way that things should be."

Stark as the inequities in District 10 appear, educators say that they are "mild" in comparison to other situations in the city. Some of the most stunning inequality, according to a report by the Community Service Society, derives from allocations granted by state legislators to school districts where they have political allies. The poorest districts in the city get approximately 90 cents per pupil from these legislative grants, while the richest districts have been given $14 for each pupil.

Newspapers in New York City have reported other instances of the misallocation of resources. "The Board of Education," wrote the *New York Post* during July of 1987, "was hit with bombshell charges yesterday that money earmarked for fighting drug abuse and illiteracy in ghetto schools was funneled instead to schools in wealthy areas."

In receipt of extra legislative funds, according to the *Post,* affluent districts were funded "at a rate 14 times greater than low-income districts." The paper said the city's poorest areas were underfunded "with stunning consistency."

The report by the Community Service Society cites

an official of the New York City Board of Education who remarks that there is "no point" in putting further money "into some poor districts" because, in his belief, "new teachers would not stay there." But the report observes that, in an instance where beginning teacher salaries were raised by nearly half, "that problem largely disappeared"—another interesting reminder of the difference money makes when we are willing to invest it. Nonetheless, says the report, "the perception that the poorest districts are beyond help still remains. . . ." Perhaps the worst result of such beliefs, says the report, is the message that resources would be "wasted on poor children." This message "trickles down to districts, schools, and classrooms." Children hear and understand this theme—they are poor investments—and behave accordingly. If society's resources would be wasted on their destinies, perhaps their own determination would be wasted too. "Expectations are a powerful force . . . ," the CSS observes.

Despite the evidence, the CSS report leans over backwards not to fuel the flames of racial indignation. "In the present climate," the report says, "suggestions of racism must be made with caution. However, it is inescapable that these inequities are being perpetrated on [school] districts which are virtually all black and Hispanic. . . ." While the report says, very carefully, that there is no "evidence" of "deliberate individual discrimination," it nonetheless concludes that "those who allocate resources make decisions over and over again which penalize the poorest districts." Analysis of city policy, the study says, "speaks to systemic bias which constitutes a conspiracy of effect. . . . Whether consciously or not, the system writes off its poorest students."

* * *

It is not only at the grade-school level that inequities like these are seen in New York City. Morris High School in the South Bronx, for example, says a teacher who has taught here more than 20 years, "does everything an inanimate object can do to keep children from being educated."

Blackboards at the school, according to the *New York Times,* are "so badly cracked that teachers are afraid to let students write on them for fear they'll cut themselves. Some mornings, fallen chips of paint cover classrooms like snow. . . . Teachers and students have come to see humor in the waterfall that courses down six flights of stairs after a heavy rain."

One classroom, we are told, has been sealed off "because of a gaping hole in the floor." In the band room, "chairs are positioned where acoustic tiles don't fall quite so often." In many places, "plaster and ceramic tile have peeled off" the walls, leaving the external brick wall of the school exposed. "There isn't much between us and the great outdoors," the principal reports.

A "landscape of hopelessness"—"burnt-out apartments, boarded windows, vacant lot upon garbage-strewn vacant lot"—surrounds the school. Statistics tell us, says the *Times,* that the South Bronx is "the poorest congressional district in the United States." But statistics cannot tell us "what it means to a child to leave his often hellish home and go to a school—his hope for a transcendent future—that is literally falling apart."

The head of school facilities for the Board of Education speaks of classrooms unrepaired years after having been destroyed by fire. "What's really sad," she notes, "is that so many kids come from places that look as bad as our schools—and we have nothing better to offer them."

A year later, when I visit Morris High, most of these

conditions are unchanged. Water still cascades down the stairs. Plaster is still falling from the walls. Female students tell me that they shower after school to wash the plaster from their hair. Entering ninth grade children at the school, I'm told, read about four years behind grade level.

From the street, the school looks like a medieval castle; its turreted tower rises high above the devastated lots below. A plaque in the principal's office tells a visitor that this is the oldest high school in the Bronx.

The first things that one senses in the building are the sweetness, the real innocence, of many of the children, the patience and determination of the teachers, and the shameful disrepair of the surroundings. The principal is unsparing in her honesty. "The first floor," she tells me as we head off to the stairwell, "isn't bad—unless you go into the gym or auditorium." It's the top two floors, she says, the fourth and fifth floors, that reveal the full extent of Morris High's neglect by New York City's Board of Education.

Despite her warning, I am somewhat stunned to see a huge hole in the ceiling of the stairwell on the school's fourth floor. The plaster is gone, exposing rusted metal bars embedded in the outside wall. It will cost as much as $50 million to restore the school to an acceptable condition, she reports.

Jack Forman, the head of the English department, is a scholarly and handsome gray-haired man whose academic specialty is British literature. Sitting in his office in a pinstripe shirt and red suspenders, his feet up on the table, he is interrupted by a stream of kids. A tiny ninth grade student seems to hesitate outside the office door. Forman invites her to come in and, after she has given him a message ("Carmen had to leave—for an emergency") and gone to her next class, his face breaks out into a smile. "She's a lovely little kid. These students live in a tough neighborhood, but they are children and I speak to them as children."

Forman says that freshman English students get a solid diet of good reading: *A Tale of Two Cities, Manchild in the Promised Land,* Steinbeck's *The Pearl,* some African fiction, a number of Greek tragedies. "We're implementing an AP course ["advanced placement"—for pre-college students] for the first time. We don't know how many children will succeed in it, but we intend to try. Our mission is to stretch their minds, to give them every chance to grow beyond their present expectations.

"I have strong feelings about getting past the basics. Too many schools are stripping down curriculum to meet the pressure for success on tests that measure only minimal skills. That's why I teach a theater course. Students who don't respond to ordinary classes may surprise us, and surprise themselves, when they are asked to step out on a stage.

"I have a student, Carlos, who had dropped out once and then returned. He had no confidence in his ability. Then he began to act. He memorized the part of Pyramus. Then he played Sebastian in *The Tempest.* He had a photographic memory. Amazing! He will graduate, I hope, this June.

"Now, if we didn't have that theater program, you have got to ask if Carlos would have stayed in school."

In a sun-drenched corner room on the top floor, a female teacher and some 25 black and Hispanic children are reading a poem by Paul Laurence Dunbar. Holes in the walls and ceiling leave exposed the structural brick. The sun appears to blind the teacher. There are no shades. Sheets of torn construction paper have been taped to windowpanes, but the glare is quite relentless. The children look forlorn and sleepy.

> I know why the caged bird sings. . . .
> It is not a carol of joy. . . .

"This is your homework," says the teacher. "Let's get on with it."

But the children cannot seem to wake up to the words. A 15-year-old boy, wearing a floppy purple hat, white jersey and striped baggy pants, is asked to read the lines.

> I know what the caged bird feels . . .
> When the wind stirs soft through the
>   springing grass,
> And the river flows like a stream of glass. . . .

A 15-year-old girl with curly long red hair and many freckles reads the lines. Her T-shirt hangs down almost to her knees.

> I know why the caged bird beats his wing
> Till its blood is red on the cruel bars.

A boy named Victor, sitting at my side, whispers the words: "I know why the caged bird beats his wing. . . . His blood is red. He wants to spread his wings."

The teacher asks the children what the poet means or what the imagery conveys. There is no response at first. Then Victor lifts his hand. "The poem is about ancient days of slavery," he says. "The bird destroys himself because he can't escape the cage."

"Why does he sing?" the teacher asks.

"He sings out of the longing to be free."

At the end of class the teacher tells me, "Forty, maybe 45 percent out of this group will graduate."

The counseling office is the worst room I have seen. There is a large blue barrel by the window.

"When it rains," one of the counselors says, "that barrel will be full." I ask her how the kids react. "They would like to see the rain stop in the office," she replies.

The counselor seems to like the kids and points to three young women sitting at a table in the middle of the room. One of them, an elegant tall girl with long dark hair, is studying her homework. She's wearing jeans, a long black coat, a black turtleneck, a black hat with a bright red band. "I love the style of these kids," the counselor says.

A very shy light-skinned girl waits by the desk. A transfer from another school, she's with her father. They fill out certain transfer forms and ask the counselor some questions. The father's earnestness, his faith in the importance of these details, and the child's almost painful shyness stay in my mind later.

At eleven o'clock, about 200 children in a top-floor room are watching Forman's theater class performing *The Creation* by James Weldon Johnson. Next, a gospel choir sings—"I once was lost and now am found"— and then a tall black student gives a powerful delivery of a much-recited speech of Martin Luther King while another student does an agonizing, slow-paced slave ballet. The students seem mesmerized. The speaker's voice is strong and filled with longing.

"One day, the sons of former slaves and the sons of former slave-owners will be able to sit down together at the table of brotherhood."

But the register of enrollment given to me by the principal reflects the demographics of continued racial segregation: Of the students in this school, 38 percent are black, 62 percent Hispanic. There are no white children in the building.

The session ends with a terrific fast jazz concert by a band composed of students dressed in black ties, crimson jackets and white shirts. A student with a small trimmed beard and mustache stands to do a solo on the saxophone. The pianist is the same young man who read the words of Martin Luther King. His solo, on a battered Baldwin, brings the students to their feet.

Victor Acosta and eight other boys and girls meet with me in the freshman counselors' office. They talk about "the table of brotherhood"—the words of Dr. King that we have heard recited by the theater class upstairs.

"We are not yet seated at that table," Victor says.

"The table is set but no one's in the chairs," says a black student who, I later learn, is named Carissa.

Alexander, a 16-year-old student who was brought here by his parents from Jamaica just a year ago, says this: "You can understand things better when you go among the wealthy. You look around you at their school, although it's impolite to do that, and you take a deep breath at the sight of all those beautiful surroundings. Then you come back home and see that these are things you do not have. You think of the difference. Not at first, it takes a while to settle in."

I ask him why these differences exist.

"Let me answer that," says Israel, a small, wiry Puerto Rican boy. "If you threw us all into some different place, some ugly land, and put white children in this building in our place, this school would start to shine. No question. The parents would say: 'This building sucks. It's ugly. Fix it up.' They'd fix it fast—no question.

"People on the outside," he goes on, "may think that we don't know what it is like for other students, but we *visit* other schools and we have eyes and we have brains. You cannot hide the differences. You see it and compare. . . .

"Most of the students in this school won't go to college. Many of them will join the military. If there's a war, we have to fight. Why should I go to war and fight for opportunities I can't enjoy—for things rich people value, for their freedom, but I do not *have* that freedom and I can't go to their schools?"

"You tell your friends, 'I go to Morris High,'" Carissa says. "They make a face. How does that make you feel?" She points to the floor beside the water barrel. "I found wild mushrooms growing in that corner."

"Big fat ugly things with hairs," says Victor.

Alexander then begins an explanation of the way that inequality becomes ensconced. "See," he says, "the parents of rich children have the money to get into better schools. Then, after a while, they begin to say, 'Well, I have this. Why not keep it for my children?' In other words, it locks them into the idea of always having something more. After that, these things—the extra things they have—are seen like an *inheritance*. They feel it's theirs and they don't understand why we should question it.

"See, that's where the trouble starts. They get used to what they have. They think it's theirs by rights because they had it from the start. So it leaves those children with a legacy of greed. I don't think most people understand this."

One of the counselors, who sits nearby, looks at me and then at Alexander. Later he says, "It's quite remarkable how much these children see. You wouldn't know it from their academic work. Most of them write poorly. There is a tremendous gulf between their skills and capabilities. This gulf, this dissonance, is frightening. I mean, it says so much about the squandering of human worth. . . ."

I ask the students if they can explain the reasons for the physical condition of the school.

"Hey, it's like a welfare hospital! You're getting it for free," says Alexander. "You have no power to complain."

"Is money really everything?" I ask.

"It's a nice fraction of everything," he says.

Janice, who is soft-spoken and black, speaks about the overcrowding of the school. "I make it my business," she says, "to know my fellow students. But it isn't easy when the classes are so large. I had 45 children in my fifth grade class. The teacher sometimes didn't know you, She would ask you, 'What's your name?'"

"You *want* the teacher to know your name," says Rosie, who is Puerto Rican. "The teacher asks me, 'Are you really in this class?' 'Yes, I've been here all semester.' But she doesn't know my name."

All the students hope to go to college. After college they have ambitious plans. One of them hopes to be a doctor. Two want to be lawyers. Alexander wants to be an architect. Carissa hopes to be a businesswoman. What is the likelihood that they will live up to these dreams? Five years ago, I'm told, there were approximately 500 freshman students in the school. Of these, only 180 survived four grades and made it through twelfth grade to graduation; only 82 were skilled enough to take the SATs. The projection I have heard for this year's ninth grade class is that 150 or so may graduate four years from now. Which of the kids before me will survive?

Rosie speaks of sixth grade classmates who had babies and left school. Victor speaks of boys who left school during eighth grade. Only one of the children in this, group has ever been a student in a racially desegregated school.

"How long will it be," I ask, "before white children and black and Hispanic children in New York will go to the same schools?"

"How long has the United States existed?" Alexander asks,

Janice says, "Two hundred years."

"Give it another two hundred years," says Alexander.

"Thank you," says Carissa.

At the end of school, Jack Forman takes me down to see the ground-floor auditorium. The room resembles an Elizabethan theater. Above the proscenium arch there is a mural, circa 1910, that must have been impressive long ago. The ceiling is crossed by wooden ribs; there are stained-glass windows in the back. But it is all in ruins. Two thirds of the stained-glass panes are missing and replaced by Plexiglas. Next to each of eight tall windows is a huge black number scrawled across the wall by a contractor who began but never finished the repairs. Chunks of wall and sections of the arches and supporting pillars have been blasted out by rot. Lights are falling from the ceiling. Chunks of plaster also hang from underneath the balcony above my head. The floor is filled with lumber, broken and upended desks, potato-chip bags, Styrofoam coffee cups and other trash. There is a bank of organ pipes, gold-colored within a frame of dark-stained wood, but there is no organ. Spilled on the floor beside my feet are several boxes that contain a "Regents Action Plan" for New York City's schools. Scattered across the floor amid the trash: "English Instructional Worksheets: 1984."

"Think what we could do with this," says Forman. "This kind of room was meant for theater and to hold commencements. Parents could enter directly from outside. The mural above the proscenium arch could be restored.

"This could be the soul of the school," he says.

"Hopefully, three years from now, when Victor is a senior, we will have this auditorium restored. That's my dream: to see him stand and graduate beneath this arch, his parents out there under the stained glass."

From my notes: "Morris High could be a wonderful place, a centerpiece of education, theater, music, every kind of richness for poor children. The teachers I've met are good and energized. They seem to love the children, and the kids deserve it. The building mocks their goodness."

Like Chicago, New York City has a number of selective high schools that have special programs and impressive up-to-date facilities. Schools like Morris High, in contrast, says the *New York Times,* tend to be "most overcrowded" and have "the highest dropout rates" and "lowest scores." In addition, we read, they receive "less money" per pupil.

The selective schools, according to the *Times,* "compete for the brightest students, but some students who might qualify lose out for lack of information and counseling." Other families, says the paper, "win admission through political influence."

The *Times* writes that these better-funded schools should not be "the preserve of an unfairly chosen elite." Yet, if the experience of other cities holds in New York City, this is what these special schools are meant to be. They are *intended* to be enclaves of superior education, private schools essentially, within the public system.

New York City's selective admissions program, says the principal of nonselective Jackson High, "has had the effect of making Jackson a racially segregated high school. . . . Simultaneously, the most 'difficult' and 'challenging' black students [have been] *encouraged* to select Jackson. . . ." The plan, she says, has had the effect of "placing a disproportionate number" of nonachieving children in one school. Moreover, she observes, students who do not meet "acceptable standards" in their chosen schools are sent back to schools like Jackson, making it effectively a dumping ground for children who are unsuccessful elsewhere.

"The gerrymandered zoning and the high school selection processes," according to a resident of the Jackson district, "create a citywide skimming policy that we compare to orange juice—our black youngsters are being treated like the sediment." The city, she says, is "not shaking the juice right." But she may be wrong. In the minds of those who have their eyes on an effective triage process—selective betterment of the most fortunate—this may be exactly the right way to shake the juice.

Unfairness on this scale is hard to contemplate in any setting. In the case of New York City and particularly Riverdale, however, it takes on a special poignance. Riverdale, after all, is not a redneck neighborhood. It has been home for many years to some of the most progressive people in the nation. Dozens of college students from this neighborhood went south during the civil rights campaigns to fight for the desegregation of the schools and restaurants and stores. The parents of those students often made large contributions to support the work of SNCC and CORE. One generation passes, and the cruelties they fought in Mississippi have come north to New York City. Suddenly, no doubt unwittingly, they find themselves opposed to simple things they would have died for 20 years before. Perhaps it isn't fair to say they are "opposed." A better word, more accurate, might be "oblivious." They do not want poor children to be harmed. They simply want the best for their own children. To the children of the South Bronx, it is all the same.

The system of selective schools in New York City has its passionate defenders. There are those who argue that these schools *deserve* the preferential treatment they receive in fiscal areas and faculty assignment because of the remarkable success that they have had with those whom they enroll. One such argument is made by the sociologist and writer Nathan Glazer.

Noting that excellent math and science teachers are in short supply in New York City, Glazer asks, "If they are scarce, is their effectiveness maximized by scattering them" to serve all children "or by their concentration" so that they can serve the high-achieving? "I think there is a good argument to be made that their effectiveness is maximized by concentration. They, like their students, have peers to talk to and work with and to motivate them." While recognizing the potential for inequity, Glazer nonetheless goes on, "I would argue that nowhere do we get so much for so little . . . than where we bring together the gifted and competent. They teach each other. They create an institution which provides them with an advantageous . . . label."

The points that Glazer makes here seem persuasive, though I think he contemplates too comfortably the virtually inevitable fact that "concentration" of the better teachers in the schools that serve the "high-achieving" necessarily requires a dilution of such teachers in the schools that serve the poorest children. While disagreeing with him on the fairness of this policy, I am not in disagreement on the question of the value of selective schools and am not proposing that such schools should simply not exist. Certain of these schools—New York's Bronx High School of Science, for instance, Boston's Latin School, and others—have distinguished histories and have made important contributions to American society.

If there were a multitude of schools *almost* as good as these in every city, so that applicants for high school could select from dozens of good options—so that even parents who did not have the sophistication or connections to assist their children in obtaining entrance to selective schools would not see their kids attending truly *bad* schools, since there would be none—then it would do little harm if certain of these schools were even better than the rest. In such a situation, kids who couldn't be admitted to a famous school such as Bronx Science might be jealous of the ones who did get in, but would not, for this reason, be condemned to third-rate education and would not be written off by the society.

But that is not the situation that exists. In the present situation, which is less a field of education options than a battlefield on which a class and racial war is being acted out, the better schools function, effectively, as siphons which draw off not only the most high-achieving and the best-connected students but their parents too; and this, in turn, leads to a rather cruel, if easily predictable, scenario: Once these students win admission to the places where, in Glazer's words, the "competent" and "gifted" "teach each other" and win "advantageous" labels, there is no incentive for their parents to be vocal on the issues that concern the students who have been excluded. Having obtained what they desired, they secede, to a degree, from the political arena. The political effectiveness of those who have been left behind is thus depleted. Soon enough, the failure of their children and the chaos, overcrowding and low funding of the schools that they attend confirm the wisdom of those families who have fled to the selective schools. This is, of course, exactly what a private school makes possible; but public schools in a democracy should not be allowed to fill this role.

A 16-year-old student in the South Bronx tells me that he went to English class for two months in the fall of 1989 before the school supplied him with a textbook. He spent the entire year without a science text. "My mother offered to help me with my science, which was hard for me," he says, "but I could not bring home a book."

In May of 1990 he is facing final exams, but, because the school requires students to pass in their textbooks one week prior to the end of the semester, he is forced to study without math and English texts.

He wants to go to college and he knows that math and English are important, but he's feeling overwhelmed, especially in math. He asked his teacher if he could come in for extra help, but she informed him that she didn't have the time. He asked if he could come to school an hour early, when she might have time to help him, but security precautions at the school made this impossible.

Sitting in his kitchen, I attempt to help him with his math and English. In math, according to a practice test he has been given, he is asked to solve the following equation: "$2x - 2 = 14$. What is x?" He finds this baffling. In English, he is told he'll have to know the parts of speech. In the sentence "Jack walks to the store," he is unable to identify the verb.

He is in a dark mood, worried about this and other problems. His mother has recently been diagnosed as having cancer. We leave the apartment and walk downstairs to the street. He's a full-grown young man, tall and quiet and strong-looking; but out on the street, when it is time to say good-bye, his eyes fill up with tears.

In the fall of the year, he phones me at my home. "There are 42 students in my science class, 40 in my English class—45 in my home room. When all the kids show up, five of us have to stand in back."

A first-year English teacher at another high school in the Bronx calls me two nights later: "I've got five classes—42 in each! We have no textbooks yet. I'm using my old textbook from the seventh grade. They're doing construction all around me so the noise is quite amazing. They're actually *drilling* in the hall outside my room. I have more kids than desks in all five classes.

"A student came in today whom I had never seen. I said, 'We'll have to wait and see if someone doesn't come so you can have a chair.' She looked at me and said, 'I'm leaving.'"

The other teachers tell her that the problem will resolve itself. "Half the students will be gone by Christmastime, they say. It's awful when you realize that the school is *counting* on the failure of one half my class. If they didn't count on it, perhaps it wouldn't happen. If I *began* with 20 students in a class, I'd have lots more time to spend with each of them. I'd have a chance to track them down, go to their homes, see them on the weekends. . . . I don't understand why people in New York permit this."

One of the students in her class, she says, wrote this two-line poem for Martin Luther King:

> He tried to help the white and black.
> Now that he's dead he can't do jack.

Another student wrote these lines:

America the beautiful,
Who are you beautiful for?

"Frequently," says a teacher at another crowded high school in New York, "a student may be in the wrong class for a term and never know it." With only one counselor to 700 students system-wide in New York City, there is little help available to those who feel confused. It is not surprising, says the teacher, "that many find the experience so cold, impersonal and disheartening that they decide to stay home by the sad warmth of the TV set."

According to a recent study issued by the State Commissioner of Education, "as many as three out of four blacks" in New York City "and four out of five Latinos fail to complete high school within the traditional four-year period." The number of students of all races who drop out between ninth and twelfth grades, and do not return, and never finish school, remains a mystery in New York City. The *Times* itself, at various points, has offered estimates that range from 25 percent to nearly twice that high—a range of numbers that suggests how inconsistent and perplexing school board estimates appear even to seasoned journalists. Sara Rimer of the *New York Times* pegged the rate of those who do not graduate at 46 percent in 1990—a figure that seems credible because it is consistent with the numbers for most other cities with large nonwhite student populations. Including those who drop out during junior high—numbers not included in the dropout figures offered by the New York City Board of Education—it may be that roughly half of New York City's children do not finish school.

The school board goes to great extremes to understate these numbers, and now and then the press explains why numbers coming from the central office are not necessarily to be believed. Number-juggling by school boards—for example, by devising "a new formula" of calculation to appease the public by appearing to show progress—is familiar all over the nation. The *Times,* for instance, notes in another article that, while the "official" dropout rate "has fallen from 45 percent to 29.2 percent," watchdog groups say that the alleged "improvement" stems from "changes in the way the number has been calculated." School boards, moreover, have a vested interest in low-balling dropout figures since the federal and state aid that they receive is pegged to actual attendance.

Listening to children who drop out of school, we often hear an awful note of anonymity. "I hated the school. . . . I never knew who my counselor was," a former New York City student says. "He wasn't available for me. . . . I saw him once. One ten-minute interview. . . . That was all."

Chaos and anonymity overtake some of the elementary schools as well. "A child identified as a chronic truant," reports an official of the Rheedlen Foundation, a child welfare agency in New York City, "might be reported by the teacher—or he might not. Someone from the public school attendance office might try to contact the parents and might be successful, or he might not. The child might attend school again. Probably not." Several children of my acquaintance in the New York City schools were truant for eight months in 1988 and 1989 but were never phoned or visited by school attendance officers.

"We have children," says one grade-school principal, "who just disappear from the face of the earth."

This information strikes one as astonishing. How does a child simply "disappear" in New York City? Efficiency in information transfer—when it comes to stock transactions, for example—is one of the city's best-developed skills. Why is it so difficult to keep track of poor children? When the school board loses track of hundreds of poor children, the explanations given by the city point to "managerial dilemmas" and to "problems" in a new computer system. The same dilemmas are advanced as explanations for the city's inability to get books into classrooms in sufficient numbers for the class enrollments, or to paint the walls or keep the roofs from leaking. But managerial dilemmas never quite suffice to justify these failures. A city which is home to some of the most clever and aggressive and ingenious men and women in the world surely could devise more orderly and less humiliating ways to meet the needs of these poor children. Failure to do so rests in explanations other than a flawed administration, but the city and, particularly, its press appear to favor the administrative explanation. It defuses anger at injustice and replaces it with irritation at bureaucracy.

New York City manages expertly, and with marvelous predictability, whatever it considers humanly important. Fax machines, computers, automated telephones and even messengers on bikes convey a million bits of data through Manhattan every day to guarantee that Wall Street brokers get their orders placed, confirmed, delivered, at the moment they demand. But leaking roofs cannot be fixed and books cannot be gotten into Morris High in time to meet the fall enrollment. Efficiency in educational provision for low-income children, as in health care and most other elementals of existence, is secreted and doled out by our municipalities as if it were a scarce resource. Like kindness, cleanliness and promptness of provision, it is not secured by gravity of need but by the cash, skin color and class status of the applicant.

At a high school in Crown Heights, a neighborhood of Brooklyn, "bathrooms, gymnasiums, hallways and closets" have been converted into classrooms, says the

New York Times. "We have no closets—they're classrooms now," says the principal of another school. "We went to a school," says Robert Wagner, former president of the city's Board of Education, "where there were five Haitian youngsters literally [having classes] in a urinal."

At P.S. 94 in District 10, where 1,300 children study in a building suitable for 700, the gym has been transformed into four noisy, makeshift classrooms. The gym teacher improvises with no gym. A reading teacher, in whose room "huge pieces of a ceiling" have collapsed, according to the *Times,* "covering the floor, the desks and the books," describes the rain that spills in through the roof. "If society gave a damn about these children," says the teacher, "they wouldn't let this happen." These are the same conditions I observed in Boston's segregated schools a quarter-century ago. Nothing has changed.

A class of third grade children at the school has four different teachers in a five-month span in 1989. "We get dizzy," says one child in the class. The only social worker in the school has 30 minutes in a week to help a troubled child. Her caseload holds the names of nearly 80 children. The only truant officer available, who splits her time between this and three other schools in District 10—the district has ten truant officers, in all, for 36,000 children—is responsible for finding and retrieving no less than 400 children at a given time.

When a school board hires just *one* woman to retrieve 400 missing children from the streets of the North Bronx, we may reasonably conclude that it does not particularly desire to find them. If 100 of these children startled us by showing up at school, moreover, there would be no room for them in P.S. 94. The building couldn't hold them.

Many of these problems, says the press again, may be attributed to inefficiency and certain very special bureaucratic difficulties in the New York City system. As we have seen, however, comparable problems are apparent in Chicago, and the same conditions are routinely found in other systems serving mainly nonwhite children. The systems and bureaucracies are different. What is consistent is that all of them are serving children who are viewed as having little value to America.

One way of establishing the value we attribute to a given group of children is to look at the medical provision that we make for them. The usual indices of school investment and performance—class size, teacher salaries and test results—are at best imperfect tools of measurement; but infant survival rates are absolute.

In Central Harlem, notes the *New York Times,* the infant death rate is the same as in Malaysia. Among black children in East Harlem, it is even higher: 42 per thousand, which would be considered high in many Third World nations. "A child's chances of surviving to age five," notes New Jersey Senator Bill Bradley, "are better in Bangladesh than in East Harlem." In the South Bronx, says the author of a recent study by the nonprofit United Hospital Fund of New York City, 531 infants out of 1,000 require neonatal hospitalization—a remarkable statistic that portends high rates of retardation and brain damage. In Riverdale, by contrast, only 69 infants in 1,000 call for such attention.

What is promised these poor children and their parents, says Professor Eli Ginzberg of Columbia University, is "an essential level" of care as "distinct from optimal." Equity, he states, is "out of the question." In a similar way, the *New York Times* observes, a lower quality of education for poor children in New York, as elsewhere in America, is "accepted as a fact." Inequality, whether in hospitals or schools, is simply not contested. Any suggestion that poor people in New York will get the same good health care as the rich or middle class, says Dr. Ginzberg, is "inherently nonsensical."

The *New York Times* describes some public hospitals in which there is "no working microscope" to study sputum samples, no gauze or syringes "to collect blood samples." A couple of years ago, says a physician at the city's Bellevue Hospital, "we were running out of sutures in the operating room." Two years before, Harlem Hospital ran out of penicillin.

"Out-and-out racism, which in our city and our society is institutionalized," said David Dinkins in 1987, a year before he was elected mayor, "has allowed this to go on for years."

But the racial explanation is aggressively rejected by the medical establishment. The *Journal of the American Medical Association*, for example, seeking to explain the differences in care provided to the white and non-white, speculates that "cultural differences" in patients' attitudes toward modern care may be involved. White people, says the *Journal*, "may prefer a more technological approach . . . ."

A doctor at Cook County Hospital in Chicago has another explanation. "I think," he says, "there's a different subjective response on the part of doctors. . . ." And, in explanation of the fact that white patients in cardiac care are two to three times as likely as black patients to be given bypass surgery, he wonders whether white physicians may be "less inclined to invest in a black patient's heart" than in the heart of a "white, middle-class executive" because the future economic value of the white man, who is far more likely to return to a productive job, is often so much higher. Investment strategies in education, as we've seen, are often framed in the same terms: "How much is it worth investing in *this* child as opposed to *that* one? Where will we see the best return?" Although respectable newspapers rarely pose the question in these chilling terms, it is clear that certain choices have been made: Who shall be educated? Who shall live? Who is likely to return the most to our society?

A doctor who has worked for many years in the South Bronx notes that views like these are masked by our apparently benevolent attempts to rectify the damage that we have permitted: "Once these babies, damaged by denial of sufficient health care for their mothers, have been born impaired, we hook them up to tubes and place them on a heated table in an isolette and do our very best to save their lives. It seems that we do not want them to die. Much is made in press reports of our provision for these infants; it may even be that we are prone to praise ourselves for these expensive efforts. But, like the often costly salvage programs of teen-age remediation for the children we have first denied the opportunity for health care, then for preschool, then for equal education, these special wards for damaged infants are provisions of obligatory mercy which are needed only as a consequence of our refusal to provide initial justice."

Health officials sometimes fend off criticism of this nature by assuring us that better facilities or more elaborate surgical procedures offered to rich patients do not necessarily pay off in every case, just as we are often told that higher funding for the schools attended by more affluent children does not necessarily imply superior education. What may be at stake among the wealthy, says the AMA, is "overutilization."

Overutilization is a fact of life in modern medicine—and it raises costs for all prospective patients over the long run—but one feels a troubling uneasiness about the way in which this argument is introduced. "It is," says the doctor I have cited, "an intriguing explanation.

Perhaps, these people seem to say, the point is not that blacks receive too little but that whites receive too much. The second point may be correct, but there is something that I find insidious about the way this point is used. You could also argue, I suppose, that children at expensive high schools do not really profit from their access to so many books, so many foreign languages, so many high-paid teachers, and may even suffer from exposure to so many guidance counselors. We have the right to raise our eyebrows, nonetheless, when 'overutilization' by the very rich has been permitted to continue at the very time that we are told to question whether it much matters. If it doesn't matter, cancel it for everybody. Don't give to them, deny it to us, then ask us to believe that it is not significant."

One consequence of medical and early educational denial is the virtual destruction of the learning skills of many children by the time they get to secondary school. Knowing one is ruined is a powerful incentive to destroy the learning opportunities for other children, and the consequence in many schools is nearly uncontrollable disruption.

Two years ago, in order to meet this and other problems, New York City's Office of School Safety started buying handcuffs. Some 2,300 pairs were purchased for a system that contains almost 1,000 schools: an average of two pairs of handcuffs for each school. "It is no doubt possible," the weekly *New York Observer* editorializes, "to obtain improvements in discipline and even in test scores and dropout rates" by "turning schools into disciplinary barracks." But the paper questions whether such a regimen is ideal preparation for life in a democratic nation.

Handcuffs, however, may be better preparation

than we realize for the lives that many of these adolescent kids will lead. According to the New York City Department of Corrections, 90 percent of the male inmates of the city's prisons are the former dropouts of the city's public schools. Incarceration of each inmate, the department notes, costs the city nearly $60,000 every year.

Handcuffs draw the attention of the press because they are a graphic symbol of so many other problems. But far more damaging, I am convinced, are the more subtle manacles of racial patterns in assignment and school tracking. Few things can injure a child more, or do more damage to the child's self-esteem, than to be locked into a bottom-level track as early as the first or second grade. Add to this the squalor of the setting and the ever-present message of a child's racial isolation, and we have in place an almost perfect instrument to guarantee that we will need more handcuffs and, no doubt, more prisons.

The slotting of black children into lower tracks, according to the Public Education Association of New York, is a familiar practice in the city: "Classes for the emotionally handicapped, neurologically impaired, learning disabled and educable mentally retarded are disproportionately black. . . . Classes for the speech, language, and hearing impaired are disproportionately Hispanic." Citywide, the association adds, fewer than 10 percent of children slotted in these special tracks will graduate from school. Nationwide, black children are three times as likely as white children to be placed in classes for the mentally retarded but only half as likely to be placed in classes for the gifted: a well-known statistic that should long since have aroused a sense of utter shame in our society. Most shameful is the fact that no such outrage can be stirred in New York City.

This is the case with almost every aspect of the degradation of poor children in New York. Even the most thorough exposition of the facts within the major organs of the press is neutralized too frequently by context and a predilection for the type of grayish language that denies the possibilities for indignation. Facts are cited. Editorials are written. Five years later, the same facts are cited once again. There is no sense of moral urgency; and nothing changes.

The differences between school districts and *within* school districts in the city are, however, almost insignificant compared to those between the city and the world of affluence around it—in Westchester County, for example, and in largely prosperous Long Island.

Even in the suburbs, nonetheless, it has been noted that a differential system still exists, and it may not be surprising to discover that the differences are once again determined by the social class, parental wealth, and sometimes race, of the schoolchildren. A study, a few years ago, of 20 of the wealthiest and poorest districts of Long Island, for example, matched by location and size of enrollment, found that the differences in per-pupil spending were not only large but had approximately doubled in a five-year period. Schools, in Great Neck, in 1987, spent $11,265 for each pupil. In affluent Jericho and Manhasset the figures were, respectively, $11,325 and $11,370. In Oyster Bay the figure was $9,980. Compare this to Levittown, also on Long Island but a town of mostly working-class white families, where per-pupil spending dropped to $6,900. Then compare these numbers to the spending level in the town of Roosevelt, the poorest district in the county, where the schools are 99 percent nonwhite and where the figure dropped to $6,340. Finally, consider New York City, where, in the same year, $5,590 was invested in each pupil—less than half of what was spent in Great Neck. The pattern is almost identical to that which we have seen outside Chicago.

Again, look at Westchester County, where, in the same year, the same range of discrepancies was found. Affluent Bronxville, an attractive suburb just north of the Bronx, spent $10,000 for each pupil. Chappaqua's yearly spending figure rose above $9,000. Studying the chart again, we locate Yonkers—a blue-collar town that is predominantly white but where over half the student population is nonwhite—and we find the figure drops to $7,400. This is not the lowest figure, though. The lowest-spending schools within Westchester, spending a full thousand dollars less than Yonkers, serve the suburb of Mount Vernon, where three quarters of the children in the public schools are black.

"If you're looking for a home," a realtor notes, "you can look at the charts for school expenditures and use them to determine if your neighbors will be white and wealthy or, conversely, black or white but poor."

Newsday, a Long Island paper, notes that these comparisons are studied with great interest by home-buyers. Indeed, the paper notes, the state's exhaustive compilation, "Statistical Profiles of Public School Districts," has unexpectedly become a small best-seller. People who want to know if public schools in areas where they are planning to buy homes are actually as good as it is claimed in real-estate brochures, according to *Newsday,* now can use the "Statistical Profiles" as a more authoritative source. Superintendents in some districts say the publication, which compares student performance, spending, staff and such in every state school system, "will be useful for home-buyers." For real-estate agents in the highest-rated districts, the appearance of this publication is good news. It helps to elevate the value of the homes they have for sale.

In effect, a circular phenomenon evolves: The richer districts—those in which the property lots and houses are more highly valued—have more revenue, derived from taxing land and homes, to fund their public schools. The reputation of the schools, in turn, adds to the value of their homes, and this, in turn, expands the tax base for their public schools. The fact that they can levy lower taxes than the poorer districts, but exact more money, raises values even more; and this, again, means further funds for smaller classes and for higher teacher salaries within their public schools. Few of the children in the schools of Roosevelt or Mount Vernon will, as a result, be likely to compete effectively with kids in Great Neck and Manhasset for admissions to the better local colleges and universities of New York state. Even fewer will compete for more exclusive Ivy League admissions. And few of the graduates or dropouts of those poorer systems, as a consequence, are likely ever to earn enough to buy a home in Great Neck or Manhasset.

The New York State Commissioner of Education cautions parents not to make "the judgment that a district is good because the scores are good, or bad because the scores are bad." This, we will find, is a recurrent theme in public statements on this issue, and the commissioner is correct, of course, that overemphasis on test scores, when the differences are slight, can be deceptive. But it may be somewhat disingenuous to act as if the larger differences do not effectively predict success or failure for large numbers of schoolchildren. Certainly home-buyers will be easily convinced that schools in Jericho, third-highest-spending district on Long Island, where the dropout rate is an astonishing and enviable "zero" and where all but 3 percent of seniors go to college, are likely to be "good" compared to those of New York City, which spends only half as much per pupil and where only half the students ever graduate.

An apparent obligation of officials in these situations is to shelter the recipients of privilege from the potential wrath of those who are less favored. Officials manage, in effect, to broadcast a dual message. To their friends they say, in private, "This is the best place to buy a home. These are the best schools. These are the hospitals. These are the physicians." For the record, however, they assure the public that these numbers must not be regarded as implying any drastic differentials.

"The question," says the New York State Commissioner, is not how good the test scores look, but "how well is the district doing by the children it enrolls?" This will bring to mind the statement of New Trier High School's former head of student services. ("This school is right," he said, "for this community." It wouldn't, however, be "right" for everyone.) It does not require much political sophistication to decode these statements—no more than it requires to discern what is at stake when scholars at conservative foundations tell us that black children and white children may have "different learning styles" and require "different strategies" and maybe "different schools."

The commissioner's question—"How well is the district doing by the children it enrolls?"—sounds reasonable. But the answers that are given to that question, as we know, will be determined by class expectations. The schools of the South Bronx—not many, but a few at least—are "doing well" by future typists, auto mechanics, office clerks and factory employees. The schools of Great Neck are "doing well" by those who will someday employ them.

There is a certain grim aesthetic in the almost perfect upward scaling of expenditures from poorest of the poor to richest of the rich within the New York City area: $5,590 for the children of the Bronx and Harlem, $6,340 for the nonwhite kids of Roosevelt, $6,400 for the black kids of Mount Vernon, $7,400 for the slightly better-off community of Yonkers, over $11,000 for the very lucky children of Manhasset, Jericho and Great Neck. In an ethical society, where money was apportioned in accord with need, these scalings would run almost in precise reverse.

The point is often made that, even with a genuine equality of schooling for poor children, other forces still would militate against their school performance. Cultural and economic factors and the flight of middle-income blacks from inner cities still would have their consequences in the heightened concentration of the poorest children in the poorest neighborhoods. Teenage pregnancy, drug use and other problems still would render many families in these neighborhoods all but dysfunctional. Nothing I have said within this book should leave the misimpression that I do not think these factors are enormously important. A polarization of this issue, whereby some insist upon the primacy of school, others upon the primacy of family and neighborhood, obscures the fact that both are elemental forces in the lives of children.

The family, however, differs from the school in the significant respect that government is not responsible, or at least not directly, for the inequalities of family background. It *is* responsible for inequalities in public education. The school is the creature of the state; the family is not. To the degree, moreover, that destructive family situations may be bettered by the future acts of government, no one expects that this could happen in the years immediately ahead. Schools, on the other hand, could make dramatic changes almost overnight if fiscal equity were a reality.

If the New York City schools were funded, for example, at the level of the highest-spending suburbs of Long Island, a fourth grade class of 36 children such as those I visited in District 10 would have had *$200,000 more* invested in their education during 1987. Although a portion of this extra money would have gone into administrative costs, the remainder would have been enough to hire two extraordinary teachers at enticing salaries of $50,000 each, divide the class into *two classes* of some 18 children each, provide them with computers, carpets, air conditioning, new texts and reference books and learning games—indeed, with everything available today in the most affluent school districts—and also pay the costs of extra counseling to help those children cope with the dilemmas that they face at home. Even the most skeptical detractor of "the worth of spending further money in the public schools" would hesitate, I think, to face a grade-school principal in the South Bronx and try to tell her that this "wouldn't make much difference."

It is obvious that urban schools have other problems in addition to their insufficient funding. Administrative chaos is endemic in some urban systems. (The fact that this in itself is a reflection of our low regard for children who depend upon these systems is a separate matter.) Greater funding, if it were intelligently applied, could partially correct these problems—by making possible, for instance, the employment of some very gifted, high-paid fiscal managers who could assure that money is well used—but it probably is also true that major structural reforms would still be needed. To polarize these points, however, and to argue, as the White House has been claiming for a decade, that administrative changes are a "better" answer to the problem than equality of funding and real efforts at desegregation is dishonest and simplistic. The suburbs have better administrations (sometimes, but not always), and they also have a lot more money in proportion to their children's needs. To speak of the former and evade the latter is a formula that guarantees that nothing will be done *today* for children who have no responsibility for either problem.

To be in favor of "good families" or of "good administration" does not take much courage or originality. It is hard to think of anyone who is opposed to either. To be in favor of redistribution of resources and of racial integration would require a great deal of courage—and a soaring sense of vision—in a president or any other politician. Whether such courage or such vision will someday become transcendent forces in our nation is by no means clear.

The train ride from Grand Central Station to suburban Rye, New York, takes 35 to 40 minutes. The high school is a short ride from the station. Built of handsome gray stone and set in a landscaped campus, it resembles a New England prep school. On a day in early June of 1990, I enter the school and am directed by a student to the office.

The principal, a relaxed, unhurried man who, unlike many urban principals, seems gratified to have me visit in his school, takes me in to see the auditorium, which, he says, was recently restored with private charitable funds ($400,000) raised by parents. The crenellated ceiling, which is white and spotless, and the polished dark-wood paneling contrast with the collapsing structure of the auditorium at Morris High. The principal strikes his fist against the balcony: "They made this place extremely solid." Through a window, one can see the spreading branches of a beech tree in the central courtyard of the school.

In a student lounge, a dozen seniors are relaxing on a carpeted floor that is constructed with a number of tiers so that, as the principal explains, "they can stretch out and be comfortable while reading."

The library is wood-paneled, like the auditorium. Students, all of whom are white, are seated at private carrels, of which there are approximately 40. Some are doing homework; others are looking through the *New York Times*. Every student that I see during my visit to the school is white or Asian, though I later learn there are a number of Hispanic students and that 1 or 2 percent of students in the school are black.

According to the principal, the school has 96 computers for 546 children. The typical student, he says, studies a foreign language for four or five years, beginning in the junior high school, and a second foreign language (Latin is available) for two years. Of 140 seniors, 92 are now enrolled in AP classes. Maximum teacher salary will soon reach $70,000. Per-pupil funding is above $12,000 at the time I visit.

The students I meet include eleventh and twelfth graders. The teacher tells me that the class is reading Robert Coles, Studs Terkel, Alice Walker. He tells me I will find them more than willing to engage me in debate, and this turns out to be correct. Primed for my visit, it appears, they arrow in directly on the dual questions of equality and race.

Three general positions soon emerge and seem to be accepted widely. The first is that the fiscal inequalities "do matter very much" in shaping what a school can offer ("That is obvious," one student says) and that any loss of funds in Rye, as a potential consequence of future equalizing, would be damaging to many things the town regards as quite essential.

The second position is that racial integration—for example, by the busing of black children from the city or a nonwhite suburb to this school—would meet with strong resistance, and the reason would not simply be the fear that certain standards might decline. The reason, several students say straightforwardly, is "racial" or, as others say it, "out-and-out racism" on the part of adults.

The third position voiced by many students, but not all, is that equity is basically a goal to be desired and should be pursued for moral reasons, but "will probably make no major difference" since poor children "still would lack the motivation" and "would probably fail in any case because of other problems."

At this point, I ask if they can truly say "it wouldn't make a difference" since it's never been attempted. Several students then seem to rethink their views and say that "it might work, but it would have to start with preschool and the elementary grades" and "it might be 20 years before we'd see a difference."

At this stage in the discussion, several students speak with some real feeling of the present inequalities, which, they say, are "obviously unfair," and one student goes a little further and proposes that "we need to change a lot more than the schools." Another says she'd favor racial integration "by whatever means—including busing—even if my parents disapprove." But a contradictory opinion also is expressed with a good deal of fervor and is stated by one student in a rather biting voice: "I don't see why we should do it. How could it be of benefit to us?"

Throughout the discussion, whatever the views the children voice, there is a degree of unreality about the whole exchange. The children are lucid and their language is well chosen and their arguments well made, but there is a sense that they are dealing with an issue that does not feel very vivid, and that nothing that we say about it to each other really matters since it's "just a theoretical discussion." To a certain degree, the skillfulness and cleverness that they display seem to derive precisely from this sense of unreality. Questions of unfairness feel more like a geometric problem than a matter of humanity or conscience. A few of the students do break through the note of unreality, but, when they do, they cease to be so agile in their use of words and speak more awkwardly. Ethical challenges seem to threaten their effectiveness. There is the sense that they were skating over ice and that the issues we addressed were safely frozen underneath. When they stop to look beneath the ice they start to stumble. The verbal competence they have acquired here may have been gained by building walls around some regions of the heart.

"I don't think that busing students from their ghetto to a different school would do much good," one student says. "You can take them out of the environment, but you can't take the environment out of *them*. If someone grows up in the South Bronx, he's not going to be prone to learn." His name is Max and he has short black hair and speaks with confidence. "Busing didn't work when it was tried," he says. I ask him how he knows this and he says he saw a television movie about Boston.

"I agree that it's unfair the way it is," another student says. "We have AP courses and they don't. Our classes are much smaller." But, she says, "putting them in schools like ours is not the answer. Why not put some AP classes into *their* school? Fix the roof and paint the halls so it will not be so depressing."

The students know the term "separate but equal," but seem unaware of its historical associations. "Keep them where they are but make it equal," says a girl in the front row.

A student named Jennifer, whose manner of speech is somewhat less refined and polished than that of the others, tells me that her parents came here from New York. "My family is originally from the Bronx. Schools are hell there. That's one reason that we moved. I don't think it's our responsibility to pay our taxes to provide for *them*. I mean, my parents used to live there and they wanted to get out. There's no point in coming to a place like this, where schools are good, and then your taxes go back to the place where you began."

I bait her a bit: "Do you mean that, now that you are not in hell, you have no feeling for the people that you left behind?"

"It has to be the people in the area who want an education. If your parents just don't care, it won't do any good to spend a lot of money. Someone else can't want a good life for you. You have got to want it for yourself." Then she adds, however, "I agree that everyone should have a chance at taking the same courses. . . ."

I ask her if she'd think it fair to pay more taxes so that this was possible.

"I don't see how that benefits me," she says.

It occurs to me how hard it would have been for anyone to make that kind of statement, even in the wealthiest suburban school, in 1968. Her classmates would have been unsettled by the voicing of such undisguised self-interest. Here in Rye, in 1990, she can say this with impunity. She's an interesting girl and I reluctantly admire her for being so straightforward.

Max raises a different point. "I'm not convinced," he says, "that AP courses would be valued in the Bronx. Not everyone is going to go to college."

Jennifer picks up on this and carries it a little further. "The point," she says, "is that you cannot give an equal chance to every single person. If you did it, you'd be changing the whole economic system. Let's be honest. If you equalize the money, someone's got to be shortchanged. I don't doubt that children in the Bronx are getting a bad deal. But do we want *everyone* to get a mediocre education?"

"The other point," says Max, "is that you need to match the money that you spend to whether children in the school can profit from it. We get twice as much as kids in the South Bronx, but our school is *more* than twice as good and that's because of who is here. Money isn't the whole story. . . ."

"In New York," says Jennifer, "rich people put their kids in private school. If we equalize between New York and Rye, you would see the same thing happen here. People would pull out their kids. Some people do it now. So it would happen a lot more."

An eleventh grader shakes her head at this. "Poor children need more money. It's as simple as that," she says. "Money comes from taxes. If we have it, we should pay it."

It is at this point that a boy named David picks up on a statement made before. "Someone said just now that this is not our obligation, our responsibility. I don't think that that's the question. I don't think you'd do it, pay more taxes or whatever, out of obligation. You would do it just because . . . it is unfair the way it is." He falters on these words and looks a bit embarrassed. Unlike many of the other students who have spoken, he is somewhat hesitant and seems to choke up on his words. "Well, it's easy for me to be sitting here and say I'd spend my parents' money. I'm not working. I don't earn the money. I don't need to be conservative until I do. I can be as open-minded and unrealistic as I want to be. You can be a liberal until you have a mortgage."

I ask him what he'd likely say if he were ten years older. "Hopefully," he says, "my values would remain the same. But I know that having money does affect you. This, at least, is what they tell me."

Spurred perhaps by David's words, another student says, "The biggest tax that people pay is to the federal government. Why not take some money from the budget that we spend on armaments and use it for the children in these urban schools?"

A well-dressed student with a healthy tan, however, says that using federal taxes for the poor "would be like giving charity," and "charitable things have never worked. . . . Charity will not instill the poor with self-respect."

Max returns to something that he said before: "The environment is everything. It's going to take something more than money." He goes on to speak of inefficiency and of alleged corruption in the New York City schools. "Some years ago the chancellor was caught in borrowing $100,000 from the schools. I am told that he did not intend to pay it back. These things happen too much in New York. Why should we pour money in, when they are wasting what they have?"

I ask him, "Have we *any* obligations to poor people?"

"I don't think the burden is on us," says Jennifer again. "Taxing the rich to help the poor—we'd be getting nothing out of it. I don't understand how it would make a better educational experience for me."

"A child's in school only six hours in a day," says Max. "You've got to deal with what is happening at home. If his father's in the streets, his mother's using crack . . . how is money going to make a difference?"

David dismisses this and tells me, "Here's what we should do. Put more money into preschool, kindergarten, elementary years. Pay college kids to tutor inner-city children. Get rid of the property tax, which is too uneven, and use income taxes to support these schools. Pay teachers more to work in places like the Bronx. It has to come from taxes. Pay them extra to go into the worst schools. You could forgive their college loans to make it worth their while."

"Give the children Head Start classes," says another student. "If they need more buildings, give them extra money so they wouldn't need to be so crowded."

"It has got to come from taxes," David says again.

"I'm against busing," Max repeats, although this subject hasn't been brought up by anybody else in a long while.

"When people talk this way," says David, "they are saying, actually—" He stops and starts again: "They're saying that black kids will never learn. Even if you spend more in New York. Even if you bring them here to Rye. So what it means is—you are writing people off. You're just dismissing them. . . ."

"I'd like it if we had black students in this school," the girl beside him says.

"It seems rather odd," says David when the hour is up, "that we were sitting in an AP class discussing whether poor kids in the Bronx deserve to get an AP class. We are in a powerful position."

In his earnestness and in his willingness to search his conscience, David reminds me of some of the kids I knew during the civil rights campaigns of the mid-1960s. Standing here beside him and his teacher, it occurs to me that many students from this town, much like those in Riverdale, were active in those struggles. Hundreds of kids from neighborhoods like these exposed themselves to all the dangers and the violence that waited for young volunteers in rural areas of Mississippi.

Today, after a quarter of a century, black and white children go to the same schools in many parts of Mississippi—the public schools of Mississippi are, in fact, far more desegregated now than public schools in New York City—but the schools are very poor. In 1987, when a child in Great Neck or Manhasset was receiving education costing some $11,000, children in Neshoba County, Mississippi, scene of many of the bloodiest events during the voter registration drives of 23 years before, received some $1,500 for their education. In equally poor Greene County, Mississippi, things got so bad in the winter of 1988 that children enrolled at Sand Hill Elementary School had to bring toilet paper, as well as writing paper, from their homes because, according to the *Jackson Daily News,* "the school has no money for supplies." In the same year, *Time* magazine described conditions in the Mississippi town of Tunica. The roof of a junior high school building in the district had "collapsed" some years before, the magazine reported, but the district had no money for repairs. School desks were "split" and textbooks were "rotting," said *Time.* "Outside, there is no playground equipment."

At Humphreys County High School, in the Mississippi Delta, the science lab has no equipment except a tattered periodic table. "The only air conditioning," says a recent visitor, "is a hole in the roof." In June and September, when the temperature outside can reach 100 degrees, the school is "double hot," according to the principal. Children graduating from the school, he says, have little to look forward to except low-paid employment at a local catfish plant.

Until 1983, Mississippi was one of the few states with no kindergarten program and without compulsory attendance laws. Governor William Winter tried that year to get the legislature to approve a $60-million plan to upgrade public education. The plan included early childhood education, higher teacher salaries, a better math and science program for the high schools, and compulsory attendance with provisions for enforcement. The state's powerful oil corporations, facing a modest increase in their taxes to support the plan, lobbied vigorously against it. The Mid-Continent Oil and Gas Association began a television advertising campaign to defeat the bill, according to a *Newsweek* story.

"The vested interests are just too powerful," a state legislator said. Those interests, according to *Newsweek,* are "unlikely" to rush to the aid of public schools that serve poor children.

It is unlikely that the parents or the kids in Rye or Riverdale know much about realities like these; and, if they do, they may well tell themselves that Mississippi is a distant place and that they have work enough to do to face inequities in New York City. But, in reality, the plight of children in the South Bronx of New York is almost as far from them as that of children in the farthest reaches of the South.

All of these children say the Pledge of Allegiance every morning. Whether in the New York suburbs, Mississippi, or the South Bronx, they salute the same flag. They place their hands across their hearts and join their voices in a tribute to "one nation indivisible" which promises liberty and justice to all people. What is the danger that the people in a town like Rye would face if they resolved to make this statement true? How much would it really harm their children to compete in a fair race?

CHAPTER 4

Children of the City Invincible: Camden, New Jersey

"Money," writes the *Wall Street Journal,* "doesn't buy better education. . . . The evidence can scarcely be clearer."

The paper notes that student achievement has been static in the nation while per-pupil spending has increased by $1,800 in five years, after adjusting for inflation. "The investment," says the *Journal,* "hasn't paid off."

What the *Journal* does not add is that per-pupil spending grew at the same rate in the suburbs as it did in urban districts, and quite frequently at faster rates, thereby preventing any catch-up by the urban schools. Then, too, the *Journal* does not tell its readers that the current average figure masks disparities between the schools that spend above $12,000 (Rye, New York, for instance) and the ones that spend less than $3,000. Many of the poorest schools today spend less than the average district spent ten years ago.

"Increasing teachers' salaries doesn't mean better schooling," continues the *Journal*. "More experienced teachers don't mean better schooling. Hiring teachers with advanced degrees doesn't improve schooling. . . ."

The *Journal* returns to this idea at every opportunity. "Big budgets don't boost achievement," it announces in another article. "It's parental influence that counts." Money, in fact, the paper says, is "getting a bad name. . . . Indeed, our fixation on numbers—spending per pupil, teacher salaries, class size—may only be distracting us from more fundamental issues. . . . It is even possible to argue that schools themselves don't matter much, at least compared with parental influence. . . . Cash alone can't do the trick. . . . The U.S. has already tried that. . . . It has failed. . . ."

If this is so, one wants to ask, how do we explain those affluent districts where high spending coincides with high achievement? The *Journal*'s answer is that, in these cases, it is not money spent by parents, but the value system that *impels* them to spend money, which is the decisive cause of high achievement in their schools. The *Journal* does not explain how it distinguishes between a parent's values and the cash expenditures that they allegedly inspire. It does not tell its readers that poor districts, where impoverished parent values are supposedly to blame for poor performance, often tax themselves at higher rates than do surrounding suburbs. Nor does it tell us why the wealthy districts, where so many of its readers live, keep on investing so much money in their schools. Nor does it exhort them to do otherwise.

The *Journal* expands upon the theme that higher spending brings "diminishing returns." After a certain point, it says, it makes only a "slight" difference. This is an argument which, if valid, ought to be applied first to control the spending at the upper limits—in the schools that spend $12,000 on each child, for example. Instead, it is employed to caution against wasting further money in the schools where less than half that much is spent. So an argument which, if it is applicable at all, applies most naturally to wealthy schools is used instead to further limit options for poor children.

There is a parallel in this to arguments that we have heard in New York City in regard to health facilities that serve the rich and poor. There, too, we were told by doctors that the more exhaustive services provided to rich patients may not represent superior health care but a form of "overutilization"—again the theory of "diminishing returns." But here again it is not argued that the rich should therefore be denied this luxury, if that is what it is, but only that it shouldn't be extended to poor people. Affluent people, it has often been observed, seldom lack for arguments to deny to others the advantages that they enjoy. But it is going a step further for the *Wall Street Journal* to pretend that they are not advantages.

In disparaging the value of reducing class size in the cities, the newspaper makes this interesting detour: "If deep cuts can be made—reducing large classes by perhaps half—solid benefits may accrue, and research suggests that even smaller cuts can help the performance of young children in particular. But, as a universal principle, the idea that smaller classes automatically mean more learning doesn't hold water."

This pile-up of unassailables protects the *Journal* against logical rebuttal. The use of several qualifying terms—"as a universal principle" and "automatically"— creates a cushion of apparent reason for these statements, but, of course, we are not speaking about universal principles but about specific applications; nor need a change be automatic to be beneficial. What is most disarming, and seductive, in this argument is that it reasons from an insufficient premise: Small cuts won't help. Deep cuts will; but these the *Journal* has ruled out. What if the *Journal* turned it around and worded it like this: "Meager reductions in class size will not make much difference; but cutting the size of classes in Chicago to the class size of Winnetka would be fair and it would do some good. This is what we therefore recommend." The *Journal* doesn't say that. To speak this way would indicate that we might have one set of expectations for all children.

"The usual reduction in class size," says the *Journal*— from 30 to 24, for instance—"isn't enough to make a difference." If this were really true, and if the *Journal* wanted to help the poorest children of Chicago, the logical solution would appear to be to cut their class size even more—perhaps to 17, as in Winnetka. This is a change that even the *Journal*'s editors concede to be worthwhile. But this is a degree of equity the *Journal* does not entertain. It contemplates a minor change and then concludes that it would make only a minor difference.

In actual fact, as every teacher of small children knows, the difference even from 30 kids to 24 would be a blessing in most cases, if some other needed changes came at the same time. But the *Journal* does not speak of several changes. The search is for the one change that will cost the least and bring the best return. "Changing parent values" is the ideal answer to this search because, if it were possible, it would cost nothing and, since it isn't really possible, it doesn't even need to be attempted. Isolating one thing and then telling us that this alone won't do much good and, for this reason, ought not to be tried, is a way of saying that the children of the poor will have to choose one out of seven things rich children take for granted—and then, as a kind of final curse upon their dreams, that any one of those seven things will not make a difference. Why not offer them all seven things?

Ironically, such research as exists is not entirely clear about the benefits of smaller class size to rich children, but very clear about its payoff to the poor. So what the *Journal*'s editors do again is to extrapolate a theme ("diminishing returns") that might be accurately applied to the well-financed schools attended by *their* children, then apply it only to the schools that serve the poor.

After several columns of such qualified and, at certain moments, seemingly well-balanced reasoning, the paper finally casts away its reservations to drive home its central point. "If money can't buy happiness," the final sentence of the editorial reads, "neither can it buy learning."

Thus it is that the progression moves from the unassailable to the self-serving. It will be noted that the *Journal* never says that money "does not matter." This would be implausible to those who read the *Wall Street Journal* to acquire knowledge about making money. What it says is that it matters "much less than we think," or that it is less important than "some other factors," or that it is "not the only factor," or that it is not the "fundamental" factor, or that it will not show instantaneous results, or that money used to lower class size will not matter if this is the only change, or if class size isn't lowered very much. Out of this buildup of discouraging and cautionary words, a mood of cumulative futility is gradually formed. At length it is transformed into a crystal of amused denunciation of the value of equality itself.

Camden, New Jersey, is the fourth-poorest city of more than 50,000 people in America. In 1985, nearly a quarter of its families had less than $5,000 annual income. Nearly 60 percent of its residents receive public assistance. Its children have the highest rate of poverty in the United States.

Once a commercial and industrial center for the southern portion of New Jersey—a single corporation, New York Shipyards, gave employment to 35,000 people during World War II—Camden now has little industry. There are 35,000 jobs in the entire city now, and most of them don't go to Camden residents. The largest employer, RCA, which once gave work to 18,000 people, has about 3,000 jobs today, but only 65 are held by Camden residents. Camden's entire property wealth of $250 million is less than the value of just one casino in Atlantic City.

The city has 200 liquor stores and bars and 180 gambling establishments, no movie theater, one chain supermarket, no new-car dealership, few restaurants other than some fast-food places. City blocks are filled with burnt-out buildings. Of the city's 2,200 public housing units, 500 are boarded up, although there is a three-year waiting list of homeless families. As the city's aged sewers crumble and collapse, streets cave in, but there are no funds to make repairs.

What is life like for children in this city?

To find some answers, I spent several days in Camden in the early spring of 1990. Because the city has no hotel, teachers in Camden arranged for me to stay nearby in Cherry Hill, a beautiful suburban area of handsome stores and costly homes. The drive from Cherry Hill to Camden takes about five minutes. It is like a journey between different worlds.

On a stretch of land beside the Delaware River in the northern part of Camden, in a neighborhood of factories and many abandoned homes, roughly equidistant from a paper plant, a gelatine factory and an illegal dumpsite, stands a school called Pyne Point Junior High.

In the evening, when I drive into the neighborhood to find the school, the air at Pyne Point bears the smell of burning trash. When I return the next day I am hit with a strong smell of ether, or some kind of glue, that seems to be emitted by the paper factory.

The school is a two-story building, yellow brick, its windows covered with metal grates, the flag on its flagpole motionless above a lawn that has no grass. Some 650 children, 98 percent of whom are black or Latino, are enrolled here.

The school nurse, who walks me through the building while the principal is on the phone, speaks of the emergencies and illnesses that she contends with. "Children come into school with rotting teeth," she says. "They sit in class, leaning on their elbows, in discomfort. Many kids have chronic and untreated illnesses. I had a child in here yesterday with diabetes. Her blood-sugar level was over 700. Close to coma level. . . ."

A number of teachers, says the nurse, who tells me that her children go to school in Cherry Hill, do not have books for half the students in their classes. "Black teachers in the building ask me whether I'd put up with this in Cherry Hill. I tell them I would not. But some of the parents here make no demands. They don't know how much we have in Cherry Hill, so they do not know what they're missing."

The typing teacher shows me the typewriters that her students use. "These Olympia machines," she says, "should have been thrown out ten years ago. Most of them were here when I had parents of these children in my class. Some of the children, poor as they are, have better machines at home." The typewriters in the room are battered-looking. It is not a modern typing lab but a historical museum of old typewriters. "What I need are new electrics," says the teacher. When I ask her, "Why not use computers as they do in other schools?" she says, "They'd love it! We don't have the money."

I ask her if the children take this class with a career in mind. Are there any offices in Camden where they use typewriters? "I tell them, 'We are in the age of the computer,' "she replies. " 'We cannot afford to give you a computer. If you learn on these typewriters, you will find it easier to move on to computers if you ever have one.' The keyboard, I explain to them, is virtually the same."

In a class in basic mathematics skills, an eighth grade student that I meet cannot add five and two. In a sixth grade classroom, brownish clumps of plaster dot the ceiling where there once were sound-absorbing tiles. An eighth grade science class is using workbooks in a laboratory without lab equipment.

In another science class, where half of the ceiling tiles are missing and where once again there are no laboratory stations, children are being taught about the way that waves are formed. The teacher instructs them to let a drop of water fall into a glass of water and observe the circles that are formed. Following a printed lesson plan, she tells them to drop the water from successive levels—first six inches, then 12 inches, then a higher level—and "observe the consequences." The answer in her lesson plan is this: "Water forms a circle that spreads out until it reaches the circumference of container." When they drop the water from a certain level they should see the ripples spread out to the edge of the container, then return back toward the center.

The children hold eyedroppers at the levels they are told and, when the teacher tells them, they release a water drop. "Describe the phenomena," the teacher says.

Several children write down in their notebooks, "Water splashes."

The teacher insists they try again until they get the

answer in her lesson plan. I stand behind a row of children and observe them as they drop the water. The students are right: No ripples can be seen. There is a splash and nothing more.

The problem is that the children do not have the right equipment. In order to see ripples form, they need a saucer with a wide circumference. Instead, as a cost-saving measure, the school system has supplied them with cheap plastic cocktail glasses. There is so little water surface that there is no room for waves to form. The water surface shakes a bit when water drops descend from a low level. When the water-droppers are held higher, there is a faint splash. Doggedly persisting with the lesson plan, the teacher tells the children: "Hold the dropper now at 18 inches. Release one drop. Describe the consequence." Students again write "Water splashes" or "The water surface shakes."

What the science lesson is intended to deliver to the children is an element of scientific process. "Controlling for variables" is the description of this lesson in a guide prepared by the New Jersey Board of Education. But, because the children do not have appropriate equipment, there are no variables to be observed. Children in water play in a pre-kindergarten class would learn as much of scientific process as these eighth grade kids are learning. As I leave, the children are being instructed by the teacher to "review the various phenomena we have observed."

Vernon Dover, principal of Pyne Point Junior High, who joins me as I'm heading up the stairs, tells me a student was shot twice in the chest the day before. He says the boy is in a trauma unit at a local hospital.

Two boys race past us as we're standing on the stairs. They leave the building and the principal pursues them out the door. "These are older kids who ought to be in high school," he explains when I catch up with him outside. The playing field next to the school is bleak and bare. There are no goalposts and there is no sports equipment. Beyond the field is an illegal dumpsite. Contractors from the suburbs drive here, sometimes late at night, the principal says, and dump their trash behind the school. A medical lab in Haddon, which is a white suburb, recently deposited a load of waste, including hypodermic needles, in the field. Children then set fire to the trash.

In the principal's office, a fire inspector is waiting to discuss a recent fire. On the desk, as an exhibit, is a blackened bottle with a torn Budweiser label. The bottle is stuffed with paper that was soaked in kerosene. The inspector says that it was found inside the school. The principal sighs. He says there have been several recent fires. The fire alarm is of no use, he says, because there is a steam leak in the boiler room that sets it off. "The fire alarm has been dysfunctional," he says, "for 20 years. . . .

"A boy named Joselito and his brother," says the principal, "set the science room on fire. Another boy set fire to the curtains in the auditorium. He had no history of arson. He was doing well in school. . . . It puzzles me. This school may be the safest place in life for many of these children. Why do they set fires? They do these things and, when I ask them, they do not know why."

He speaks of the difficulty of retaining teachers. "Salaries are far too low," he says. "Some of my teachers have to work two jobs to pay the rent." Space, he tells me, is a problem too. "When we have to hold remedial classes in a woodshop, that's a problem." Up to 20 percent of children in the school, he says, will not go on to high school. "If 650 enter in sixth grade, I will see at least 100 disappear before ninth grade."

I ask him if desegregation with adjacent Cherry

Hill has ever been proposed. "Desegregation in New Jersey means combining black kids and Hispanics," he replies. "Kids in Cherry Hill would never be included. Do you think white people would permit their kids to be exposed to education of this nature? Desegregation? Not with Cherry Hill. It would be easy, a seven-minute ride, but it's not going to happen."

Camden High School, which I visit the next morning, can't afford facilities for lunch, so 2,000 children leave school daily to obtain lunch elsewhere. Many do not bother to return. Nonattendance and dropout rates, according to the principal, are very high.

In a twelfth grade English class the teacher is presenting a good overview of nineteenth-century history in England. On the blackboard are these words: "Idealism . . . Industrialization . . . Exploitation . . . Laissez-faire. . . ." The teacher seems competent, but, in this room as almost everywhere in Camden, lack of funds creates a shortage of materials. Half the children in the classroom have no texts.

"What impresses me," the teacher says after the class is over, "is that kids get up at all and come to school. They're old enough to know what they are coming into."

I ask, "Is segregation an accepted fact for children here?"

"You don't even dare to speak about desegregation now. It doesn't come up. Impossible. It's gone."

He's a likable man with horn-rimmed glasses, a mustache, very dark skin, sensitive eyes, a gentle smile. I ask him where he lives.

"I just moved my family out of Camden," he replies. "I grew up here and I pledged in college I'd return here, and I did. Then, a month ago, I was in school when I was told my house was broken into and cleaned out. I packed my bags.

"I'm not angry. What did I expect? Rats packed tight in a cage destroy each other. I got out. I do not plan to be destroyed."

"President Bush," says Ruthie Green-Brown, principal of Camden High, when we meet later in her office, "speaks of his 'goals' and these sound very fine. He mentions preschool education—early childhood. Where is the money? We have children coming to kindergarten or to first grade who are starting out three years delayed in their development. They have had no preschool. Only a minute number of our kids have had a chance at Head Start. This is the *most* significant thing that you can do to help an urban child if your goal is to include that urban child in America. Do we *want* that child to be included?

"These little children cry out to be cared for. Half the population of this city is 20 years old or less. Seven in ten grow up in poverty. . . .

"There is that notion out there," she goes on, "that the fate of all these children is determined from their birth. If they fail, it's something in themselves. That, I believe, is why Joe Clark got so much praise from the white media. 'If they're failing, kick 'em out!' My heart goes out to children in this city. I've worked in upper-middle-class suburban schools. I know the difference.

"I had a little girl stop in to see me yesterday. A little ninth grade girl. 'It's my lunch hour. I wanted to visit you,' she said. There is so much tenderness and shyness in some children. I told her I was glad she came to visit and I asked her to sit down. We had our sandwiches together. She looked at my desk. 'I'd like to have an office like this someday.' I said to her, 'You can!' But I was looking at this little girl and thinking to myself, 'What are the odds?'"

She speaks of the insistence of the state on a curriculum designed around a battery of tests. The test-driven curriculum, she says, established at the prodding of the former governor, Tom Kean, "is, in a sense, a product of the back-to-basics pressures of the 1980s." The results, she says, are anything but reassuring.

"In the education catch-up game, we are entrapped by teaching to the tests. In keeping with the values of these recent years, the state requires test results. It 'mandates' higher scores. But it provides us no resources in the areas that count to make this possible. So it is a rather hollow 'mandate' after all, as if you could create these things by shouting at the wind.

"If they first had given Head Start to our children *and* pre-kindergarten, *and* materials *and* classes of 15 or 18 children in the elementary grades, *and* computers *and* attractive buildings *and* enough books and supplies *and* teacher salaries sufficient to compete with the suburban schools, and then come in a few years later with their tests and test-demands, it might have been fair play. Instead, they leave us as we are, separate and unequal, underfunded, with large classes, and with virtually no Head Start, and they think that they can test our children into a mechanical proficiency.

"What is the result? We are preparing a generation of robots. Kids are learning exclusively through rote. We have children who are given no conceptual framework. They do not learn to think, because their teachers are straitjacketed by tests that measure only isolated skills. As a result, they can be given no electives, nothing wonderful or fanciful or beautiful, nothing that touches the spirit or the soul. Is this what the country wants for its black children?

"In order to get these kids to pass the tests, they've got to be divided up according to their previous test results. This is what is now described as 'homogeneous grouping.' In an urban school, the term is a misnomer. What does it do to character? The children in the highest groups become elitist, selfish, and they separate themselves from other children. We don't call it tracking, no. But tell me that the children in Math I or in Math VI don't know why they are there."

The children have to pass three tests: in reading, math and writing skills, according to a ninth grade English teacher. "They take preliminary tests before they leave eighth grade," the teacher says. "Eighty percent are failed, because of what has not been done for them in elementary school. So they enter high school labeled 'failures.' Their entire ninth grade year becomes test preparation. No illusions about education as a good thing in itself. They take the state proficiency exams in April of the ninth grade year. If they fail, they do it again in tenth grade. If they fail again, it's all remediation in eleventh grade. They must pass these tests to graduate.

"Already, in the ninth grade, kids are saying, 'If I have to do this all again, I'm leaving.' The highest dropout rate is in those first two years."

She shows me the curriculum for ninth grade writing skills: "Work-A-Text Study Program." There is no literature—in fact, there are no books. The longest passage in the "Work-A-Text" is one short paragraph immediately followed by test questions.

"The high school proficiency exam," another teacher says, "controls curriculum. It bores the children, but we have to do it or we get no money from the state."

From September to May, she says, instruction is exclusively test preparation. "Then, if we are lucky, we have two months left in May and June to teach some subject matter. Eight months for tests. Two months, maybe, to enjoy some poetry or fiction.

"The result of this regime is that the children who survive do slightly better on their tests, because that's all they study, while the failing kids give up and leave the school before they even make it to eleventh grade. The average scores look better, however, and the governor can point to this and tell the press that he is 'raising reading levels.' It isn't hard to do this if your children study nothing but the tests. What have they learned, however? They have learned that education is a brittle, abstract ritual to ready them for an examination. If they get to college they do not know how to think. They know how to pass the tests and this may get them into college, but it cannot keep them there. We see students going off to Rutgers every year. By the end of the first semester they are back in Camden. So we teach them failure. When you think of what their peers in Cherry Hill have gotten in the same years, it seems terribly unfair. I call it failure by design."

I ask her if the students see it in the way that she does, as a case of failure by design.

"Our students are innocent of the treachery of the world," she says. "They do not yet understand what is in store for them."

"My first priority, if we had equal funding," says the principal when I return to see her at the end of school, "would be the salaries of teachers. People ask me, 'Can you make a mediocre teacher better with more money?' I am speaking of the money to *attract* the teachers. In some areas where I run into shortages of staff—math and science, in particular—I get provisional teachers who are not yet certified but sometimes highly talented, exciting people. As soon as he or she becomes proficient— squat!—where is she? Out to the suburbs to earn $7,000 more. . . . So this gives you a sense perhaps of the unfairness that we face.

"I am asked to speak sometimes in towns like Princeton. I tell them, 'If you don't believe that money makes a difference, let your children go to school in Camden. *Trade* with our children—not beginning in the high school. Start when they're little, in the first or second grade.' When I say this, people will not meet my eyes. They stare down at the floor. . . .

"I have a brochure here. It is from—" she names a well-known private school. "They want me to accept a nomination as headmistress. I'm skimming through this and I see—alumni gifts, the colleges that they attend, 99 percent of children graduating, a superb curriculum. . . . The endowment of this school is $50 million. . . . You are left with no choice but to think, 'My God! Am I preparing children to compete with this? And do they even have a *chance*?' "

At night two teachers from the high school meet me at a restaurant in Cherry Hill because, they say, there is no place in Camden to have dinner. At 8:00 P.M. we drive back into Camden.

As we drive, they speak about the students they are losing. "Six hundred children enter ninth grade," says one of the teachers, Linnell Wright, who has been at Camden High School for six years. "By eleventh grade we have about 300. I am the eleventh grade adviser so I see the difference. I look out into the auditorium when the freshman class comes in. The room is full. By the time they enter the eleventh grade, the same room is half empty. The room is haunted by the presence of the children who are gone. . . .

"This," she tells me as we pass an old stone church, "is supposed to be the church attended by Walt Whitman. I don't know if he cared much for churches, but he did reside in Camden in the last years of his life." A sign on the door indicates that it is now a homeless shelter.

A block from the church, we pass two ruined houses with their walls torn out. A few blocks more and we are at the waterfront, next to the Delaware.

"That darkened building is the Campbell's plant," the other teacher, Winnefred Bullard, says. "Campbell's just announced that they'll be closing down."

On the roof of the shuttered factory is an illuminated soup can: red and white, the Campbell's logo. Now the company is leaving town. General Electric, Mrs. Bullard tells me, may be leaving too. Its RCA division had a major operation here for many years, but Mrs. Bullard says that it is virtually shut down. As we pass the RCA plant on the silent waterfront, I see the lighted symbol of that corporation too: the faithful dog attending to his master's voice. The plants are closing and the jobs are disappearing, but the old familiar symbols are still there for now.

"The world is leaving us behind in Camden," Mrs. Bullard says.

Before us, over the darkened water of the Delaware, are the brightly lighted high-rise office buildings and the new hotels and condominiums of Philadelphia. The bridges that cross the river here in Camden bear the names of Whitman and Ben Franklin. History surrounds the children growing up in Camden, but they do not learn a lot of it in school. Whitman is not read by students in the basic skills curriculum. Few children that I met at Camden High, indeed, had ever heard of him.

Before the announcement of the closing of the Campbell's plant, says Mrs. Bullard, there had been high hopes for a commercial rebirth on the waterfront of Camden. Plans for a riverfront hotel had been announced. Land had been cleared and several buildings were destroyed.

Now it is an endless parking lot. Mrs. Bullard turns the car around so that the Delaware is just behind us. A turn to the left, and one to the right, and just ahead of us there is a huge, white, modern building. It's the first new structure I have seen in Camden. Brilliantly illuminated, it resembles a hotel.

"It may be the closest we will come to a hotel in Camden," Mrs. Bullard says. "This is the new Camden County Jail."

On the street beside the jail, several black women in white gloves are making gestures with their hands to men whose faces can be seen behind the windows; "They are making conversation with their men," says Mrs. Bullard. Directly across the street is the two-story wooden house in which Walt Whitman wrote the final manuscript of *Leaves of Grass* and in which he died, in 1892. One block away, the south face of the Camden City Hall bears Whitman's words: "In a dream I saw a city invincible."

The city, Mrs. Bullard tells me, has the highest tax rate in the area. "But," she says, "in order to get more businesses to settle here, we have to give them tax relief. The result is that we don't gain anything in taxes. But, even with that, we can't attract them."

The major industries, apart from RCA and Campbell's, are a trash incinerator and a sewage-treatment plant (neither of which pay taxes to the city), scrapyards (there are ten of them) and two new prisons. A third prison, intended for North Camden near the Pyne Point neighborhood, was halted by the pressures brought by local activists. According to Father Michael Doyle, pastor of Sacred Heart Church in North Camden, "55 million gallons of the county's sewage come into Camden every day. It's processed at the treatment plant, a stone's throw from my church. Five blocks south, on the other side, they're finishing a new incinerator for the county." The incinerator tower, some 350 feet in height, rises above the church and soon will add its smoke to air already fouled by the smell of sewage.

"The stench is tremendous," says Lou Esola, an environmentalist who lives in neighboring Pennsauken. "Sacred Heart is in the midst of it. I went down to talk with Father Doyle. I stepped out of my car and saw the houses and the children and I wondered, 'How can people live here?' They would never dare to put these things in Cherry Hill. It simply would not happen."

"Anything that would reduce the property values of a town like Cherry Hill," says Father Doyle, "is sited here in Camden." In this way, he notes, the tax base for the schools of Cherry Hill remains protected while the tax base for the schools of Camden is diminished even more. Property values in the city are so low today that abandoned houses in North Camden can be purchased for as little as $1,000.

Camden, he says, once had more industry per capita than any city in the world. "The record industry had its start here. Enrico Caruso first recorded here in Camden. Now we have to settle for scrap metal, sewage treatment and incinerators. When you're on your knees, you take whatever happens to come by. . . ."

Everyone who could leave, he says, has now departed. "What is left are all the ones with broken wings. I can't tell you what it does to children to grow up amid this filth and ugliness. The toxic dangers aren't the worst. It is the aesthetic consequences that may be most damaging in the long run. What is the message that it gives to children to grow up surrounded by trash burners, dumpsites and enormous prisons? Kids I know have told me they're ashamed to say they come from Camden.

"Still, there is this longing, this persistent hunger.

People look for beauty even in the midst of ugliness. 'It rains on my city,' said an eight-year-old I know, 'but I see rainbows in the puddles.' It moved me very much to hear that from a child. But you have to ask yourself: How long will this child look for rainbows?"

I spend my final day in Camden at the city's other high school, Woodrow Wilson, which also has its difficulties in retaining students. The dropout rate at Woodrow Wilson High is 58 percent, a number that does not include the 10 to 20 percent of would-be Wilson students who drop out in junior high and therefore do not show up in official figures. Of the nearly 1,400 children who attend this school, more than 800 drop out in the course of four years. About 200 finally graduate each year. Only 60 of these kids, however, take the SATs—prerequisite for entrance to most four-year colleges.

The principal, Herbert Factor, an even-tempered white man in a soft tweed jacket who has been here for three years, takes me into a chemistry lab that has no lab equipment, just a fish tank and a single lab desk at the front, used by the teacher. The room is sweltering. "Something is wrong with the heating," says the principal. "We're right above the boiler room." He tugs at his shirt collar. "Would you want to study in this room? I'm surprised the fish don't die."

Fifty computers line the wall of a computer lab, but 30 to 40 can't be used, according to the teacher. "They were melted by the heat," she says.

"Hot as hell!" the principal remarks.

"We spend about $4,000 yearly on each student," he reports, as we are heading to the cafeteria for lunch. "The statewide average is about $5,000, but our children are competing also with the kids in places such as Cherry

Hill, which spends over $6,000, Summit, which is up to $7,000, Princeton, which is past $8,000 now. . . .

"My students also have to work much longer hours than suburban children to earn money after school. Then there is the lack of health care and the ugly poverty on every side. Nonetheless, they have to take the same tests as the kids in Cherry Hill.

"The sophomore class contains about 550 students. This includes 350 entering ninth graders, who are reading on the average at a sixth grade level, although many read much lower—some at only fourth grade level—and about 200 older kids who are held back each year because they failed the state exam. Of the 200 who make it to twelfth grade and graduate, maybe 80 to 100 go on to some further education. Of these, maybe 20 to 25 enroll in four-year colleges of any real distinction.

"How many graduate from higher education? Not even 40 percent of those who are admitted will complete a four-year program.

"For the brightest kids, the ones who have a chance at four-year college, we cannot provide an AP program. We don't have the funds or the facilities. We offer something called 'AT'—'academically talented' instruction—but it's not the same as AP classes in the suburbs. So, when they take the SATs, they're at that extra disadvantage. They've been given less but will be judged by the same tests."

In discussion of the problems that he faces, the principal of Woodrow Wilson High School differs in one interesting respect from several of the black administrators I have met. The latter, even when entirely open in the things they tell me, tend to speak with torn desires. On the one hand they want to be sure I understand how bitterly their children are denied resources given to the rich. On the other hand they want me to respect their efforts, and their teachers, and their children—they are frightened of the terribly demoralizing power of bad press reports—and also, partly out of racial pride and loyalty, they seem determined to convince me that their school is not a "dumpsite" or a "black hole" or "backwater," hoping perhaps that I will see it as a valiant effort to transcend the odds. So, on the one hand, they describe how bad things are, and, on the other hand, they paint an upbeat picture of the many hopeful programs they have instituted, typically describing them in jargon-ridden terms ("individually tailored units," "every child learning at her own pace"), often labeled with elaborate alphabetic acronyms, which differ from one city to another only in the set of letters they employ.

But it is so very human and so natural and understandable that black officials wouldn't want to see their school subjected to the pity or contempt of a white visitor. One of the most poignant things about the visits I have made to urban schools is that the principals make such elaborate preparations for my visits. In suburban schools, with few exceptions, it is not like this at all. "Go wherever you like. No need to ask permission," I am told. "Take a bunch of kids up to the library and grill them if you want." In the urban schools it is quite different. Careful schedules are arranged well in advance. The principal escorts me or assigns a trusted aide to shepherd me to the right classrooms and to steer me from the empty labs, the ugly gyms, the overcrowded rooms in which embattled substitutes attempt in vain to keep a semblance of control. Then, too, the principals are rarely willing to allow me very much unsupervised discussion with the children.

More often than not, they also seem reluctant to describe their schools as being "segregated" or, indeed, even to speak of segregation. It is as if they have assimilated racial isolation as a matter so immutable, so absolute, that it no longer forms part of their thinking. They speak of their efforts "to make this school a quality institution." The other word—"equality"—is not, it seems, a realistic part of their ambition. I am reminded often, in these visits, of the times when I would visit very poorly funded all-black southern colleges, as long ago as 1966 and 1967, and would hear the teachers speaking, with the bravest front they could present, of "making do" and "dealing with the needs of our own children." The longing voiced today, as then, by good courageous black administrators and black teachers is for something that might be at best "a little less unequal," but with inequality a given and with racial segregation an unquestioned starting point.

Sometimes I have put the matter this way in talking with a black school principal and asked the question sharply: "Are we back to *Plessy,* then?" At this point, all pretense falls away: "What do you think? Just look around the school. Should I beat my head against the wall? This is reality."

Only once, and not in Camden, did I have the opportunity to press the matter further with a black school principal. I said that I felt black principals were sometimes feeding into the desires of the white society by praising the virtues of "going it alone" as if this were a matter of their choice, not of necessity. The principal, who must go unnamed, said this: "I'm sad to hear you say that, and I'm also sad to say it, but the truth is that we are, to a degree, what you have made of us. The United States now has, in many black administrators of the public schools, precisely the defeated overseers it needs to justify this terrible immiseration. It is a tradition that goes back at least 300 years. A few of us are favored. They invite us to a White House ceremony and award us something—a 'certificate of excellence'—for our achievement. So we accept some things and we forget some other things and what we can't forget we learn how to shut out of mind and we adopt the rhetoric that is required of us and we speak of 'quality' or 'excellence'—not justice."

Questions of justice are not distant from the thoughts of Woodrow Wilson students, as I learn when six young men and women meet me for a conversation after lunch.

"I have a friend," says Jezebel, who is in the eleventh grade. "She goes to school in Cherry Hill. I go to her house and I compare the work she's doing with the work I'm doing. Each class at her school in Cherry Hill, they have the books they're s'posed to have for their grade level. Here, I'm in eleventh grade. I take American history. I have an eighth-grade book. So I have to ask, 'Well, are they three years smarter? Am I stupid?' But it's not like that at all. Because we're kids like they are. We're no different. And, you know, there are *smart* people here. But then, you know, they have that money goin' to their schools. They have a nice *clean* school to go to. They have carpets on the floors and air-conditioned rooms and brand-new books. Their old books, when they're done with them, they ship them here to us."

Books and carpets and cleanliness seem reasonable matters to complain about, but air conditioning strikes me as a luxury. I ask her if it really matters all that much.

"It gets steaming hot here in the summer. Lots of kids, on summer days, they look outside. They'd rather be outside there in the park. . . . But what I want to know is this: Why are the levels of our work so different? What we call a 'C' at our school is a 'D' in Cherry Hill. And I'm thinking, 'I can *get* it. I can work at my grade level same as them. Maybe better. I can do as well as other people. . . .' "

An eleventh grader named Luis tells me that he

went to private school before he came to Woodrow Wilson High. "If you ask me how it's different, I begin to think of books, or air conditioners, or computers. But it isn't one thing. It's a lot of things: the whole effect. The teachers at that school, they had a comfortable lounge. You go in there, with their permission, if you want to sit and get to know your teacher. The students also have a lounge. It isn't *concentrated*. It's relaxed. You drive up a slope. The school is on a hill. You go up the driveway and it's circular and like the entrance to a college campus or a nice hotel. The school is brick. A real nice-lookin' school. There is a lacrosse field. When you go to lunch you go together, not in shifts, and it's a pleasant place for lunch. My class had 15 students. And the teachers help you during class. They have the time, you know, to make sure that you understand. . . .

"In this school, they sometimes do not have the time. You know: They Xerox something. 'Here, do this.' Just hand it out. 'This is your work. Just do it. Get it in before the end of class. You'll get a grade.' And, you know, it does take time for kids to understand. And some kids, when they don't understand—they feel embarrassed. You don't want to be the only one to raise your hand and sayin' you don't understand. You sit there and say nothin'. If the teacher has the time to come around and talk to you, it's different. You're not scared to say to him, 'I didn't understand. I didn't get it.' And he helps you. And you're willing to come early on the next day and be helped some more. And, in this way, you're really *learnin'*."

I ask them: "If you had the things here that you want—new books, more computers, air conditioning, all of that—it would take a lot of money. Money has to come from taxes. Where would that money and those taxes come from?"

"If there's a surplus, say, in Cherry Hill," Luis replies, "well, you could divide that money."

"Let's say that you have $10,000," Jezebel says. "Split that sum in half: $5,000 for Cherry Hill, $5,000 for Camden."

Luis: "Make it equal. I don't mean that you should make it worse for them. They have the right to education. But we need our education too. Make it equal. Even if you have to take some funds from somewhere else. . . ."

I ask him this: "If they raise more money from their taxes out in Cherry Hill, don't they have the right to keep that money there and use it to buy things that they may want for their own school?"

"What could they possibly want," says Jezebel, "that they don't have?"

After a silence, she goes on. "Listen. They have those beautiful science labs. I've been there and I've seen them. You came to my science lab. You saw the difference. Look at this." She hands me a paperback volume with no cover and with pages falling out. "You see this book? We have to read Charles Dickens. That's the book they gave me. Pages are missing. *A Tale of Two Cities.* We don't even have enough for every student. There are just ten students in that class!" Her eyes are bright with anger. "Ten people! They had only seven books! Why are we treated like this?"

I ask her, "Did you like the book?"

"I loved it," she replies.

"I heard of a place once," says the girl beside her, "where white children and black children go to the same school. First and second graders go to one school. Third and fourth and fifth go to another. So it's mixed. Now that's been going on for years. So there are mixed families. People meet in school. When they're grown up, sometimes they marry."

I ask her, "If the governor announced that he was going to combine you with the kids from Cherry Hill— everybody goes to one school maybe for the ninth grade and the tenth grade, everybody to the other school for both their final years—what would you say?"

"As soon as it was announced, they'd start remodeling," Luis replies. "You'd see progress very fast. Parents of white children, with their money, they'd come in and say, 'We need this fixed. Our kids deserve it.' So they'd back us up, you see, and there'd be changes."

"I'd be glad," says Jezebel, "but they would never do it."

"What they'll say," says Luis, "is that it's a loss of education for their children. And that's so for now. They'd be afraid to come here. They would think the education would be less. It is. But it would be more natural to be together.

"Put it this way," he goes on. "Sooner or later, we have got to be around each other. You go to a hospital, or to a lawyer's office, and you'll see all kinds of different people. That's America. We have to live in the same world."

"I think," says Jezebel, "that it would take a war to bring us all together. Do you know how close we are to Cherry Hill? You go out from here five minutes down across the bridge. You're on the way to Cherry Hill."

"It seems the plan for now," I say, "is not to let you go to school in Cherry Hill but to try to make this a much better school. If this were done, and if the schools were equal, would that be enough?"

"I don't like that," she replies. "First, they wouldn't be equal. You know that as well as I. So long as there are no white children in our school, we're going to be cheated. That's America. That's how it is. But, even if they both were equal, you would still have students feeling, 'Well, if I'm not good enough for them, if we are going to be separate—well, I'm lower . . . somehow. . . .' You think: lower."

Luis speaks about the guidance system at the school. "This is what it's like," he says. "You go in to your counselor. He's under pressure so he acts impatient: 'What do you need?' You ask for help on college credits. They don't know. You end up choosing on your own. . . . We need people who can *tell* us what we do not know, or what we need to know. We don't know everything. But they don't have the time."

Chilly, which is the nickname of a young Cambodian girl, speaks up for the first time: "I'll give you an example. I went to my counselor. He said, 'What do you want?' I said, 'I want to be a lawyer. I don't know what courses I should take.' He told me, 'No, you cannot be a lawyer.' I said, 'Why?' He said, 'Your English isn't good.' I'm seventeen. I've been here in America four years. I want to be a lawyer. He said, 'No. You cannot be a lawyer. Look for something else. Look for an easier job.' "

Luis: "Who said that?"

Chilly: "I don't want to say his name. . . . Well, anyway, I feel so disappointed. He tells me, 'Choose another job.' He gives me all these books that list these easy jobs. He says, 'Choose something else.' I tell him that I cannot choose because I do not *know*. 'Which one do you want?' he says. I say, 'How can I know?' I can't decide my life there in just 15 minutes. . . .

"This upset me very much because, when I came to America, they said, you know, 'This is the place of opportunity.' I'd been through the war. Through all of that. And now I'm here, and, even though my English may not be so good—"

The other students grow aroused.

"Don't let him shake your confidence," says Jezebel.

Chilly: "You know, I have problems with my self-esteem. I wasn't born here. Every day I think, 'Maybe he's right. Do something else.' But what I'm thinking is that 15 minutes isn't very long for somebody to counsel you about a choice that will determine your whole life. He throws this book at me: 'Choose something else!'"

The other students side with her so warmly, and so naturally; it is as if perhaps they feel their own dreams are at risk along with hers. "I want to say this also," she goes on. "Over there, where I was from, America is very famous. People think of it like heaven. Like, go to America—you go to heaven. Because life there is hell. Then you get here and, you know, it's not like that at all.

"When I came here I thought that America was mainly a white nation. Then I came here to this school and there are no white people. I see black and Spanish. I don't see white students. I think: 'Oh, my God! Where are the white Americans?' Well, I mean it did seem strange to me that all the black and Spanish and the Asian people go to the same school. Why were they putting us together? It surprised me. And I feel so disappointed. I was thinking: 'Oh, my God!' This school, you know, is named for Woodrow Wilson. . . ."

What does money buy for children in New Jersey? For high school students in East Orange, where the track team has no field and therefore has to do its running in the hallways of the school, it buys a minimum of exercise but a good deal of pent-up energy and anger. In mostly upper-middle-income Montclair, on the other hand, it buys two recreation fields, four gyms, a dance room, a wrestling room, a weight room with a universal gym, tennis courts, a track, and indoor areas for fencing. It also buys 13 full-time physical education teachers for its 1,900 high school students. East Orange High School, by comparison, has four physical education teachers for 2,000 students, 99.9 percent of whom are black.

A physical education expert, asked to visit a grade school in East Orange, is astonished to be told that jump ropes are in short supply and that the children therefore have to jump "in groups." Basketball courts, however, "are in abundance" in these schools, the visitor says, because the game involves little expense.

Defendants in a recent suit brought by the parents of schoolchildren in New Jersey's poorest districts claimed that differences like these, far from being offensive, should be honored as the consequence of "local choice"—the inference being that local choice in urban schools elects to let black children gravitate to basketball. But this "choice"—which feeds one of the most intransigent myths about black teen-age boys—is determined by the lack of other choices. Children in East Orange cannot choose to play lacrosse or soccer, or to practice modern dance, on fields or in dance studios they do not have; nor can they keep their bodies clean in showers that their schools cannot afford. Little children in East Orange do not choose to wait for 15 minutes for a chance to hold a jump rope.

In suburban Millburn, where per-pupil spending is some $1,500 more than in East Orange although the tax rate in East Orange is three times as high, 14 different AP courses are available to high school students; the athletic program offers fencing, golf, ice hockey and lacrosse; and music instruction means ten music teachers and a music supervisor for six schools, music rooms in every elementary school, a "music suite" in high school, and an "honors music program" that enables children to work one-on-one with music teachers. Meanwhile, in an elementary school in Jersey City, seventeenth-poorest city in America, where the schools are 85 percent non-white, only 30 of 680 children can participate in instrumental music. The school provides no instruments—the children have to rent them—and the classes take place not in "music suites" but in the lunchroom or the basement of the school. Art instruction is also meager in the Jersey City schools. The entire budget for art education comes to $2.62 per child for one year—less than the price of a pad of drawing paper at a K mart store. Computer classes take place in a storage closet. This may be compared to Princeton, where the high school students work in comfortable computer areas equipped with some 200 IBMs, as well as with a hookup to Dow Jones to study stock transactions. These kinds of things are unknown to kids in Jersey City.

Academic failure rates and dropout rates are very high in Jersey City's public schools, compared, for example, to the schools of Princeton. Moreover, as a judge has noted in New Jersey, the students listed as dropouts by most urban districts "tend to be only those . . . who *tell* the school that they are leaving." Statistics offered by the schools, therefore, "greatly understate the problem," says the judge. But, even with more accurate reporting, the percentile differences in failure rates would still obscure the full dimensions of the inequalities at stake. In Jersey City, 45 percent of third grade children fail their basic-skills exams, compared to only 10 percent in Princeton. But Jersey City's 45 percentage points translate to the failure of 800 children; in Princeton, where the student population is much smaller, ten percentage points translate to only 19 children. Again, the high school dropout rate of Jersey City, 52 percent, translates to failure for some 2,500 children every four years. The corresponding rate in Princeton, less than 6 percent, translates to only 40 children. Behind the good statistics of the richest districts lies the triumph of a few. Behind the saddening statistics of the poorest cities lies the misery of many.

Overcrowding in New Jersey, as in Harlem and the Bronx, is a constant feature of the schools that serve the poorest children. In low-income Irvington, for instance, where 94 percent of students are nonwhite, 11 classes in one school don't even have the luxury of classrooms. They share an auditorium in which they occupy adjacent sections of the stage and backstage areas. "It's very difficult," says the music teacher, "to have concert rehearsals with the choir" while ten other classes try to study in the same space. "Obviously," she says, "there is a problem with sound. . . ."

"I'm housed in a coat room," says a reading teacher at another school in Irvington. "I teach," says a music teacher, "in a storage room." Two other classes, their teachers say, are in converted coal bins. A guidance counselor says she holds her parent meetings in a closet. "My problem," says a compensatory-reading teacher, "is that I work in a pantry. . . . It's very difficult to teach in these conditions."

At Irvington High School, where gym students have no showers, the gym is used by up to seven classes at a time. To shoot one basketball, according to the coach, a student waits for 20 minutes. There are no working lockers. Children lack opportunities to bathe. They fight over items left in lockers they can't lock. They fight for their eight minutes on the floor. Again, the scarcity of things that other children take for granted in America— showers, lockers, space and time to exercise—creates the overheated mood that also causes trouble in the streets. The students perspire. They grow dirty and impatient. They dislike who they are and what they have become.

The crowding of the school reflects the crowding of the streets. "It becomes striking," says a parent in another urban district, "how closely these schools reflect their communities, as if the duty of the school were to prepare a child for the life he's born to. . . . It hardly seems fair."

The crowding of children into insufficient, often squalid spaces seems an inexplicable anomaly in the United States. Images of spaciousness and majesty, of endless plains and soaring mountains, fill our folklore and our music and the anthems that our children sing. "This land is your land," they are told; and, in one of the patriotic songs that children truly love because it summons up so well the goodness and the optimism of the nation at its best, they sing of "good" and "brotherhood" "from sea to shining sea." It is a betrayal of the best things that we value when poor children are obliged to sing these songs in storerooms and coat closets.

Among the overcrowded districts of New Jersey, one of the most crowded may be Paterson. The city is so short of space that four elementary schools now occupy abandoned factories. Children at one wood-frame elementary school, which has no cafeteria or indoor space for recreation, eat lunch in a section of the boiler room. A bathroom houses reading classes. Science labs in the high schools have no microscopes; sinks do not work; and class enrollment is too high for lab capacity. At Paterson's Kennedy High School, there is one physics section for 2,200 high school students. In affluent Summit, by comparison, where the labs are well equipped, there are six physics sections for 1,100 children.

Counseling facilities are particularly scarce in Paterson. One counselor serves 3,600 children in the elementary schools. Defendants in the recent period of litigation sought to undercut the relevance of counseling comparisons by asking if it is appropriate for schools to deal with "personal" problems that low-income children bring to class. But they did not ask this question in regard to affluent children. If it is an inappropriate concern for urban schools, observers asked, why did kids in wealthy districts need so high a ratio of conselors? Once again, it strains belief to say that Paterson's parents choose not to provide their children with sufficient counseling—just as it would not be credible to say that, when their kids are physically unwell, they choose to wait all day in crowded clinics rather than pay for the consoling care and kindliness available from private doctors. Local choice, where residence is not by choice, becomes a brutal euphemism for necessity.

How little choice poor children really have is seen at East Side High in Paterson. The school is in a stolid-looking building with no campus and no lawn. The regimen within the school is much like that which we have seen within the schools of Camden. Scarcity and squalor are again compounded by the consequences of a test-curriculum that strips the child's school day down to meaningless small particles of unrelated rote instruction.

"The pressure for testing starts in elementary school," the principal reports, "and then intensifies in junior high. By the time they get to high school, preparation for the state exams controls curriculum."

According to a daily schedule given to me by Alfred Weiss, who chairs the Department of English at the school, 12 English teachers offer 60 classes in test-preparation to about 1,200 of the 2,200 students every day. I ask him what gets sacrificed in the test-preparation program.

"Literature gets lost," he says. "The driving notion here is that skills learned in isolation are more useful than skills learned in context. We need more money, but one of the dangers is that new state funds will be restricted to another stripped-down program of this nature. I mean, they'll give us funds if we will give them scores. The money will not be for education."

Paterson, he reminds me, was the home of the poet William Carlos Williams. But students at East Side High will get to know no more of William Carlos Williams than their peers at Woodrow Wilson High in Camden know about the writings of Walt Whitman.

In a basic-skills-improvement class, which, like all the English classes, takes place in the basement of the school, the textbook is the same compendium of short skill-paragraphs and brief examination questions that I saw in Camden. The classroom is dingy and gets little outside light. There are four different kinds of desks, some of them extremely old and too small for the students. The awkwardness of full-grown adolescents folding up their knees under these little desks stays in my mind afterward.

In another basic-skills class in the basement, a teacher tells me that the average reading level of the students in the school is just below sixth grade. The room, in which two classes take place simultaneously, is being used to teach the "Work-A-Text" on 12 computers. As elsewhere in the Paterson and Camden schools, computers are not used for reasoning or research—what the suburbs label "higher-order skills"—but as a toylike substitute for pen and paper.

Mr. Weiss, the English Department chairman who has led me through the school, stays very close to me and rarely smiles. An intelligent, weary-looking man with close-cropped hair, he does not realize possibly that I feel stifled by his presence. On the other hand, his presence is instructive, for his anguished manner and uncomfortable role, that of a top-rate scholar forced to shove aside all that he knows and values to atone for the results of history and poverty, embody much of the despair that filters through the classrooms and the hallways of the school. Forced by state requirements to teach an arid test-curriculum, he tells me that he feels a sense of long-ing for the literary work that led him into teaching. "I'm a New Yorker. I grew up in the South Bronx and I attended Morris High and City College. I insist that we do Shake-speare in non-basics classes. *Romeo and Juliet* in the tenth grade. *Julius Caesar* in eleventh. This woman," he says— and gestures toward a teacher—"will be doing *Caesar* next year with her students." Then, however: "I wonder what she thinks she will be doing. . . ." He throws out his hands, and winces, and then shrugs.

East Side High became well known some years ago when its former principal, a colorful and controversial figure named Joe Clark, was given special praise by U.S. Education Secretary William Bennett. Bennett called the school "a mecca of education" and paid tribute to Joe Clark for throwing out 300 students who were thought to be involved with violence or drugs.

"He was a perfect hero," says a school official who has dinner with me the next evening, "for an age in which the ethos was to cut down on the carrots and increase the sticks. The day that Bennett made his visit, Clark came out and walked the hallways with a bullhorn and a bat. If you didn't know he was a principal, you would have thought he was the warden of a jail. Bennett created Joe Clark as a hero for white people. He was on the cover of *Time* magazine. Parents and kids were held in thrall after the president endorsed him.

"In certain respects, this set a pattern for the national agenda. Find black principals who don't iden-tify with civil rights concerns but are prepared to whip black children into line. Throw out the kids who cause you trouble. It's an easy way to raise the average scores. Where do you put these kids once they're expelled? You build more prisons. Two thirds of the kids that Clark threw out are in Passaic County Jail.

"This is a very popular approach in the United States today. Don't provide the kids with a new building. Don't provide them with more teachers or more books or more computers. Don't even breathe a whisper of desegregation. Keep them in confinement so they can't subvert the education of the suburbs. Don't permit them 'frills' like art or poetry or theater. Carry a bat and tell them they're no good if they can't pass the state exam. Then, when they are ruined, throw them into prison. Will it surprise you to be told that Paterson destroyed a library because it needed space to build a jail?"

Clark has now left East Side High and taken to the lecture circuit. East Side High is virtually unchanged. The only difference, one that is regarded with much favor by some teachers, is that Clark's successor does not wield a bat. He is also less inclined to blame the students for the consequences of their poverty and racial isolation. He would like to see a new school building and would like to hire many more school counselors and outreach workers. Most of all, he says, "I'd like to put real money into preschool education and the elementary years. Children drop out in elementary school. They simply formalize that process here."

Outside his office, as I leave, I see a poster that announces an upcoming game. The basketball team is called the East Side Ghosts. On an adjoining wall there is a U.S. flag. Next to the flag, and written in the colors of the flag, there is this sign: "The American Dream Is Alive and Well at East Side High."

Reassurances like these are not required in the schools of Cherry Hill and Princeton. The American dream is not a slogan but a day-to-day reality in schools like these.

In Cherry Hill, for instance, according to a recent survey in *New Jersey Monthly* magazine, future scientists can choose from "14 offerings in the physical sciences department." There is "a greenhouse" for students interested in horticulture. "Future doctors have 18 biology electives. . . ." In 1988, we read, "the school's wind ensemble traveled to the Soviet Union to perform."

In a section devoted to Princeton, we are told: "Future musicians have the use of seven well-appointed 'music suites'. . . . Carpeted hallways encourage students with free periods to curl up and study in a corner. . . . Computer-equipped subject-related study halls [are] open throughout the day [and] manned by faculty. . . ." The ratio of counselors to students is one to 150, not up to New Trier's level (one to 24) but better than New York City, where the ratio is one to 700, and better than that of the Camden high school in which Chilly and her classmates had to fight for 15 minutes yearly with a guidance counselor. Again, there is the added detail that supplies an extra touch of elegance to life at Princeton High: Three years ago, we are told, parents in Princeton raised $187,000—from outside sources—so that the choir and orchestra could travel to Vienna to perform in concert.

One thinks of the school in Jersey City where 650 of 680 children are denied the instrumental music class and where that program, such as it is, must take place in a basement. What would it do for the motivation of the children in this school to practice in a "music suite"—of all extraordinary things!—and with the dream of traveling someday to perform in Moscow or Vienna? How might carpeted hallways calm the tensions of the at-risk pupils of East Orange?

In summarizing differences in yearly spending that

make possible these differences in educational provision, we have not considered certain other matters like the one-time costs of capital outlay (school construction, for example) and the size and value of school buildings. Matters like these—including floor-space measurements—were introduced by plaintiffs in the arguments that led to the Supreme Court finding in *Brown* v. *Board of Education.* A century ago, in *Plessy* v. *Ferguson,* the same kinds of comparisons were introduced.

If the court should ever be disposed to look at matters of this sort again, it might be persuaded to consider a comparison between an elementary school in Paterson and one in nearby Wayne. The school in Wayne, which is a white community, is 33 years old and holds 323 children. The school in Paterson is 60 years old and holds 615 children. The first school has 395 square feet per child, the second 87 square feet. The first school has 40,000 square feet of playing area, the second 3,000 square feet. The kindergarten in the first school holds 15 to 18 children. A room the same size in the second school holds 60 children divided into two groups of 30 each and separated only by a row of file cabinets. The kindergarten in the first school has a climbing apparatus for the children, as a judge observed during the course of recent litigation, "and many things to be played with." The kindergarten in the second school has "no play equipment."

"Why," asks the judge, "should this type of disparity be permitted?"

It has recently become a matter of some interest to the press and to some academic experts to determine whether it is race or class that is the major factor in denial of these children. The question always strikes me as a scholar's luxury. To kindergarten children in the schools of Paterson or Camden, it can hardly matter very much to know if the denial they experience is caused by their skin color or their destitution, but now and then an answer of some vividness and clarity has been provided. Several of New Jersey's schools have literally run out of classrooms in some recent years and have gone with hat in hand to the suburban districts and "attempted to rent space" from them, according to court papers. They were thwarted in these efforts, says the court, even with the state's awareness that "the suburban districts' refusal was based on race." The state, says the court, "allowed suburban resistance" to these rentals "under circumstances which, if true, [are] particularly troubling."

For example, when Asbury Park—predominantly nonwhite—asked to rent facilities in a white district, the white district was willing to take only "a small number of students" and insisted that they "be kept separate." Similarly, the schools of Irvington, where 92 percent of children are nonwhite, tried to rent rooms for their children in three suburbs, all of which were white, when building shortages left children without schools. "The schools sought by Irvington were vacant," the court notes. "The districts simply did not want [the] children."

In Paterson, the court observes, after a fire in which a wood-frame elementary school burned to the ground, leaving 1,100 children with no school, the city tried to rent a vacant school from nearby Wayne. The state refused to order Wayne to take the children. Suburban Fairlawn, an upper-middle-class community, finally agreed to let the children have a vacant building, but it did so with insulting stipulations—for example, that the children must be bused "at certain hours" and only "by certain routes."

This testimony, says the court, "was extremely upsetting."

* * *

The class-action suit that brought these issues to the notice of the public was filed in 1981 by parents of school-children in East Orange, Camden, Irvington and Jersey City. The case succinctly crystallizes many of the issues we have seen in other cities; and the findings of the trial judge, which run for some 600 pages, are evocative and saddening.

In finding in favor of the plaintiffs, in a ruling handed down in August 1988, Judge Stephen L. Lefelt takes notice of the plaintiffs' claim that New Jersey operates two separate and unequal public education systems, then makes this observation: The state "did not dispute the existence of disparities" but argued that "different types of programs are the result of local choice and needs." According to the state, "each district . . . is free to address the educational needs of its children in any manner it sees fit. . . . To the extent that program choices exercised by local districts are deemed inappropriate . . . , defendants claim that they are caused by local mismanagement. . . ."

However, asks the court, "is it local control that permits suburban wealthy districts to have schools located on spacious campuses surrounded by grass, trees and playing fields" while "urban district schools [are] cramped by deserted buildings, litter-strewn vacant lots and blacktop parking lots?" It is local control, continues the court, that permits Paterson to offer its 5,000 nonwhite high school students no other vocal music options than a gospel choir "while South Brunswick offers 990 students a concert choir, women's ensemble and a madrigal group?" Is it local control "that results in some urban districts conducting science instruction . . . in science rooms where water is not running" while suburban districts offer genuine science programs in elaborate laboratories?

The court concedes that certain programs—those

for "the academically talented," for instance—may have more demand in wealthier districts, but it also notes that hundreds of academically talented students live in the poor districts too but are denied these programs. "It seems to me," writes the judge, "that students with similar abilities and needs should be treated substantially equally."

The court notes that the highest-spending districts have "twice as many art, music, and foreign-language teachers . . . , 75 percent more physical education teachers . . . , 50 percent more nurses, school librarians, guidance counselors and psychologists . . . and 60 percent more personnel in school administration than the low-spending districts."

Noting a statewide mandate for school libraries with at least 6,000 volumes in each school, the court points to the Washington Elementary School in Irvington, which has only 300 books. "Why should not all districts have similar library facilities?" asks the court.

Wealthy districts downgrade the importance of these inequalities, the court observes. But, when one of the wealthier suburbs asked the state's permission to back out of a cross-busing plan with a poor district, it cited the district's "old and dilapidated buildings, lack of adequate equipment and materials [and] lack of science programs."

Why, asks the court, "should the gifted urban science students be taught in a manner which has been recognized by science educators as inferior? Why should urban districts not have microscopes . . . ?" Why are classes "larger in urban elementary schools than in suburban schools? Why are there more teaching staff per pupil in [rich] districts?" If "local differences" are genuinely the issue, asks the court, why are there fewer early-intervention programs in the urban districts, where the need is most acute?

Again and again the court poses the question: "Why is this so?"

The court asks the superintendent of affluent South Brunswick to assess the impact on his district, were it to be funded at the level of low-income Trenton. The superintendent tells the court that such a cut would be an "absolute disaster." He says that he "would quit" before he would accept it. If such a cut were made, he says, class size would increase about 17 percent; nursing, custodial and other staff would have to be reduced; the district would stop purchasing computers and new software; it would be unable to paint the high school, would cut back sports, drop Latin and German, and reduce supplies to every school. "We would have a school district," he says, "that is as mediocre as some that exist, that don't have money enough to spend for some of the things I just eliminated. And our kids would . . . get shortchanged, as these kids in these cities are getting shortchanged. And I'm convinced that they're shortchanged."

The New Jersey constitution, says the court in its decision, requires that all students be provided with "an opportunity to compete fairly for a place in our society. . . . Pole vaulters using bamboo poles even with the greatest effort cannot compete with pole vaulters using aluminum poles."

In our contemporary society, the court goes on, "money purchases almost everything. . . . Children in high-wealth communities enjoy high levels of expenditures and other educational inputs, and children in low-wealth communities receive low levels of school expenditures and inputs. This pattern is not related to the educational characteristics of the children in these districts. In fact . . . , given the characteristics of student bodies in urban and suburban districts, one would expect expenditure rates to be exactly opposite to what they are."

The state's justification for these disparate conditions, says the court, "can be characterized as the need to protect against further diminishment of local control." But the court notes that local control is "already seriously undermined" in a number of ways—for example, by the state's assumption of the right to take control of local districts which it judges to be poorly managed, an action that the state has taken several times, most recently in Paterson and Jersey City.

Defendants also argue, says the court, that, until the urban districts show that they can "wisely use the vast sums they now receive, no additional funds should be provided." No testimony, however, says the court, has been provided to affirm "that high-spending districts are spending [money] wisely." Under the defendants' argument, "wealthy districts can continue to spend as much money as they wish. Poor districts will go on pretty much as they have. . . . If money is inadequate to improve education, the residents of poor districts should at least have an equal opportunity to be disappointed by its failure."

Equal protection, in any case, the court observes, does not require efficiency but substantial comparability. "The record demonstrates that poor urban school districts are unable to achieve comparability because of defects in the funding system. . . ." Therefore, says the court, "I conclude that the defendants' local control, associational rights and efficiency justifications are outweighed by the educational rights of children residing in poor urban districts. There is sufficient proof in this record . . . to find that plaintiffs have also proved a violation of the equal protection clause of the New Jersey constitution."

In his final words, the judge asks how we may discern the benefits that might be gained from a more equitable system. "How do you evaluate [the benefit of] retaining a few students who would have dropped out? How do you weight the one student who becomes a successful artist and creates works that provide enjoyment for thousands of people? How do you cost-out the student who learns to enjoy reading and thereby adds excitement to what otherwise would be a rather ordinary existence? How important to society are flexible, imaginative and inventive citizens? I cannot even guess. Suffice it to say that I opt for providing equal opportunity to all our children, no matter where they may live."

Two years after these words were written, a high court in New Jersey affirmed the lower court's decision. In its ruling, the Supreme Court of New Jersey noted the defendants' argument that "education currently offered in these poorer . . . districts is tailored to the students' present need" and that "these students simply cannot now benefit from the kind of vastly superior course offerings found in the richer districts." If, said the court, the argument here is that "these students simply cannot make it, the constitutional answer is, give them a chance. The constitution does not tell them that, since more money will not help, we will give them less; that, because their needs cannot be fully met, they will not be met at all. It does not tell them they will get the minimum, because that is all they can benefit from." There would, said the court, "be little short of a revolution in the suburban districts" if the course of study in those districts were as barren as the course of study found in these poor cities.

Noting that the equalizing formula for state assistance to the local districts had, in fact, been "counter-equalizing" and had widened the disparities between the rich and poor, the Supreme Court said, "The failure has gone on too long. . . . The remedy must be systemic."

The sweeping nature of the court's decision led the press to speculate that efforts might at last be undertaken to apportion educational resources in more equitable ways, and a newly elected Democratic governor, Jim Florio, appeared to favor a substantial transformation of the funding scheme. Opposition, however, surfaced rapidly and murmurs of a tax revolt have now been heard across the state. Newspapers have been flooded with the letters of suburban residents protesting the redistribution of resources. Taking state money from the towns that have high property values to prop up the urban schools, says one letter-writer, will "bring mediocrity to every classroom in the state." Putting more money into the poor districts, says another letter-writer, "won't change anything. . . . Money is not the answer. . . . It has to begin in the home." A letter-writer from affluent Fair Lawn compares the plan for fiscal equity to Eastern European communism. "Everything in a free society," says another man, who calls himself a former liberal, "is not supposed to be equal." An assemblyman from a suburban district doubts that giving Camden extra money will improve its schools. "How about providing values instead?" he asks.

The superintendent of affluent West Orange, faced with the threat of running his school district on the same lean budget as East Orange, Paterson and Camden, says, "I cannot comprehend that. . . . I can't believe that anybody will permit that to occur." The fulfillment of the dream of equity for the poor districts, says the *New York Times,* is seen by richer districts as a "nightmare."

The *Wall Street Journal* applauds the thousands of New Jersey residents who have jammed the streets of the state capital in protest of the threatened plan, and the *Journal* hopefully anticipates "a California-style tax revolt." Popular talk-show hosts take up the cause. Phone calls aired on several radio stations voice a raw contempt for the capacities of urban children ("money will not help these children") but predict the imminent demise of education in the richer districts if their funding is cut back. Money, the message seems to be, is crucial to rich districts but will be of little difference to the poor.

Whatever the next step that may be taken in New Jersey, no one believes that people in Princeton, Millburn, Cherry Hill and Summit are prepared to sacrifice the extra edge their children now enjoy. The notion that every child in New Jersey might someday be given what the kids in Princeton now enjoy is not even entertained as a legitimate scenario. In the recent litigation, the defendants went so far as to deride attempts to judge one district by the other's standards. Comparing what was offered in the poorest districts to the academic offerings in Princeton was unfair, they charged, because, they said, the programs offered in the schools of Princeton were "extraordinary."

The state's defense, in essence, was that Princeton was so far beyond the range of what poor children had the right to hope for that it ought to be left out of the discussion. Princeton's excellence, according to this reasoning, positions it in a unique location outside questions of injustice. The court dismissed this logic without comment; but the fact that such an argument could actually be made by educated people is profoundly troubling.

For children who were plaintiffs in the case, meanwhile, it is too late to hope for vindication. None of them are still in school and many have already paid a high price for the long delay in litigation.

"It took a judge seven years and 607 pages," notes the *Philadelphia Inquirer,* "to explain why children in New

Jersey's poor cities deserve the same basic education as kids in the state's affluent suburbs." But the Camden boy who was lead plaintiff in the case, the paper adds, "would have a hard time reading the decision." Raymond Abbott, whose name is affixed to the decision, is today a 19-year-old high school dropout with the reading skills of a child in the seventh grade. A learning-disabled student who spent eight years in the Camden public schools, his problems were never diagnosed and he was passed on each year from grade to grade. During the years in which he was in school, says the *Inquirer,* Camden "was unable to afford science, art, music or physical education teachers" for the children in its elementary schools and lacked the staff to deal with learning disabilities. On the day that the decision came down from the court, Abbott, now a cocaine addict, heard the news of his belated vindication from a small cell in the Camden County Jail.

The decision might have meant more to him, the *Inquirer* writes, "if it had come . . . when there was still a chance to teach him something." Except for "an occasional letter, written in a childish scrawl," his mother says that she no longer hears from him. "I was prepared for a long battle," she reports, "but not for seven or eight years."

What may be learned from the rebuttals made by the defendants in New Jersey and from the protests that were sparked by the decision of the court? Much of the resistance, it appears, derives from a conservative anxiety that equity equates to "leveling." The fear that comes across in many of the letters and the editorials in the New Jersey press is that democratizing opportunity will undermine diversity and even elegance in our society and that the best schools will be dragged down to a sullen norm, a mediocre middle ground of uniformity. References to Eastern European socialism keep appearing in these letters. Visions of Prague and Moscow come to mind: Equity means shortages of toilet tissue for all students, not just for the black kids in New Jersey or in Mississippi. An impoverished vision of America seems to prevail in these scenarios.

In this respect, the advocates of fiscal equity seem to be more confident about American potentials than their adversaries are. "America," they say, "is wealthy, wise, ingenious. We can give terrific schools to *all* our children. The nation is vast. There is sufficient air for all our kids to draw into their lungs. There is plenty of space. No child needs to use a closet for a classroom. There is enough money. No one needs to ration crayons, books or toilet paper." If they speak of leveling at all, they speak of "leveling up." Their adversaries call it "leveling down." They look at equity for all and see it spelling excellence for none.

This, then, is the dread that seems to lie beneath the fear of equalizing. Equity is seen as dispossession. Local autonomy is seen as liberty—even if the poverty of those in nearby cities robs them of all meaningful autonomy by narrowing their choices to the meanest and the shabbiest of options. In this way, defendants in these cases seem to polarize two of the principles that lie close to the origins of this republic. Liberty and equity are seen as antibodies to each other.

Again there is this stunted image of our nation as a land that can afford one of two dreams—liberty or equity—but cannot manage both. There is some irony in this as well. Conservatives are generally the ones who speak more passionately of patriotic values. They are often the first to rise up to protest an insult to the flag. But, in this instance, they reduce America to something rather tight and mean and sour, and they make the flag less beautiful than it should be. They soil the flag in telling us to fly it over ruined children's heads in ugly segregated schools. Flags in these schools hang motionless and gather dust, often in airless rooms, and they are frequently no cleaner than the schools themselves. Children in a dirty school are asked to pledge a dirtied flag. What they learn of patriotism is not clear.

One other contradiction may be noted here. Marilyn Morheuser, a 67-year-old former nun who was the lead attorney for the plaintiffs in New Jersey and prepared and tried the case as part of a nonprofit team, speaks of the vast sums of money the defendants spent to hire expensive expert witnesses to try to undermine the plaintiffs' suit. This, she says—like virtually every other action of the wealthy suburbs in this instance—demonstrates that those who question commonsense ideas about the worth of spending money to create a better education for poor children have no doubts about the usefulness of spending money for the things that they desire.

"Is it possible that the defendants in these cases do not sense the irony," she asks, "of spending so much money to obtain the services of experts to convince the court that money isn't the real issue? These contradictions do not seem to trouble them at all. But do they really ask us to believe that laws of economics, which control all other aspects of our lives in this society, somehow cease to function at the schoolhouse door? Do they think poor people will believe this?"

CHAPTER 5

The Equality of Innocence:
Washington, D.C.

Most academic studies of school finance, sooner or later, ask us to consider the same question: "How can we achieve more equity in education in America?" A variation of the question is a bit more circumspect: "How can we achieve both equity and excellence in education?" Both questions, however, seem to value equity as a desired goal. But, when the recommendations of such studies are examined, and when we look as well at the solutions that innumerable commissions have proposed, we realize that they do not quite mean "equity" and that they have seldom asked for "equity." What they mean, what they prescribe, is *something that resembles equity but never reaches it:* something close enough to equity to silence criticism by approximating justice, but far enough from equity to guarantee the benefits enjoyed by privilege. The differences are justified by telling us that equity must always be "approximate" and cannot possibly be perfect. But the imperfection falls in almost every case to the advantage of the privileged.

In Maryland, for instance, one of several states in which the courts have looked at fiscal inequalities between school districts, an equity suit filed in 1978, although unsuccessful, led the state to reexamine the school funding system. When a task force set up by the governor offered its suggestions five years later, it argued that 100 percent equality was too expensive. The goal, it said, was *75 percent equality*—meaning that the poorest districts should be granted no less than three quarters of the funds at the disposal of the average district. But, as the missing 25 percent translates into differences of input (teacher pay, provision of books, class size, etc.), we discover it is just enough to demarcate the difference between services appropriate to different social classes, and to formalize that difference in their destinies.

"The equalized 75 percent," says an educator in one of the state's low-income districts, "buys just enough to keep all ships afloat. The unequal 25 percent assures that they will sail in opposite directions."

It is a matter of national pride that every child's ship be kept afloat. Otherwise our nation would be subject to the charge that we deny poor children public school. But what is now encompassed by the one word ("school") are two very different kinds of institutions that, in function, finance and intention, serve entirely different roles. Both are needed for our nation's governance. But children in one set of schools are educated to be governors; children in the other set of schools are trained for being governed. The former are given the imaginative range to mobilize ideas for economic growth; the latter are provided with the discipline to do the narrow tasks the first group will prescribe.

Societies cannot be all generals, no soldiers. But, by

our schooling patterns, we assure that soldiers' children are more likely to be soldiers and that the offspring of the generals will have at least the option to be generals. If this is not so, if it is just a matter of the difficulty of assuring perfect fairness, why does the unfairness never benefit the children of the poor?

"Children in a true sense," writes John Coons of Berkeley University, "are all poor" because they are dependent on adults. There is also, he says, "a sameness among children in the sense of [a] substantial uncertainty about their potential role as adults." It could be expressed, he says, "as an equality of innocence." The equality of adults, by comparison, "is always problematical; even social and economic differences among them are plausibly ascribed to their own deserts. . . . In any event, adults as a class enjoy no presumption of homogeneous virtue and their ethical demand for equality of treatment is accordingly attenuated. The differences among children, on the other hand, cannot be ascribed even vaguely to fault without indulging in an attaint of blood uncongenial to our time."

Terms such as "attaint of blood" are rarely used today, and, if they were, they would occasion public indignation; but the rigging of the game and the acceptance, which is nearly universal, of uneven playing fields reflect a dark unspoken sense that other people's children are of less inherent value than our own. Now and then, in private, affluent suburbanites concede that certain aspects of the game may be a trifle rigged to their advantage. "Sure, it's a bit unjust," they may concede, "but that's reality and that's the way the game is played. . . .

"In any case," they sometimes add in a refrain that we have heard now many times, "there's no real evidence that spending money makes much difference in the out-come of a child's education. We have it. So we spend it. But it's probably a secondary matter. Other factors—family and background—seem to be a great deal more important."

In these ways they fend off dangers of disturbing introspection; and this, in turn, enables them to give their children something far more precious than the simple gift of pedagogic privilege. They give them uncontami-nated satisfaction in their victories. Their children learn to shut from mind the possibility that they are winners in an unfair race, and they seldom let themselves lose sleep about the losers. There are, of course, unusual young people who, no matter what their parents tell them, do become aware of the inequities at stake. We have heard the voices of a few such students in this book. But the larger numbers of these favored children live with a remarkable experience of ethical exemption. Cruelty is seldom present in the thinking of such students, but it is contained within insouciance.

Sometimes the residents of affluent school districts point to certain failings in their own suburban schools, as if to say that "all our schools" are "rather unsuccess-ful" and that "minor differentials" between urban and suburban schools may not therefore be of much signifi-cance. "You know," said the father of two children who had gone to school in Great Neck, "it isn't just New York. We have our problems on Long Island too. My daugh-ter had some high school teachers who were utterly inept and uninspired. She has had a devil of a time at Sarah Lawrence. . . ." He added that she had friends who went to private school and who were given a much better prep-aration. "It just seems terribly unfair," he said.

Defining unfairness as the difficulty that a Great Neck graduate encounters at a top-flight private college, to which any child in the South Bronx would have given her right arm to be admitted, strikes one as a way of rendering the term so large that it means almost nothing. "What is unfair," he is saying in effect, "is what I *determine* to be unfair. What I find unfair is what affects my child, not somebody else's child in New York."

Competition at the local high school, said another Great Neck parent, was "unhealthy." He described the toll it took on certain students. "Children in New York may suffer from too little. Many of our children suffer from too much." The loss of distinctions in these statements serves to blur the differences between the inescapable unhappiness of being human and the needless misery created by injustice. It also frees the wealthy from the obligation to concede the difference between inconvenience and destruction.

Poor people do not need to be reminded that the contest is unfair. "My children," says Elizabeth, a friend of mine who lives in a black neighborhood of Boston, "know very well the system is unfair. They also know that they are living in a rich society. They see it on TV, and in advertisements, and in the movies. They see the president at his place in Maine, riding around the harbor in his motor boat and playing golf with other wealthy men. They know that men like these did not come out of schools in Roxbury or Harlem. They know that they were given something extra. They don't know exactly what it is, but they have seen enough, and heard enough, to know that men don't speak like that and look like that unless they have been fed with silver spoons—and went to schools that had a lot of silver spoons and other things that cost a lot. . . .

"So they know this other world exists, and, when

you tell them that the government can't find the money to provide them with a decent place to go to school, they don't believe it and they know that it's a *choice* that has been made—a choice about how much they matter to society. They see it as a message: 'This is to tell you that you don't much matter. You are ugly to us so we crowd you into ugly places. You are dirty so it will not hurt to pack you into dirty places.' My son says this: 'By doing this to you, we teach you how much you are hated.' I like to listen to the things my children say. They're not sophisticated so they speak out of their hearts."

One of the ideas, heard often in the press, that stirs the greatest sense of anger in a number of black parents that I know is that the obstacles black children face, to the extent that "obstacles" are still conceded, are attributable, at most, to "past injustice"—something dating maybe back to slavery or maybe to the era of official segregation that came to its close during the years from 1954 to 1968—but not, in any case, to something recent or contemporary or ongoing. The nostrum of a "past injustice"—an expression often spoken with sarcasm—is particularly cherished by conservatives because it serves to undercut the claim that young black people living now may have some right to preferential opportunities. Contemporary claims based on a "past injustice," after all, begin to seem implausible if the alleged injustice is believed to be a generation, or six generations, in the past. "We were not alive when these injustices took place," white students say. "Some of us were born to parents who came here as immigrants. None of these things are our responsibility, and we should not be asked to suffer for them."

But the hundreds of classrooms without teachers in Chicago's public schools, the thousands of children without classrooms in the schools of Irvington and Paterson and East Orange, the calculated racial segregation of the children in the skating rink in District 10 in New York City, and the lifelong poisoning of children in the streets and schools of East St. Louis are not matters of anterior injustice. They are injustices of 1991.

Over 30 years ago, the city of Chicago purposely constructed the high-speed Dan Ryan Expressway in such a way as to cut off the section of the city in which housing projects for black people had been built. The Robert Taylor Homes, served by Du Sable High, were subsequently constructed in that isolated area as well; realtors thereafter set aside adjoining neighborhoods for rental only to black people. The expressway is still there. The projects are still there. Black children still grow up in the same neighborhoods. There is nothing "past" about most "past discrimination" in Chicago or in any other northern city.

In seeking to find a metaphor for the unequal contest that takes place in public school, advocates for equal education sometimes use the image of a tainted sports event. We have seen, for instance, the familiar image of the playing field that isn't level. Unlike a tainted sports event, however, a childhood cannot be played again. We are children only once; and, after those few years are gone, there is no second chance to make amends. In this respect, the consequences of unequal education have a terrible finality. Those who are denied cannot be "made whole" by a later act of government. Those who get the unfair edge cannot be later stripped of what they've won. Skills, once attained—no matter how unfairly— take on a compelling aura. Effectiveness seems irrefutable, no matter how acquired. The winners in this race *feel* meritorious. Since they also are, in large part, those who govern the discussion of this issue, they are not disposed to cast a cloud upon the means of their ascent.

People like Elizabeth are left disarmed. Their only argument is justice. But justice, poorly argued, is no match for the acquired ingenuity of the successful. The fruits of inequality, in this respect, are self-confirming.

There are "two worlds of Washington," the *Wall Street Journal* writes. One is the Washington of "cherry blossoms, the sparkling white monuments, the magisterial buildings of government. . . , of politics and power." In the Rayburn House Office Building, the *Journal* writes, "a harpist is playing Schumann's 'Traumerei,' the bartenders are tipping the top brands of Scotch, and two huge salmons sit on mirrored platters." Just over a mile away, the other world is known as Anacostia.

In an elementary school in Anacostia, a little girl in the fifth grade tells me that the first thing she would do if somebody gave money to her school would be to plant a row of flowers by the street. "Blue flowers," she says. "And I'd buy some curtains for my teacher." And she specifies again: "Blue curtains."

I ask her, "Why blue curtains?"

"It's like this," she says. "The school is dirty. There isn't any playground. There's a hole in the wall behind the principal's desk. What we need to do is first rebuild the school. Another color. Build a playground. Plant a lot of flowers. Paint the classrooms. Blue and white. Fix the hole in the principal's office. Buy doors for the toilet stalls in the girls' bathroom. Fix the ceiling in this room. It looks like somebody went up and peed over our heads. Make it a beautiful clean building. Make it *pretty*. Way it is, I feel ashamed."

Her name is Tunisia. She is tall and thin and has big glasses with red frames. "When people come and see our school," she says, "they don't say nothing, but I know what they are thinking."

"Our teachers," says Octavia, who is tiny with red sneakers and two beaded cornrows in her hair, "shouldn't have to eat here in the basement. I would like for them to have a dining room. A nice room with a salad bar. Serve our teachers big thick steaks to give them energy."

A boy named Gregory tells me that he was visiting in Fairfax County on the weekend. "Those neighborhoods are different," Gregory reports. "They got a golf course there. Big houses. Better schools."

I ask him why he thinks they're better schools.

"We don't know why," Tunisia says. "We are too young to have the information."

"You live in certain areas and things are different," Gregory explains.

Not too long ago, the basement cafeteria was flooded. Rain poured into the school and rats appeared. Someone telephoned the mayor: "You've got dead rats here in the cafeteria."

The principal is an aging, slender man. He speaks of generations of black children lost to bitterness and failure. He seems worn down by sorrow and by anger at defeat. He has been the principal since 1959.

"How frustrating it is," he says, "to see so many children going hungry. On Fridays in the cafeteria I see small children putting chicken nuggets in their pockets. They're afraid of being hungry on the weekend."

A teacher looks out at her class: "These children don't smile. Why should they learn when their lives are so hard and so unhappy?"

Seven children meet me in the basement cafeteria. The flood that brought the rats is gone, but other floods have streaked the tiles in the ceiling.

The school is on a road that runs past several boarded buildings. Gregory tells me they are called "pipe" houses. "Go by there one day—it be vacant. Next day, they bring sofas, chairs. Day after that, you see the junkies going in."

I ask the children what they'd do to get rid of the drugs.

"Get the New Yorkers off our streets," Octavia says. "They come here from New York, perturbed, and sell our children drugs."

"Children working for the dealers," Gregory explains.

A teacher sitting with us says, "At eight years old, some of the boys are running drugs and holding money for the dealers. By 28, they're going to be dead."

Tunisia: "It makes me sad to see black people kill black people."

"Four years from now," the principal says when we sit down to talk after the close of school, "one third of the little girls in this fifth grade are going to be pregnant."

I look into the faces of these children. At this moment they seem full of hope and innocence and expectation. The little girls have tiny voices and they squirm about on little chairs and lean way forward with their elbows on the table and their noses just above the table's surface and make faces at each other and seem mischievous and wise and beautiful. Two years from now, in junior high, there may be more toughness in their eyes, a look of lessened expectations and increasing cynicism. By the time they are 14, a certain rawness and vulgarity may have set in. Many will be hostile and embittered by that time. Others will coarsen, partly the result of diet, partly self-neglect and self-dislike. Visitors who meet such girls in elementary school feel tenderness; by junior high, they feel more pity or alarm.

But today, in Anacostia, the children are young and whimsical and playful. If you hadn't worked with kids like these for 20 years, you would have no reason to feel sad. You'd think, "They have the world before them."

"The little ones come into school on Monday," says the teacher, "and they're hungry. A five-year-old. Her laces are undone. She says, 'I had to dress myself this morning.' I ask her why. She says, 'They took my mother off to jail.' Their stomachs hurt. They don't know why. We feed them something hot because they're hungry."

I ask the children if they go to church. Most of them say they do. I ask them how they think of God.

"He has a face like ours," Octavia says.

A white face or a black face?

"Mexican," she says.

Tunisia: "I don't know the answer to that question."

"When you go to God," says Gregory, "He'll remind you of everything you did. He adds it up. If you were good, you go to Heaven. If you were selfish, then He makes you stand and wait awhile—over there. Sometimes you get a second chance. You need to wait and see."

We talk about teen-agers who get pregnant. Octavia explains: "They want to be like rock stars. Grow up fast." She mentions a well-known singer. "She left school in junior high, had a baby. Now she got a swimming pool and car."

Tunisia says, "That isn't it. Their lives are sad."

A child named Monique goes back to something we discussed before: "If I had a lot of money, I would give it to poor children."

The statement surprises me. I ask her if the children in this neighborhood are poor. Several children answer, "No."

Tunisia (after a long pause): "We are all poor people in this school."

The bell rings, although it isn't three o'clock. The children get up and say good-bye and start to head off to the stairs that lead up from the basement to the first floor. The principal later tells me he released the children early. He had been advised that there would be a shooting in the street this afternoon.

I tell him how much I liked the children and he's obviously pleased. Tunisia, he tells me, lives in the Capital City Inn—the city's largest homeless shelter. She has been homeless for a year, he says; he thinks that this may be one reason she is so reflective and mature.

Delabian Rice-Thurston, an urban planner who has children in the D.C. schools, says this: "We did a comparison of schools in Washington and schools out in the suburbs. A group of business leaders went with us. They found it sobering. One of them said, 'If anybody thinks that money's not an issue, let the people in Montgomery County put their children in the D.C. schools. Parents in Montgomery would riot.'"

She runs through a number of the schools they visited in Washington: "There was a hole in the ceiling of a classroom on the third floor of the Coolidge School. They'd put a 20-gallon drum under the hole to catch the rain. The toilets at the Stevens School were downright unpleasant. But, if you really want to see some filth, you go to the Langston School. You go down into the basement—to the women's toilet. I would not go to the bathroom in that building if my life depended on it.

"Go to Spingarn. It's a high school in the District. The time we visited, it was a hot, humid day in June. It was steaming up there on the third floor. Every window on one side had been nailed shut. A teacher told me that a child said to her, 'This school ain't shit.' She answered him, 'I have to teach you here. We both know what it is.'

"If you're rich in Washington, you try to send your kids to private school. Middle-class people sometimes put their kids in certain public schools. Parents in those neighborhoods raise outside money so their kids get certain extras. There are boundaries for school districts, but some parents know the way to cross the borders. The poorer and less educated parents can't. They don't know how.

"The D.C. schools are 92 percent black, 4 percent white, 4 percent Hispanic and some other ethnics. There is no discussion of cross-busing with the suburbs. People in Montgomery and Fairfax wouldn't hear of it. It would mean their children had to cross state borders. There is regional cooperation on a lot of other things. We have a regional airport, a regional public-transit system, and a regional sewage-disposal system. Not when it comes to education.

"Black people did not understand that whites would go to such extremes to keep our children at a distance. We never believed that it would come to this: that they would flee our children. Mind you, many of these folks are government officials. They are setting policy for the entire nation. So their actions, their behavior, speak to something more than just one system.

"If you're black you have to understand—white people would destroy their schools before they'd let our children sit beside their children. They would leave their homes and sell them for a song in order not to live with us and see our children socializing with their children. And if white people want the central city back someday, they'll get it. If they want to build nice homes along the Anacostia River, they'll get Anacostia too. We'll be sent off to another neighborhood, another city."

Poor people in the District, she explains, want very much to keep the middle-class children, white and black, from fleeing from the city's schools. In order to keep them, they are willing to accept a dual system in the District, even while recognizing that the better schools, the so-called "magnet schools," for instance, will attract the wealthier children and will leave more concentrated numbers of the poorest children in the poorest schools. In other words, she says, in order not to have an all-poor system with still less political and fiscal backing than they have today, they will accept the lesser injustice of two kinds of schools within one system. Even within a single school, they will accept a dual track—essentially, two separate schools within one building.

This compromise would not be needed if the city were not isolated from the suburbs in the first place. A similar dynamic is at stake in New York City and Chicago, where, as we have seen, at least two separate systems coexist disguised as one. If the urban schools were not so poor, if there were no ghetto and therefore no ghetto system, people wouldn't be obliged to make this bleak accommodation. But once a city of primarily poor people has been isolated and cut off, the poorest of the poor will often acquiesce in this duality out of the fear of losing some of the side-benefits of having less-poor people in the system.

So it is a loser's strategy: "Favor the most fortunate among us or they'll leave us too. Then we will have even fewer neighbors who can win political attention for our children." There is always the example of a place like Paterson or East St. Louis, where almost all residents are poor. These pitiful trade-offs would not be required if we did not have a dual system in the first place. But one dual system (city versus suburbs) almost inevitably creates a second dual system (city-poor versus city-less-than-poor).

So it is that inequality, once it is accepted, grows contagious.

"Like soldiers who have seen too much combat," writes the *New York Times,* "increasing numbers of children in the nation's capital" are beginning to show "battle fatigue." Psychologists tell of children "who talk of death" while parents speak of children "who cry uncontrollably" and "keep the shades drawn in their rooms."

"We're seeing more and more kids who are simply overwhelmed," says a doctor at a local hospital, "not unlike people who have experienced shell shock."

Another physician calls them "children under siege." They are, he says, "always suspicious . . . fatalistic and impulsive." They live surrounded by the vivid symbols of their undesirable status: drugs and death, decay and destitution.

Soon after my visit to the elementary school in Anacostia, the press described the efforts of the District of Columbia to round up its prostitutes and ship them to Virginia. Two dozen prostitutes, according to one report, were "herded" by policemen from the sidewalks of the downtown area and forced to "hoof it" along Fourteenth Street to a bridge over the Potomac River, "This is the fourth commodity the District exports to Virginia," said a Virginia congressman. "We get all the sludge, all the garbage, most of the prisoners and now their prostitutes." One commodity, however, was effectively resisted. As observers noted, black children from the District were successfully kept out of the Virginia schools.

A few weeks later, at a housing project in a crowded neighborhood of Anacostia, a little girl named Harper and her mother talk to me about the neighborhood while standing on the front steps of their house. Nearby, a group of men stand in a semicircle looking at a car that has been set on blocks. The hood is up and auto parts are spread out on the street. A number of boys in bare feet, some in sneakers, stand around the men, while others watch from the adjacent stoops. A boy who may be six years old is holding a baby girl, perhaps his sister, in his arms.

In back of the building, in a narrow lane, about a dozen men are lined against the wall. Every so often a car comes by and stops. A brief transaction is concluded. Then the car moves on. A game of dice is going on outside the kitchen door.

Above our heads a helicopter circles in the sky. As the tempo of drug-dealing rises in the lane, the helicopter's passes grow more frequent. Now and then it banks and dives, then soars up in the sky.

"It's like being in a battle zone," says Harper's mother. "Cops above us. People up to no good on the ground. . . ."

The helicopter's roar becomes an intermittent background to the children's afternoon. Dozens of men on every side are doing nothing.

"What do you do with a former slave," asks Congressman Augustus Hawkins when I meet him the next day, "when you no longer need his labor?"

Harper and four friends of hers go with me to a neighborhood McDonald's. While we eat, they talk about their school. Harper describes the paddle that her teacher uses when the children misbehave. "Teacher makes you stand and bend across the desk," she says.

Another child, named Rebecca, climbs from her chair and shows me how she stands and bends when she is beaten. "Man!" she says. "That thing eats up your butt."

At some point, whenever I'm with children of this

age, I try to gain some sense of what they love the most or what they think is beautiful. I ask them this question: "What is the most beautiful thing in the entire world that you can think of?"

Harper says, "A baby fox."

I ask her why.

"A baby fox," she answers, "has soft reddish hair, a sweet expression, and a bushy tail."

"Butterflies are beautiful," Rebecca says.

"Daffodils and roses and sunflowers and a big old lemon cake and silky underwear and Gucci suedes," another child says.

"A wedding is also beautiful," says Harper.

Surprised by this, I ask what kind of wedding she would like.

"A wedding in a big old church," she says. "A pretty dress, all pearly white, with diamonds in my hair."

"In your hair," I ask, "or in your ears?"

"Sprinkly diamonds, sprinkled in my hair," the little girl replies. Then she goes on: "Have my honeymoon at Disneyland. Go to Nebraska after that. Live in a big white house and have a swimming pool shaped like my name."

I ask if she wants children.

"No," she says. "No children. Have a weddin', buy a house, then put my husband out so I can live with someone that I like." She bursts into a smile.

The fourth girl at the table is a somewhat awkward seventh grader who has scarcely spoken up to now. Dressed in black shorts, a black jersey and black shoes, she's not as playful as the others.

"Heaven is beautiful," she suddenly remarks.

Harper, however, screws up her face at this. "Why you want to go to Heaven when you still got time to be alive?"

Like many teachers and some journalists, I do my best to steer the conversation into channels that I somehow think will be "significant." But my careful plans are easily subverted by these lively little girls. The children's thoughts dart off in all directions. Without warning, the conversation shifts to drugs.

"This man in my neighborhood," Rebecca suddenly reports, "he's a tiny, tiny, little man. . . ." After a pause in which she seems to lose her thought, she starts again: "This man is a midget. Name is Tony Africa. Everybody knows this little man is a drug addict. If you go outside at night, 'round ten o'clock, you see him sometimes crawling in the dirt."

Harper introduces me to an expression I have never heard. "Name for what this little, little man is doing is called geeking," she explains. "Geeking is—you crawl along the street and look for rocks. You look for rocks that other people spill. You crawl along your knees. . . ."

"Night-time," says Rebecca, "you see people with no money lunchin' off each other. Lunchin' is—you breathe somebody else's air."

"Get excited!" Harper tells me. "Take their clothes off! Start to dance!"

"Ice cream man sells condoms," says the quieter, older girl.

I ask the children, "Is that true?"

"Ice cream man sells condoms in the project," she replies.

"This man, name is Hollywood," Rebecca says. "He ain't a man and ain't a lady. He's a man but dresses like a lady. Don't use drugs. He drinks. Get him a bottle of Cisco [reinforced sweet wine], he starts to dance! 'I don't need no man or woman! I don't need no condom or no nothin'!'"

"When he's drunk," says Harper, "he starts barkin'

like a dog. Go down on the ground and barks and then he's eatin' off this woman's feet."

"Name of this woman is Passion Flower," says Rebecca.

Although the things they talk about are anything but cheerful, they are animated and excited as they speak, and there is the playfulness of nine-year-olds within their voices. Harper is one of the most beautiful little girls I've ever seen. She's wearing blue-jean jumper-shorts and a white T-shirt and barrettes that look like daisies in her hair. She squirms about within her chair. Her feet, in clean blue sneakers, do not reach the floor. Rebecca, who is leaning on her elbows, holds her hands against her cheeks and squeezes them together so she looks a little like a minnow with its mouth against the wall of an aquarium.

The other child at the table is a teen-age boy, Rebecca's older brother. He speaks very little and seems somewhat bored. There is also a degree of sullenness about his words. I have to ask a question twice before he looks at me and gives an answer. The three fourth graders, on the other hand, are spirited and clear.

"The little ones," says Harper's mother later on, "are innocent. They run their mouths because they see a lot, but they don't know exactly what it means. The older ones, they know enough to guard their words." A degree of caution is a matter of survival at their age, she says.

At 8:00 P.M., the street in front of Harper's house is filled with adolescents and with many older men who seem to have more occupation now than in the listless afternoon. Inside her house I tell her mother that I'm thirsty, and she offers me a glass of ice-cold water. Through the kitchen doorway in the back I see some of the same men as before against the wall.

In the quiet living room Harper's mother gestures

to the men out in the lane. "Some of those men out there will be in jail tonight," she says.

As I prepare to leave, a cop car rolls up to the door. Two officers get out, one white, one black, both with handcuffs on their belts, and head out to the rear.

Night after night, on television, Americans can watch police or federal agents rounding up black men and black teen-agers. The sight of white policemen breaking down the doors of houses, black people emerging with their heads bent low in order to avoid the television cameras, has become a form of prime-time television entertainment in America. The story that is told by television cameras is a story of deformity. The story that is not told is the lifelong deformation of poor children by their own society and government. We hear of an insatiable attraction to consumer goods like sneakers, stereos and video recorders. The story that we do not hear is of the aggressive marketing of these commodities in neighborhoods where very poor black people live: neighborhoods where appetites for purchasable mediocrity are easily inflamed because there sometimes is so little that is rich and beautiful to offer competition. Once these children learn that lovely and transcendent things are not for them, it may be a little easier to settle for the cheaper satisfactions.

The manufacture of desire for commodities that children of low income can't afford also pushes them to underground economies and crime to find the money to appease the longings we have often fostered. Here, too, market forces are available to push them into further degradation. Gambling and prostitution have been centered now for many decades in black neighborhoods. Heroin sales to whites as well as blacks were centered in Boston's black South End and Roxbury as long ago as

1945. Today in Roxbury, as in the South Bronx and in Anacostia, eight-year-olds can watch the cars of people from the suburbs cruising through their neighborhoods in search of drugs.

"You couldn't permit this sort of thing," a journalist in Boston said, "unless you saw these children and their parents as a little less than human." There is some evidence that this is now the case. Not long ago, after the press in Boston had reported that black and Hispanic newborns had been dying at three times the rate of newborn whites, the *Boston Globe* said it was flooded with phone calls and letters. Few of them, said the paper, were compassionate. Many described the infants as "inferior" and "leeches." Their mothers were called "moral-less." Others called them "irresponsible pigs." The infants, said the *Globe,* were described as "trash that begets trash."

The press in Washington, New York and Boston has been filled with stories about drug use by black adolescents during recent months. Deaths by violence in Roxbury and Dorchester, where most of Boston's nonwhite people live, are now reported almost weekly. The *Globe* reports 170 shootings in two months. A psychiatrist whom I have known for many years speaks of the ways this violence is viewed and understood by his suburban neighbors: "When they hear of all these murders, all these men in prison, all these women pregnant with no husbands, they don't buy the explanation that it's poverty, or public schools, or racial segregation. They say, 'We didn't have much money when we started out, but we led clean and decent lives. We did it. Why can't they?' I try to get inside that statement. So I ask them what they mean. What I hear is something that sounds very much like a genetic answer: 'They don't have it.' What they mean is lack of brains, or lack of drive, or lack of willingness to work. Something like that. Whatever it is, it sounds almost inherent. Some of them are less direct. They don't say genetics; what they talk about is history. 'This is what they have become, for lots of complicated reasons. Slavery, injustice or whatever.' But they really do believe it when they say that this is what they have *become,* that this is what they *are.* And they don't believe that better schools or social changes will affect it very much. So it comes down to an explanation that is so intrinsic, so immutable, that it might as well be called genetic. They see a slipshod deviant nature—violence, lassitude, a reckless sexuality, a feverish need to over-reproduce—as if it were a character *imprinted* on black people. The degree to which this racial explanation is accepted would surprise you."

Of the recent rise in crack addiction in the Boston ghetto, he says this: "People see it as another form of reckless self-indulgence. I find this explanation puzzling. The gratification it affords is so short-lived, so pitiful and meager, in comparison to the depression that ensues— and the depression is so deep and so long-lasting—that it's just not credible to call it an indulgence. Suicide, as you know, is not particularly high in black communities, not at least the way that it is commonly defined. But crack addiction strikes me sometimes as a kind of 'covert' suicide. For many, many people in a neighborhood like Roxbury, the savor has gone out of life. I believe that many of these youths are literally *courting* death—enticing it into their presence. . . .

"Look at any other group of people in despair. Look at the Native Americans, for instance. They're out there on those barren reservations, bleak and empty places, not so different really from these burnt-out stretches of the Bronx or Dorchester. What do they do? They drink themselves to death. A third of the babies on some reservations are brain-damaged from their mothers' drinking.

Physicians used to say, 'The Indians are predisposed to being alcoholics.' Would they say that black teen-agers, then, are predisposed to crack addiction? Obviously the common bond is their oppressive lives."

He spoke about some recent crimes in Roxbury: "There is an element about it that is literally macabre. It's like a welcoming of evil. People on the outside look at this and they see savages instead of human beings. Physicians I know refuse to go into those areas. Even in the middle of the day they will not do it."

A black South African social scientist says this of the in-turned violence and hate among the people living in that country's settlements: "If you degrade people's self-respect on a daily basis, over centuries, you are bound to produce monsters. . . ." People ruled by the needs of the flesh, she says, are systematically separated from their spirit. Political anger is turned in against one's wife or children. It is, she says, "the way that animals behave."

Press discussion of these matters rarely makes much reference to the segregated, poorly funded, overcrowded schools in which these children see their early dreams destroyed. The indignation of the press is concentrated on the poor behavior of the ghetto residents; the ghetto itself, the fact that it is *still* there as a permanent disfigurement on the horizon of our nation, is no longer questioned. Research experts want to know what can be done about the values of poor segregated children; and this is a question that needs asking. But they do not ask what can be done about the values of the people who have segregated these communities. There is no academic study of the pathological detachment of the very rich, although it would be useful to society to have some understanding of these matters.

People ask me, "Is it safe to visit in these neighborhoods in Anacostia?"

I answer, "Safe for an adult to visit? Children live their whole lives in these neighborhoods! If it isn't safe for you, it isn't safe for them." But the truth is that it isn't safe either for those who live there or for those who visit.

In the summer sometimes in New York, groups of restless black teen-agers wander through the steamy streets of midtown neighborhoods and stand outside the doors of stores like Tiffany's or Saks Fifth Avenue. The clothing and behavior of these adolescents seem particularly offensive to some people. "They wear expensive sneakers," says a woman living on the East Side of Manhattan, "and they use their food allowance to buy stereo receivers. Then they bring these things downtown and blast their music at us on Fifth Avenue. Why should we be paying with our taxes for their sneakers and their gold chains and their crack addictions?" I am sure New Yorkers are familiar with this kind of statement. I have heard the same reaction also in downtown Chicago.

Her words bring back a memory from 1965. An eight-year-old, a little boy who is an orphan, goes to the school to which I've been assigned. He talks to himself and mumbles during class, but he is never offered psychiatric care or counseling. When he annoys his teacher, he is taken to the basement to be whipped. He isn't the only child in the class who seems to understand that he is being ruined, but he is the child who first captures my attention. His life is so hard and he is so small; and he is shy and still quite gentle. He has one gift: He draws delightful childish pictures, but the art instructor says he "muddies his paints." She shreds his work in front of the class. Watching this, he stabs a pencil point into his hand.

Seven years later he is in the streets. He doesn't use drugs. He is an adolescent alcoholic. Two years later he has a child that he can't support and he does not pretend to try. In front of Lord & Taylor he is seen in a long leather coat and leather hat. To affluent white shoppers he is the embodiment of evil. He laughs at people as they come out of the store; his laugh is like a pornographic sneer. Three years later I visit him in jail. His face is scarred and ugly. His skull is mapped with jagged lines where it was stitched together poorly after being shattered with a baseball bat. He does not at all resemble the shy child that I knew ten years before. He is regarded as a kind of monster now. He was jailed for murdering a white man in a wheelchair. I find him a lawyer. He is given 20 years.

To any retrospective pleas that I may make on his behalf, I hear a stock reply: "How much exactly does a person have the right to ask? We did not leave this child in the street to die. We put him in a foster home. We did not deny him education. We assigned him to a school. Yes, you can tell us that the school was segregated, dirty, poorly funded, and the books were torn and antiquated, and the teachers unprepared. Nonetheless, it was a school. We didn't give him nothing. He got something. How much does a person have the right to ask?"

A New York City social worker makes this observation: "It's very important that the city has some nonwhite people as administrators of the schools and homeless shelters and the welfare offices. It is unmistakable that many of these jobs are now reserved for nonwhite personnel. Do you notice how these cities look for black men, in particular, to be the heads of the police, the welfare and the schools? The presence of a white man at the head of a large urban system that is warehousing black children would be quite suggestive and provocative. An effort is made to find a suitable black person. Failing that, an Asian or Hispanic."

Placing a black person in control of an essentially

apartheid system—whether that system is a city or its welfare apparatus or its public schools—seems to serve at least three functions. It offers symbolism that protects the white society against the charges of racism. It offers enforcement, since a black official is expected to be even more severe in putting down unrest than white officials. It offers scapegoats: When the situation is unchanged, he or she may be condemned, depending on the situation, for corruption or ineptitude or lack of vision, for too much (or for too little) flair or energy or passion.

It is the truly gifted black officials who seem often in the most unenviable role; and this is the case especially in public education. Some of these people pay an awful price for the symbolic role they fill: a symbolism that at times appears to freeze their personalities and drain them of their normal warmth and humor.

There is a familiar pattern now in many cities. Typically, when prospective superintendents are first interviewed, they are told that they will be expected to fulfill specific "goals," and sometimes nowadays, in keeping with the growing business ethos of the schools, such goals (or, as they're often called, "objectives") are specifically enumerated: raise the test scores so many points and lower dropout rates by certain specified percentages. In order to persuade the press that they can do the job, they have to voice a confidence that bears no possible connection to their powers. Most, in privacy, must wonder why they should be able to arrest a failure rate that several able predecessors could not seriously alter. They know the nation does not plan to do away with a divided and unequal education system that is still in place nearly four decades after *Brown*. But their hiring depends upon this show of confidence. So a certain note of unreality is present.

Once hired, often in a burst of press enthusiasm,

they find themselves asphyxiated by the bureaucratic chaos they inherit and by the realities of class and race they must confront. Soon enough, the press outgrows its first inflated expectations. Impatience surfaces. Before long, they are treated as embarrassments and, sometimes, as pariahs.

An experienced superintendent was recuited some years ago to come to Boston. I'd known him for a decade prior to that time and found him an engaging man with high ideals and a disarming sense of humor. All of his humor disappeared within a month of taking up his job in Boston. Business leaders grew impatient when the reading scores refused to rise, the dropout figures to decline. Politicians grew sarcastic, then abusive. He was condemned severely now for lacking a "politically attractive" personality; and it is the truth that he seemed tight and tense and often had the cautious smile of a man who was afraid of falling off a ledge into a sea of hopelessness. At last the *Boston Globe*'s most influential columnist declared the system "leaderless." The superintendent, he said, "is a proven incompetent who would have been fired long ago if he were white."

At approximately the same time, in New York, a parallel situation was unfolding. A black administrator, Richard Green, had been recruited from a system in the Midwest. He came to New York with extravagant praise, welcomed by the press and business leaders. Soon enough, he started to incur the criticism that he was too cautious, too methodical, and not sufficiently aggressive. Dropout rates did not appreciably decline. Reading scores did not appreciably improve. New York City's schools still had only one half as much to spend as those in the rich suburbs. Selective schools still drained away the better pupils and the better teachers, leaving the poorest children even more shortchanged. Violence surrounded and invaded many of the poorest schools. He soon began to have the stricken look of someone who could barely breathe; and this, I later learned, was literally true. He was asthmatic and the asthma now became acute and chronic. Facing an audience of business leaders or the press, he held an inhaler in his hand and often held it to his mouth when he was in discomfort. During a period of special tension in the spring of 1989, he suffered an attack of asthma and died suddenly.

"The most striking thing about him . . . ," writes a journalist for *New York Magazine*, "was how *constricted* he seemed, physically and figuratively. . . . He would speak in word clouds, imprecise, clichéd and formal, his inhaler clutched tightly in his hand. When I put the notebook away—and no longer was an official emissary of the white media—he literally seemed to breathe easier." People like Dr. Green, says the reporter, "insistently moral black men and women working to overcome 400 years of stereotyping, are the most poignant victims. . . . They are the tightrope walkers, holding their breath as they perform in midair with only a slender strand of support—ever fearful that even the smallest mistake will prove cataclysmic."

The casualty rate is high among such superintendents. Boston has had nine superintendents in two decades. Black superintendents have been released or "not renewed" in half-a-dozen cities in the past 12 months. The Hispanic superintendent of the San Francisco schools has recently announced his resignation with two years still pending on his contract. As I write, 18 of the nation's 47 largest systems have no permanent leader at their helm. It is an almost literally untenable position. This may be the case because, no matter how the job may be described, it is essentially the job of mediating an injustice.

The city of Detroit has had a black administration for close to two decades. But the city is poor and mainly black and its school system, which is 89 percent black, is so poorly funded that three classes have to share a single set of books in elementary schools. "It's not until the sixth grade," the *Detroit Free Press* reports, "that every student has a textbook. . . ." At MacKenzie High School in Detroit, courses in word processing are taught without word processors. "We teach the keyboard . . . so, if they ever get on a word processor, they'd know what to do," a high school teacher says. Students ask, "When are we going to get to use computers?" But, their teacher says, the school cannot afford them. Of an entering ninth grade class of 20,000 students in Detroit, only 7,000 graduate from high school, and, of these, only 500 have the preparation to go on to college. Educators in Detroit, the *New York Times* reports, say that "the financial pressures have reached the point of desperation."

In 1988, according to a survey by the *Free Press,* the city spent some $3,600 yearly on each child's education. The suburban town of Grosse Pointe spent some $5,700 on each child. Bloomfield Hills spent even more: $6,250 for each pupil. Birmingham, at $6,400 per pupil, spent the most of any district in the area.

"Kids have no choice about where they're born or where they live," says the superintendent of another district, which has even less to spend per pupil than Detroit. "If they're fortunate [enough] to [have been] born in . . . Birmingham, that's well and good." Their opportunities, he says, are very different if they're born in a poor district.

His words, according to the *Free Press,* echo mounting criticism of a funding scheme "that has created an educational caste system." But equalizing plans that might address the problem, says the paper, have been bitterly opposed by wealthy districts, some of which deride these plans as "Robin Hood" solutions. "It would take money out and send it to Detroit . . . ," a teacher in one of the wealthy districts says.

Former Michigan Governor James Blanchard's educational adviser says that higher funding levels do not "necessarily" improve a public school.

As the *Free Press* notes, however, many educators have opposed a funding shift because they fear that "it would benefit large urban districts" like Detroit.

Thus, as in New Jersey, equal funding is opposed for opposite reasons: either because it won't improve or benefit the poorer schools—not "necessarily," the governor's assistant says—or because it *would* improve and benefit those schools but would be subtracting something from the other districts, and the other districts view this as unjust.

Race appears to play a role in this as well, according to the Speaker of the Michigan House of Representatives. People in affluent Farmington, he says, "are not going to vote for more taxes so the poor black kids in Ypsilanti can get . . . better reading programs."

A rural superintendent seems to justify the Speaker's explanation. "I'm concerned," he says, that, if the funding of the schools is changed, "you'll get most of the money going to Saginaw, Flint, Detroit"—all three being cities where the public schools are heavily nonwhite. The racial point, however, isn't generally expressed.

"Despite a lot of pious rhetoric about equality of opportunity . . . ," writes Christopher Jencks, "most parents want their children to have a more than equal chance of success"—which means, inevitably, that they want others, not all others but some others, to have less than equal chances. This is the case in health care, for example—where most wealthy people surely want to give their children something better than an equal choice of being born alive and healthy, and have so apportioned health resources to assure this—and it is the case in education too.

Test scores in math and reading in America are graded not against an absolute standard but against a "norm" or "average." For some to be above the norm, others *have* to be below it. Preeminence, by definition, is a zero-sum matter. There is not an ever-expanding pie of "better-than-average" academic excellence. There can't be. Two thirds of American children can never score above average. Half the population has to score below the average, and the average is determined not by local or state samples but by test results for all Americans. We are 16,000 districts when it comes to opportunity but one nation when it comes to the determination of rewards.

When affluent school districts proudly tell their parents that the children in the district score, for instance, "in the eightieth percentile," they are measuring local children against children everywhere. Although there is nothing invidious about this kind of claim—it is a natural thing to advertise if it is true—what goes unspoken is that this preeminence is rendered possible (or, certainly, *more* possible) by the abysmal scores of others.

There is good reason, then, as economist Charles Benson has observed, that "discussion about educational inequalities is muted." People in the suburbs who deplore *de facto* segregation in the cities, he observes, "are the ones who have a major stake in preserving the lifetime advantages that their privileged, though tax-supported, schools offer their children." The vocal elements of the community, he says, "find it hard to raise their voices on the one issue over which, in the present scheme of things, they can lose most of all."

The issue was forced dramatically in Michigan in 1975 when a U.S. district court, finding the schools of metropolitan Detroit both "separate" and "unequal," and observing that desegregation could not be achieved within the geographical limits of Detroit, ordered a metropolitan desegregation plan. The plan required the integration of the quarter-million children of Detroit with some 500,000 children, most of whom were white, in 53 suburban districts. Among these white suburban districts were Grosse Pointe and Birmingham.

The case, *Milliken* v. *Bradley,* was appealed to the Supreme Court. The court's five-man majority, which overruled the district court's decision, included all four justices that President Richard Nixon had appointed. The court decided that the metropolitan desegregation plan was punitive to the white suburbs and that Detroit would have to scramble to desegregate as best it could, within the city limits, by scattering its rapidly diminishing white student population among the larger numbers of black children—a directive, according to Richard Kluger, author of *Simple Justice,* that was "certain" to accelerate white flight out of the city. "More troubling," he writes, the court "denied the organic cohesiveness of metropolitan regions and the responsibility of satellites for the problems of the urban core around which they economically and often culturally revolved." Chief Justice Warren Burger, writing the majority opinion, said that no official acts by the suburban districts had contributed to the discrimination faced by children in Detroit and that interdistrict plans would threaten local choice and local governance.

In his dissent, Justice Byron White observed that

the majority had failed to state why remedies to racial segregation ought to stop at district lines. Nothing in *Brown* v. *Board of Education* had imposed such a constraint. "It was the state, after all," writes Kluger, that was prohibited by the Fourteenth Amendment from denial of equal protection to all citizens; and the *Brown* decision had established that school segregation constituted such denial. The courts, said Justice White, "must be free to devise workable remedies against the political entity with . . . effective power" and, in this case, that entity was not Detroit but Michigan. School districts, says Kluger, paraphrasing Justice White, "are not sovereign entities but merely creatures chartered by the state" and the state therefore should have been ordered to devise an interdistrict remedy.

Justice William Douglas, who dissented also, said that this decision, in conjunction with a Texas case decided two years earlier, in which the court refused to intervene to grant low-income districts fiscal equity, "means that there is no violation" of the Fourteenth Amendment even though "the schools are segregated" and "the black schools are not only 'separate' but 'inferior.' " We are now, he said, "in a dramatic retreat" from *Plessy* v. *Ferguson.* The Texas case had approved unequal schools. The present case accepted segregated schools. Between the two decisions, blacks were now worse off than under *Plessy.*

Justice Thurgood Marshall, who had litigated *Brown* v. *Board of Education* 20 years before, expanded these points further. After "20 years of small, often difficult steps" toward equal justice, Marshall said, "the Court today takes a giant step backwards. . . . Our nation, I fear, will be ill-served by the Court's refusal to remedy separate and unequal education. . . ." The majority's decision, he said, was "a reflection of a perceived public mood that we have gone far enough in enforcing the Constitution's guarantee of equal justice" rather than a product of neutral principles of law. "In the short run, it may seem to be the easier course to allow our great metropolitan areas to be divided up . . . into two cities—one white, the other black—but it is a course, I predict, our people will ultimately regret. I dissent."

The combined effect of this decision and the finding in the Texas case two years before, both by the same five-to-four majority, was to lock black children in Detroit into the situation that we see today. If only one of the concurring justices had accepted the opinions of the four dissenting judges (the fourth dissenting voice was that of Justice William Brennan), an entire generation of black children in such cities as East Orange, Paterson, Detroit and East St. Louis might have had an opportunity for very different adult lives; but this was not to be.

Having successfully defended its suburban children against forced desegregation with the children of Detroit, Michigan set out in the next years to demonstrate that it could make the segregated schools a little less unequal by providing a per-pupil "minimum" of funding aid to every district; as has been the case in other states, however, Michigan pegged the minimum so low as to perpetuate the inequalities. In 1988 the average minimum guarantee was $2,800—less than half of what the richest districts had available. More important, however, was the fact that the state minimum, which was expected to be assured by legislative allocations, was dependent on the whim of legislators and on shifts in economic trends. While local revenues in wealthy towns like Birmingham and Grosse Pointe were secure, state assistance for the poorer districts wavered with state revenues; and the richer districts, well endowed with locally raised funds, had little stake in fighting to sustain state revenues. When recession hit the state from 1979 to 1983, school went on as normal in Grosse Pointe while poorer areas dependent on state aid were decimated. Some districts, according to the *Free Press,* "were threatened with virtual shutdown."

This, again, is a familiar situation. In Massachusetts, in recent months, unexpected shortfalls in state revenues have forced administrators of one poorly funded system to project class size as high as 50. The low-middle-income town in which I live predicts class size of up to 40. In the neighboring city of Lawrence, where 200 eighth grade children are reduced to sharing 30 books, 280 of the system's veteran teachers have been given notice. In low-income Malden, Massachusetts, where the student population is now heavily nonwhite, the *Boston Globe* reports the schools are "reeling" after 50 teachers were laid off and 25 high school courses cut—including AP classes. Fifteen children with special needs are crammed into a former bathroom while 200 children pack the gym to have "a motionless physical education class." Seventh grade science classes, says the *Globe,* "study the earth's atmosphere" in a room that has no sink or windows— or, as one boy puts it, "without basic elements." Meanwhile, in New Bedford, Massachusetts, also heavily nonwhite, the schools have given notice to 120 teachers. Springfield has given notice to one quarter of its faculty— Worcester to one third of its schoolteachers.

Some of these teachers, we are told, will be rehired at the final moment in the fall. But nobody knows who they will be or whether they'll be teaching the same subjects they teach now, or even whether they'll be teaching in the same schools at the same grade levels. It isn't surprising that morale is low among these teachers or that the best of them are looking for work elsewhere.

In Massachusetts as in Michigan, therefore, it is not so much the final numbers as the chaos that afflicts these systems in the interim that does the greatest damage to the state of mind of teachers and the operation of the schools. Even where the actual difference in per-pupil spending between districts is not vast, the poorer districts—waiting often up to the last minute to receive part of their budget from the state—find themselves repeatedly held hostage to decisions of suburban legislators who have no direct stake in the interests of low-income children. Typically, at the end of June, such districts find themselves unable to commit resources to the programs they intend to launch the following September. Supplies are not ordered. Teachers are left hanging without contracts. Summer workshops to prepare the academic team for a new program, a computer workshop for example, are postponed or canceled.

"We had executive-order cuts in school aid during the course of a school year," a Detroit official says, leading to sudden staff cuts, class disruptions, bigger classes. Any notion that such problems have diminished is refuted by statistics offered by the *Free Press*: About 20 percent of Michigan's general revenues went to aid the local schools from 1976 to 1981. Today, in the climate of retrenchment that has favored local self-reliance over state assistance, only 11 percent of tax-raised statewide revenue goes to the local schools. "Thus," says the paper, "the spending gap [has] widened. . . ."

"You don't step up to a problem by redistributing what's there," protests the superintendent of one of the better-funded districts. But it is hard to know what else there is to redistribute—other than "what's there"—since residents of this district have opposed additional state taxes.

The Birmingham superintendent puts it this way:

"The Detroit schools need more money. The solution is not to take it from Birmingham and Bloomfield Hills." And, again, one wonders where else one would take it from if not from where it is.

The Ann Arbor superintendent ridicules what he describes as "simple-minded solutions [that attempt] to make things equal."

But, of course, the need is not "to make things equal." He would be correct to call this "simple-minded." Funding and resources should be equal to the needs that children face. The children of Detroit have greater needs than those of children in Ann Arbor. They should get more than children in Ann Arbor, more than kids in Bloomfield Hills or Birmingham. Calling ethics "simple-minded" is consistent with the tendency to label obvious solutions, that might cost us something, unsophisticated and to favor more diffuse solutions that will cost us nothing and, in any case, will not be implemented.

Two years ago, George Bush felt prompted to address this issue. More spending on public education, said the president, isn't "the best answer." Mr. Bush went on to caution parents of poor children who see money "as a cure" for education problems. "A society that worships money . . . ," said the president, "is a society in peril."

The president himself attended Phillips Academy in Andover, Massachusetts—a school that spends $11,000 yearly on each pupil, not including costs of room and board. If money is a wise investment for the education of a future president at Andover, it is no less so for the child of poor people in Detroit. But the climate of the times does not encourage this belief, and the president's words will surely reinforce that climate.

CHAPTER 6

The Dream Deferred, Again, in San Antonio

When low-income districts go to court to challenge the existing system of school funding, writes John Coons, the natural fear of the conservative is "that the levelers are at work here sapping the foundations of free enterprise."

In reality, he says, there is "no graver threat to the capitalist system than the present cyclical replacement of the 'fittest' of one generation by their artificially advantaged offspring. Worse, when that advantage is proffered to the children of the successful *by the state*, we can be sure that free enterprise has sold its birthright. . . . To defend the present public school finance system on a platform of economic or political freedom is no less absurd than to describe it as egalitarian. In the name of all the values of free enterprise, the existing system [is] a scandal."

There is something incongruous, he goes on, about "a differential of any magnitude" between the education of two children, "the sole justification for which is an imaginary school district line" between those children. The reliance of our public schools on property taxes and the localization of the uses of those taxes "have combined to make the public school into an educator for the educated rich and a keeper for the uneducated poor. There exists no more powerful force for rigidity of social class and the frustration of natural potential. . . ."

The freedom claimed by a rich man, he says, "to give his child a preferential education, and thereby achieve the transmission of advantage by inheritance, denies the children of others the freedom inherent in the notion of free enterprise." Democracy "can stand certain kinds and amounts" of inherited advantage. "What democracy cannot tolerate is an aristocracy padded and protected by the state itself from competition from below. . . ." In a free enterprise society, he writes, "differential provision by the public school marks the intrusion [of] heresy, for it means that certain participants in the economic race are hobbled at the gate—and hobbled by the public handicapper."

According to our textbook rhetoric, Americans abhor the notion of a social order in which economic privilege and political power are determined by hereditary class. Officially, we have a more enlightened goal in sight: namely, a society in which a family's wealth has no relation to the probability of future educational attainment and the wealth and station it affords. By this standard, education offered to poor children should be at least as good as that which is provided to the children of the upper-middle class.

If Americans had to discriminate directly against other people's children, I believe most citizens would find this morally abhorrent. Denial, in an active sense, of other people's children is, however, rarely necessary in this nation. Inequality is mediated for us by a taxing system that most people do not fully understand and seldom scrutinize. How this system really works, and how it came into existence, may enable us to better understand the difficulties that will be confronted in attempting to revise it.

The basic formula in place today for education finance is described as a "foundation program." First introduced during the early 1920s, the formula attempts to reconcile the right of local districts to support and govern their own schools with the obligation of the state to lessen the extremes of educational provision between districts. The former concern derives from the respect for liberty—which is defined, in this case, as the freedom of the district to provide for its own youth—and from the belief that more efficiency is possible when the control of local schools is held by those who have the greatest stake in their success. The latter concern derives from the respect for equal opportunity for all schoolchildren, regardless of their parents' poverty or wealth.

The foundation program, in its pure form, operates somewhat like this: (1) A local tax upon the value of the homes and businesses within a given district raises the initial funds required for the operations of the public schools. (2) In the wealthiest districts, this is frequently enough to operate an adequate school system. Less affluent districts levy a tax at the same rate as the richest district—which assures that the tax burden on all citizens is equally apportioned—but, because the property is worth less in a poor community, the revenues derived will be inadequate to operate a system on the level of the richest district. (3) The state will then provide sufficient funds to lift the poorer districts to a level ("the foundation") roughly equal to that of the richest district.

If this formula were strictly followed, something close to revenue equality would be achieved. It would still not satisfy the greater needs of certain districts, which for instance may have greater numbers of retarded, handicapped, or Spanish-speaking children. It would succeed in treating districts, but not children, equally. But even this degree of equal funding has not often been achieved.

The sticking point has been the third and final point listed above: what is described as the "foundation." Instead of setting the foundation at the level of the richest district, the states more frequently adopt what has been called "a low foundation." The low foundation is a level of subsistence that will raise a district to a point at which its schools are able to provide a "minimum" or "basic" education, but not an education on the level found in the rich districts. The notion of a "minimum" (rather than a "full") foundation represents a very special definition of the idea of equality. It guarantees that every child has "an equal minimum" but not that every child has the same. Stated in a slightly different way, it guarantees that every child has a building called "a school" but not that what is found within one school will bear much similarity, if any, to that which is found within another.

The decision as to what may represent a reasonable "minimum" (the term "sufficient" often is employed) is, of course, determined by the state officials. Because of the dynamics of state politics, this determination is in large part shaped by what the richer districts judge to be "sufficient" for the poorer; and this, in turn, leads to the all-important question: "sufficient" for what purpose? If the necessary outcome of the education of a child of low income is believed to be the capability to enter into equal competition with the children of the rich, then the foundation level has to be extremely high. If the necessary outcome is, however, only the capacity to hold some sort of job—perhaps a job as an employee of the person who was born in a rich district—then the foundation could be very "minimal" indeed. The latter, in effect, has been the resolution of this question.

This is not the only factor that has fostered inequality, however. In order to win backing from the wealthy districts for an equalizing plan of any kind, no matter how inadequate, legislatures offer the rich districts an incentive. The incentive is to grant some portion of state aid to *all* school districts, regardless of their poverty or wealth. While less state aid is naturally expected to be given to the wealthy than the poor, the notion of giving something to all districts is believed to be a "sweetener" that will assure a broad enough electoral appeal to raise the necessary funds through statewide taxes. As we have seen in several states, however, these "sweeteners" have been so sweet that they sometimes ended up by deepening the preexisting inequalities.

All this leads us to the point, acknowledged often by school-finance specialists but largely unknown to the public, that the various "formulas" conceived—and reconceived each time there is a legal challenge—to achieve some equity in public education have been almost total failures. In speaking of the equalizing formula in Massachusetts, for example, the historian Joel Weinberg makes this candid observation: "The state could actually have done as well if it had made no attempt to relate its support system to local ability [i.e., local wealth] and distributed its 'largesse' in a completely random fashion"—as, for example, "by the State Treasurer throwing checks from an airplane and allowing the vagaries of the elements to distribute them among the different communities." But even this description of a "random" distribution may be generous. If the wind had been distributing state money in New Jersey, for example, it might have left most disparities unchanged, but it would not likely have increased disparities consistently for 20 years, which *is* what the state formula has done without exception.

The contest between liberty and equity in education has, in the past 30 years, translated into the competing claims of local control, on the one hand, and state (or federal) intervention on the other. Liberty, school conservatives have argued, is diminished when the local powers of school districts have been sacrificed to centralized control. The opposition to desegregation in the South, for instance, was portrayed as local (states') rights as a sacred principle infringed upon by federal court decisions. The opposition to the drive for equal funding in a given state is now portrayed as local (district) rights in opposition to the powers of the state. While local control may be defended and supported on a number of important grounds, it is unmistakable that it has been historically advanced to counter equity demands; this is no less the case today.

As we have seen, the recent drive for "schools of excellence" (or "schools of choice") within a given district carries this historic conflict one step further. The evolution of a dual or tripartite system in a single district, as we have observed in New York City and Chicago, has counterposed the "freedom" of some parents to create some enclaves of selective excellence for their own children against the claims of equity made on behalf of all the children who have been excluded from these favored schools. At every level of debate, whether it is states' rights versus federal intervention, local district versus state control, or local school versus the district school board, the argument is made that more efficiency accrues from local governance and that equity concerns enforced by centralized authority inevitably lead to waste and often to corruption. Thus, "efficiency" joins "liberty" as a rhetorical rebuttal to the claims of equal opportunity and equal funding. "Local control" is the sacred principle in all these arguments.

Ironically, however, as we saw in the New Jersey situation, "local control" is readily ignored when state officials are dissatisfied with local leadership. A standard reaction of state governors, when faced with what they judge to be ineptitude at local levels, is to call for less—and not more—local governance by asking for a state takeover of the failing district. The liberty of local districts, thus, is willingly infringed on grounds of inefficiency. It is only when equal funding is the issue that the sanctity of district borders becomes absolute.

But this is not the only way in which the states subvert local control. They do it also by prescription of state guidelines that establish uniform curricula for all school districts, by certifying teachers on a statewide basis, and—in certain states like Texas, for example—by adopting textbooks on a statewide basis. During the past decade, there have also been conservative demands for national controls—a national teachers' examination, for example, and a national examination for all students— and we have been told that the commanding reason for these national controls is an alleged decline in national competitiveness against Japan and other foreign nations: a matter that transcends the needs or wishes of a local state or district. The national report that launched the recent "excellence" agenda bore the title "A Nation at Risk." It did not speak of East St. Louis, New York City or Winnetka. Testing of pupils is, in a sense, already national. Reading scores are measured "at," "above," or else "below" a national norm. Children, whether in Little Rock, Great Neck, or the Bronx, compete with all American children when they take the college-entrance tests. Teacher preparation is already standardized across the nation. Textbooks, even before the states began adoptions, were homogenized for national consumption. With the advent of TV instruction via satellite, national education will be even more consistent and, in large part, uncontested.

Then too, of course, the flag in every classroom is the same. Children do not pledge allegiance to the flag of Nashua, New Hampshire, or to that of Fargo, North Dakota. The words of the pledge are very clear: They pledge allegiance to "one nation indivisible" and, in view of what we've seen of the implacable divisions that exist and are so skillfully maintained, there is some irony in this. The nation is hardly "indivisible" where education is concerned. It is at least two nations, quite methodically divided, with a fair amount of liberty for some, no liberty that justifies the word for many others, and justice—in the sense of playing on a nearly even field—only for the kids whose parents can afford to purchase it.

We may ask again, therefore, what "local governance" in fact implies in public education. The local board does not control the manufacture of the textbooks that its students use. It does not govern teacher preparation or certification. It does not govern political allegiance. It does not govern the exams that measure math and reading. It does not govern the exams that will determine or prohibit university admissions. It does not even really govern architecture. With few exceptions, elementary schools constructed prior to ten years ago are uniform boxes parted by a corridor with six rooms to the left, six to the right, and maybe 12 or 24 more classrooms in the same configuration on the floor or floors above.

What the local school board *does* determine is how clean those floors will be; how well the principal and teachers will be paid; whether the classrooms will be adequately heated; whether a class of 18 children will have 18 textbooks or whether, as in some cities we have seen, a class of 30 children will be asked to share the use of 15 books; whether the library is stocked with up-to-date encyclopedias, computers, novels, poetry, and dictionaries or whether it's used instead for makeshift classrooms, as in New York City; whether the auditorium is well equipped for real theatrical productions or whether, as in Irvington, it must be used instead to house 11 classes; whether the gymnasium is suitable for indoor games or whether it is used for reading classes; whether the playground is equipped with jungle gyms and has green lawns for soccer games and baseball or whether it is a bleak expanse of asphalt studded with cracked glass.

If the school board has sufficient money, it can exercise some real control over these matters. If it has very little money, it has almost no control; or rather it has only negative control. Its freedom is to choose which of the children's needs should be denied. This negative authority is all that local governance in fact implies in places such as Camden and Detroit. It may be masked by the apparent power to advance one kind of "teaching style," one "approach," or one "philosophy" over another. But, where the long-standing problems are more basic (adequate space, sufficient teachers for all classrooms, heating fuel, repair of missing windowpanes and leaking roofs and toilet doors), none of the pretended power over tone and style has much meaning. Style, in the long run, is determined by the caliber and character of teachers, and this is an area in which the poorest schools have no real choice at all.

Stephen Lefelt, the judge who tried the legal challenge in New Jersey, concluded from the months of testimony he had heard, that "local control," as it is presently interpreted to justify financial inequality, denies poor districts *all* control over the things that matter most in education. So, in this respect, the age-old conflict between liberty and equity is largely nonexistent in this setting. The wealthy districts have the first and seldom think about the second, while the very poor have neither.

In surveying the continuing tensions that exist between the claims of local liberty and those of equity in public education, historians have noted three distinguishable trends within this century. From the turn of the century until the 1950s, equity concerns were muted and the courts did not intrude much upon local governance. From 1954 (the year in which *Brown* v. *Board of Education* was decided) up to the early 1970s, equity concerns were more pronounced, although the emphasis was less on economic than on racial factors. From the early 1970s to the present, local control and the efficiency agenda have once again prevailed. The decisive date that scholars generally pinpoint as the start of the most recent era is March 21 of 1973: the day on which the high court overruled the judgment of a district court in Texas that had found the local funding scheme unconstitutional—and in this way halted in its tracks the drive to equalize the public education system through the federal courts.

We have referred to the Texas case above. It is time now to examine it in detail.

A class-action suit had been filed in 1968 by a resident of San Antonio named Demetrio Rodriguez and by other parents on behalf of their own children, who were students in the city's Edgewood district, which was very poor and 96 percent nonwhite. Although Edgewood residents paid one of the highest tax rates in the area, the district could raise only $37 for each pupil. Even with the "minimum" provided by the state, Edgewood ended up with only $231 for each child. Alamo Heights, meanwhile, the richest section of the city but incorporated as a separate schooling district, was able to raise $412 for each student from a lower tax rate and, because it also got state aid (and federal aid), was able to spend $543 on each pupil. Alamo Heights, then as now, was a predominantly white district.*

The difference between spending levels in these districts was, moreover, not the widest differential to be found in Texas. A sample of 110 Texas districts at the time showed that the ten wealthiest districts spent an average of three times as much per pupil as the four poorest districts, even with the funds provided under the state's "equalizing" formula.

Late in 1971, a three-judge federal district court in San Antonio held that Texas was in violation of the equal protection clause of the U.S. Constitution. "Any mild equalizing effects" from state aid, said the court, "do not benefit the poorest districts."

It is this decision which was then appealed to the Supreme Court. The majority opinion of the high court, which reversed the lower court's decision, noted that, in order to bring to bear "strict scrutiny" upon the case, it must first establish that there had been "absolute deprivation" of a "fundamental interest" of the Edgewood children. Justice Lewis Powell wrote that education is

---

*Per-pupil expenditures presented here, as elsewhere in this book, are not adjusted for inflation.

not "a fundamental interest" inasmuch as education "is not among, the rights afforded explicit protection under our Federal Constitution." Nor, he wrote, did he believe that "absolute deprivation" was at stake. "The argument here," he said, "is not that the children in districts having relatively low assessable property values are receiving no public education; rather, it is that they are receiving a poorer quality education than that available to children in districts having more assessable wealth." In cases where wealth is involved, he said, "the Equal Protection Clause does not require absolute equality. . . ."

Attorneys for Rodriguez and the other plaintiffs, Powell wrote, argue "that education is itself a fundamental personal right because it is essential to the exercise of First Amendment freedoms and to intelligent use of the right to vote. [They argue also] that the right to speak is meaningless unless the speaker is capable of articulating his thoughts intelligently and persuasively. . . . [A] similar line of reasoning is pursued with respect to the right to vote.

"Yet we have never presumed to possess either the ability or the authority to guarantee . . . the most *effective* speech or the most *informed* electoral choice." Even if it were conceded, he wrote, that "some identifiable quantum of education" is a prerequisite to exercise of speech and voting rights, "we have no indication . . . that the [Texas funding] system fails to provide each child with an opportunity to acquire the basic minimal skills necessary" to enjoy a "full participation in the political process."

This passage raised, of course, some elemental questions. The crucial question centered on the two words "minimal" and "necessary." In the words of O. Z. White of Trinity University in San Antonio: "We would always want to know by what criteria these terms had been defined. For example, any poor Hispanic child who could spell three-letter words, add and subtract, and memorize the names and dates of several presidents would have been viewed as having been endowed with 'minimal' skills in much of Texas 50 years ago. How do we update those standards? This cannot be done without the introduction of subjective notions as to what is needed in the present age. Again, when Powell speaks of what is 'necessary' to enjoy what he calls 'full participation' in the nation's politics, we would want to know exactly what he has in mind by 'full' participation. A lot of wealthy folks in Texas think the schools are doing a sufficiently good job if the kids of poor folks learn enough to cast a vote—just not enough to cast it in their own self-interest. They might think it fine if kids could write and speak— just not enough to speak in ways that make a dent in public policy. In economic terms, a lot of folks in Alamo Heights would think that Edgewood kids were educated fine if they had all the necessary skills to do their kitchen work and tend their lawns. How does Justice Powell settle on the level of effectiveness he has in mind by 'full participation'? The definition of this term is at the essence of democracy. If pegged too low, it guarantees perpetuation of disparities of power while still presenting an illusion of fair play. Justice Powell is a human being and his decision here is bound to be subjective. When he tells us that the Edgewood kids are getting all that's 'full' or 'necessary,' he is looking at the world from Alamo Heights. This, I guess, is only natural. If he had a home here, that is where he'd likely live.

"To a real degree, what is considered 'adequate' or 'necessary' or 'sufficient' for the poor in Texas is determined by the rich or relatively rich; it is decided in accord with their opinion of what children of the poor are fitted to become, and what their social role should be. This role has always been equated with their usefulness to us; and this consideration seems to be at stake in almost all reflections on the matter of the 'minimal' foundation offered to schoolchildren, which, in a sense, is only a metaphor for 'minimal' existence. When Justice Powell speaks of 'minimal' skills, such as the capacity to speak, but argues that we have no obligation to assure that it will be the 'most effective' speech, he is saying something that may seem quite reasonable and even commonplace, but it is something that would make more sense to wealthy folks in Alamo than to the folks in Edgewood."

Powell, however, placed great emphasis on his distinction between "basic minimal" skills, permitting some participation, and no skills at all, which might deny a person all participation; and he seemed to acquiesce in the idea that some inequity would always be inevitable. "No scheme of taxation . . . ," he wrote, "has yet been devised which is free of all discriminatory impact."

In any case, said Justice Powell in a passage that anticipates much of the debate now taking place, "experts are divided" on the question of the role of money in determining the quality of education. Indeed, he said, "one of the hottest sources of controversy concerns the extent to which there is a demonstrable correlation between educational expenditures and the quality of education."

In an additional comment that would stir considerable reaction among Texas residents, Powell said the district court had been in error in deciding that the Texas funding system had created what is called "a suspect class"—that is to say, an identifiable class of unjustly treated people. There had been no proof, he said, that a poor district such as Edgewood was necessarily inhabited mainly or entirely by poor people and, for this reason, it could not be said that poverty was the real cause of deprivation, even if there *was* real deprivation. There

is, said Powell, "no basis . . . for assuming that the poorest people . . . are concentrated in the poorest districts."
Nor, he added, is there "more than a random chance that
racial minorities are concentrated" in such districts.

Justice Thurgood Marshall, in his long dissent,
challenged the notion that an interest, to be seen as "fundamental," had to be "explicitly or implicity guaranteed"
within the Constitution. Thus, he said, although the right
to procreate, the right to vote, the right to criminal appeal
are not guaranteed, "these interests have nonetheless
been afforded special judicial consideration . . . because
they are, to some extent, interrelated with constitutional
guarantees." Education, Marshall said, was also such a
"related interest" because it "directly affects the ability of
a child to exercise his First Amendment interests both as
a source and as a receiver of information and ideas. . . .
[Of] particular importance is the relationship between
education and the political process."

Marshall also addressed the argument of Justice
Powell that there was no demonstrated "correlation between poor people and poor districts." In support of this
conclusion, Marshall wrote, the majority "offers absolutely no data—which it cannot on this record. . . ." Even,
however, if it were true, he added, that *all* individuals
within poor districts are not poor, the injury to those who
are poor would not be diminished. Nor, he went on, can
we ignore the extent to which state policies contribute to
wealth differences. Government zoning regulations, for
example, "have undoubtedly encouraged and rigidified
national trends" that raise the property values in some
districts while debasing them in others.

Marshall also challenged the distinction, made
by Justice Powell, between "absolute" and "relative"
degrees of deprivation, as well as Powell's judgment that
the Texas funding scheme, because it had increased the

funds available to local districts, now provided children
of low income with the "minimum" required. "The Equal
Protection Clause is not addressed to . . . minimal suf-
ficiency," said Marshall, but to equity; and he cited the
words of *Brown* to the effect that education, "where the
State has undertaken to provide it, is a right which must
be made available to all on equal terms."

On Justice Powell's observation that some experts
questioned the connection between spending and the
quality of education, Marshall answered almost with
derision: "Even an unadorned restatement of this con-
tention is sufficient to reveal its absurdity." It is, he said,
"an inescapable fact that if one district has more funds
available per pupil than another district," it "will have
greater choice" in what it offers to its children. If, he
added, "financing variations are so insignificant" to quality, "it is difficult to understand why a number of our
country's wealthiest school districts," which, he noted,
had no obligation to support the Texas funding scheme,
had "nevertheless zealously pursued its cause before this
Court"—a reference to the *amicus* briefs that Bloomfield
Hills, Grosse Pointe and Beverly Hills had introduced in
their support of the defendants.

On the matter of local control, Marshall said this:
"I need not now decide how I might ultimately strike
the balance were we confronted with a situation where
the State's sincere concern for local control inevitably
produced educational inequality. For, on this record, it
is apparent that the State's purported concern with local
control is offered primarily as an excuse rather than as
a justification for interdistrict inequality. . . . [If] Texas
had a system truly dedicated to local fiscal control one
would expect the quality of the educational opportunity
provided in each district to vary with the decision of the
voters in that district as to the level of sacrifice they wish

to make for public education. In fact, the Texas scheme produces precisely the opposite result." Local districts, he observed, *cannot* "choose to have the best education in the State" because the education offered by a district is determined by its wealth—"a factor over which local voters [have] no control."

If, for the sake of local control, he concluded, "this court is to sustain interdistrict discrimination in the educational opportunity afforded Texas schoolchildren, it should require that the State present something more than the mere sham now before us. . . ."

Nonetheless, the court's majority turned down the suit and in a single word—"reversed"—Justice Powell ended any expectations that the children of the Edgewood schools would now be given the same opportunities as children in the richer districts. In tandem with the *Milliken* decision two years later, which exempted white suburban districts from participating in desegregation programs with the cities, the five-to-four decision in *Rodriguez* ushered in the ending of an era of progressive change and set the tone for the subsequent two decades which have left us with the present-day reality of separate and unequal public schools.

Unlike the U.S. Constitution, almost all state constitutions are specific in their references to public education. Since the decision in the Texas case, therefore, the parents of poor children have been centering their legal efforts on the various state courts, and there have been several local victories of sorts. In the absence of a sense of national imperative, however, and lacking the unusual authority of the Supreme Court, or the Congress, or the president, local victories have tended to deliver little satisfaction to poor districts. Even favorable decisions have led frequently to lengthy exercises of obstruction in the legislative process, eventuating often in a rearrangement of the old state "formula" that merely reconstructs the old inequities.

There is another way, however, in which legal victories have been devalued by the states, and this is seen most vividly in California. Even before the Texas case had been reversed, parents from Southern California had brought suit in the state courts, alleging that the funding system was unconstitutional because of the wide differential between funding for the children of the rich and poor. At the time of the trial, for example, Baldwin Park, a low-income city near Los Angeles, was spending $595 for each student while Beverly Hills was able to spend $1,244, even though the latter district had a tax rate less than half that of the former. Similar inequities were noted elsewhere in the state.

The court's decision found the California scheme a violation of both state *and* federal constitutions. For this reason, it was not affected by the later finding in the Texas case. In 1974 a second court decision ordered the state legislature to come up with a different system of school funding. A new system was at last enacted in the spring of 1977. As soon as Californians understood the implications of the plan—namely, that funding for most of their public schools would henceforth be approximately equal—a conservative revolt surged through the state. The outcome of this surge, the first of many tax revolts across the nation in the next ten years, was a referendum that applied a "cap" on taxing and effectively restricted funding for *all* districts. Proposition 13, as the tax cap would be known, may be interpreted in several ways. One interpretation was described succinctly by a California legislator: "This is the revenge of wealth against the poor. 'If the schools must actually be equal,' they are saying, 'then we'll undercut them all.' "

It is more complex than that, but there is an element of truth in this assessment and there is historic precedent as well. Two decades earlier, as U.S. Commissioner of Education Francis Keppel had observed, voters responded to desegregation orders in the South by much the same approach. "Throughout much of the rural South," he wrote, "desegregation was accompanied by lowering the tax base for [the] public schools [while] granting local and state tax exemptions for [a parallel system of private white] academies. . . ."

Today, in all but 5 percent of California districts, funding levels are within $300 of each other. Although, in this respect, the plaintiffs won the equity they sought, it is to some extent a victory of losers. Though the state ranks eighth in per capita income in the nation, the share of its income that now goes to public education is a meager 3.8 percent—placing California forty-sixth among the 50 states. Its average class size is the largest in the nation.

These developments in California, which may soon be replicated in some other states as local courts begin to call for equitable funding of the schools, tell us much about the value we assign to "excellence." If excellence must be distributed in equitable ways, it seems, Americans may be disposed to vote for mediocrity.

Meanwhile, for the children of the rich and very rich in California, there is still an open door to privileged advancement. In the affluent school districts, tax-exempt foundations have been formed to channel extra money into local schools. Afternoon "Super Schools" have been created also in these districts to provide the local children with tutorials and private lessons. And 5 percent of

California's public schools remain outside the "spread" ($300) that exists between the other districts in official funding. The consequence is easily discerned by visitors. Beverly Hills still operates a high school that, in academic excellence, can rival those of Princeton and Winnetka. Baldwin Park still operates a poorly funded and inferior system. In Northern California, Oakland remains a mainly nonwhite, poor and troubled system while the schools that serve the Piedmont district, separately incorporated though it is surrounded on four sides by Oakland, remains richly funded, white, and excellent. The range of district funding in the state is still extremely large: The poorest districts spend less than $3,000 while the wealthiest spend more than $7,000.

For those of the affluent who so desire, there are also private schools; and because the tax cap leaves them with more money, wealthy parents have these extra funds available to pay for private school tuition—a parallel, in certain ways, to the developments that Keppel outlined in the South after the *Brown* decision.

The lesson of California is that equity in education represents a formidable threat to other values held by many affluent Americans. It will be resisted just as bitterly as school desegregation. Nor is it clear that even an affirmative decision of the high court, if another case should someday reach that level, would be any more effective than the California ruling in addressing something so profoundly rooted in American ideas about the right and moral worth of individual advancement at whatever cost to others who may be less favored by the accident of birth.

Despite the evidence, suburbanites sometimes persist in asking what appears at first a reasonable question:

"So long as every child has a guarantee of education, what harm can it really be to let us spend a little more? Isn't this a very basic kind of freedom? And is it fair to tell us that we *cannot* spend some extra money if we have it?"

This sentiment is so deeply held that even advocates for equity tend to capitulate at this point. Often they will reassure the suburbs: "We don't want to take away the good things that you have. We just want to lift the poorer schools a little higher." Political accommodation, rather than conviction, dictates this approach because, of course, it begs the question: Since every district is competing for the same restricted pool of gifted teachers, the "minimum" assured to every district is immediately devalued by the district that can add $10,000 more to teacher salaries. Then, too, once the richest districts go above the minimum, school suppliers, textbook publishers, computer manufacturers adjust their price horizons—just as teachers raise their salary horizons— and the poorest districts are left where they were before the minimum existed.

Attorneys in school-equalization suits have done their best to understate the notion of "redistribution" of resources. They try instead, wherever possible, to speak in terms that seem to offer something good for everyone involved. But this is a public relations approach that blurs the real dynamics of a transfer of resources. No matter what devices are contrived to bring about equality, it is clear that they require money-transfer, and the largest source of money is the portion of the population that possesses the *most* money. When wealthy districts indicate they see the hand of Robin Hood in this, they are clear-sighted and correct. This is surely why resistance to these suits, and even to court orders, has been so intense and so ingeniously prolonged. For, while, on a lofty level, wealthy districts may be fighting in defense of a superb abstraction—"liberty," "local control," or such—on a mundane level they are fighting for the right to guarantee their children the inheritance of an ascendant role in our society.

There is a deep-seated reverence for fair play in the United States, and in many areas of life we see the consequences in a genuine distaste for loaded dice; but this is not the case in education, health care, or inheritance of wealth. In these elemental areas we want the game to be unfair and we have made it so; and it will likely so remain.

Let us return, then, for a final time to San Antonio—not to the city of 1968, when the *Rodriguez* case was filed, but to the city of today. It is 23 years now since Demetrio Rodriguez went to court. Things have not changed very much in the poor neighborhoods of Texas. After 23 years of court disputes and numerous state formula revisions, per-pupil spending ranges from $2,000 in the poorest districts to some $19,000 in the richest. The minimum foundation that the state allows the children in the poorest districts—that is to say, the funds that guarantee the minimal basic education—is $1,477. Texas, moreover, is one of the ten states that gives no financial aid for school construction to the local districts.

In San Antonio, where Demetrio Rodriguez brought his suit against the state in 1968, the children of the poor still go to separate and unequal schools.

"The poor live by the water ditches here," said O. Z. White as we were driving through the crowded streets on a hot day in 1989. "The water is stagnant in the ditches now but, when the rains come, it will rise quite fast—it flows south into the San Antonio River. . . .

"The rich live on the high ground to the north. The higher ground in San Antonio is Monte Vista. But the very rich—the families with old money—live in the section known as Alamo Heights."

Alamo Heights, he told me, is a part of San Antonio. "It's enclosed by San Antonio but operated as a separate system. Dallas has a similar white enclave known as Highland Park, enclosed on four sides by the Dallas schools but operated as a separate district. We call these places 'parasite districts' since they give no tax support to the low-income sections.

"Alamo Heights is like a different world. The air is fresher. The grass is greener. The homes are larger. And the schools are richer."

Seven minutes from Alamo Heights, at the corner of Hamilton and Guadalupe, is Cassiano—a low-income housing project. Across the street from Cassiano, tiny buildings resembling shacks, some of them painted pastel shades, house many of the children who attend the Cooper Middle School, where 96 percent of children qualify by poverty for subsidized hot lunches and where 99.3 percent are of Hispanic origin. At Cooper, $2,800 is devoted to each child's education and 72 percent of children read below grade level. Class size ranges from 28 to 30. Average teacher salary is $27,000.

In Alamo Heights, where teachers average $31,000, virtually all students graduate and 88 percent of graduates go on to college. Classes are small and $4,600 is expended yearly on each child.

Fully 10 percent of children at the Cooper Middle School drop out in seventh and eighth grades. Of the survivors, 51 percent drop out of high school.

In 1988, Alamo Heights spent an average of $46 per pupil for its "gifted" program. The San Antonio Independent District, which includes the Cooper Middle School, spent only $2 for each child for its "gifted" program. In the Edgewood District, only $1 was spent per child for the "gifted" program.

Although the property tax in Alamo Heights yielded $3,600 for each pupil, compared to $924 per pupil in the San Antonio district and only $128 in Edgewood, Alamo Heights also received a share of state and federal funds—almost $8,000 yearly for a class of 20 children. Most of this extra money, quite remarkably, came to Alamo Heights under the "equalizing" formula.

Some hope of change was briefly awakened in the fall of 1989 when front-page headlines in the *New York Times* and other leading papers heralded the news that the school funding system in the state of Texas had been found unconstitutional under state law. In a nine-to-zero decision, the state supreme court, citing what it termed "glaring disparities" in spending between wealthy and poor districts, said that the funding system was in violation of the passage in the Texas constitution that required Texas to maintain an education system for "the general diffusion of knowledge" in the state. The court's decision summarized some of the most extreme inequities: District spending ranged from $2,112 to $19,333. The richest district drew on property wealth of $14 million for each student while the poorest district drew on property worth only $20,000 for each student. The 100 wealthiest districts taxed their local property, on the average, at 47 cents for each $100 of assessed worth but spent over $7,000 for each student. The 100 poorest districts had an average tax rate more than 50 percent higher but spent less than $3,000 for each student. Speaking of the "evident intention" of "the framers of our [Texas] Constitution to provide equal educational advantages for all," the court said, "Let there be no misunderstanding. A remedy is long overdue." There was no reference this time to the U.S. Constitution.

Stories related to the finding dominated the front page and the inside pages of the *San Antonio Express-News.* "Students cheered and superintendents hugged lawyers in an emotional display of joy," the paper said. In the library of John F. Kennedy High School in the Edgewood district, Demetrio Rodriguez put his hand on his chest to fight back tears as students, teachers and community leaders cheered his vindication and their victory. As the crowd rose to applaud the 64-year-old man, Rodriguez spoke in halting words: "I cried this morning because this is something that has been in my heart. . . . My children will not benefit from it. . . . Twenty-one years is a long time to wait." Rodriguez, a sheet-metal worker at a nearby U.S. Air Force base, had lived in San Antonio for 30 years. "My children got caught in this web. It wasn't fair . . . but there is nothing I can do about it now." The problem, he said to a reporter, should have been corrected 20 years before.

In an editorial that day, the paper said that what the court had found "should have been obvious to anyone" from the beginning.

The Edgewood superintendent, who had been the leader in the latest round of litigation, spoke of the attacks that he had weathered in the course of years. He had been a high school principal in 1974 when the original *Rodriguez* finding had been overruled by the U.S. Supreme Court. "It was like somebody had died . . . ," he said. In the years since, he had gone repeatedly to the state capital in Austin, where he was met by promises from legislators that they would "take care of it," he said. "More and more task forces studied education," he recalled, while another generation of poor children entered and passed through the Edgewood schools. At length, in 1984, Edgewood joined with seven other poor school districts and brought suit against the state and 48 rich districts. The suit was seen by some as a class war, he said. He was accused of wanting to take away the "swimming pools," the "tennis courts" and "carpeted football fields" from wealthy districts. "They'd say I was being Robin Hood . . . ," he said. The district, he assured reporters, was not looking to be given swimming pools. All the district wanted was "to get us up to the average. . . ." Children in Edgewood, he said, had suffered most from being forced to lower their horizons. "Some of the students don't . . . know how to dream. . . . They have accepted [this]," he said, as if it were "the way [that] things should be."

The governor of Texas, who had opposed the suit and often stated he was confident the court would find against the claims of the poor districts, told the press of his relief that the Supreme Court hadn't mandated an immediate solution. "I am extremely pleased," he said, "that this is back in the hands of the legislature. . . ."

The chairman of the Texas Railroad Commission, who was running for governor as a Republican, voiced his concern that people might use this court decision to impose an income tax on Texas.

The U.S. Secretary of Education, Lauro Cavazos, came to Texas and provided fuel for those who sought to slow down implementation of the court's decision. "First," he said, "money is clearly not the answer. . . ." Furthermore, he said, "there is a wide body of research" to support that view and, he added, in apparent disregard of the conclusions of the court, "the evidence here in Texas corroborates those findings." He then went on to castigate Hispanic parents for not caring about education.

Meanwhile, the press observed that what it termed "the demagoguery" of "anti-tax vigilantes" posed another threat. "Legions of tax protestors" had been mobilized, a local columnist said. It was believed that they would do their best to slow down or obstruct the needed legislative action. Others focused on the likelihood that wealthy people would begin to look outside the public schools. There were already several famous private schools in Texas. Might there soon be several more?

Predictions were heard that, after legislative red tape and political delays, a revised state formula would be developed. The court would look it over, voice some doubts, but finally accept it as a reasonable effort. A few years later, O. Z. White surmised, "we'll discover that they didn't do the formula 'exactly' right. Edgewood probably will be okay. It's been in the news so it will have to be a showpiece of improvement. What of the children in those other districts where the poor Hispanic families have no leaders, where there isn't a Rodriguez? Those are the ones where children will continue to be cheated and ignored.

"There's lots of celebration now because of the decision. Wait a year. Watch and see the clever things that people will contrive. You can bet that lots of folks are thinking hard about this 'Robin Hood' idea. Up in Alamo Heights I would expect that folks have plenty on their minds tonight. I don't blame them. If I lived in Alamo Heights, I guess I'd be doing some hard thinking too. . . .

"We're not talking about some abstraction here. These things are serious. If all of these poor kids in Cassiano get to go to real good schools—I mean, so they're educated *well* and so they're smart enough to go to colleges and universities—you have got to ask who there will be to trim the lawns and scrub the kitchen floors in

Alamo Heights. Look at the lights up there. The air is nice and clean when you're up high like that in Texas. It's a different world from Guadalupe. Let me tell you something. Folks can hope, and folks can try, and folks can dream. But those two worlds are never going to meet. Not in my life. Not in yours. Not while any of these little kids in Cassiano are alive. Maybe it will happen someday. I'm not going to be counting."

Around us in the streets, the voices of children filled the heavy air. Teen-age girls stood in the doorways of the pastel houses along Guadalupe while the younger children played out in the street. Mexican music drifted from the houses and, as evening came to San Antonio, the heat subsided and there was a sense of order and serenity as people went about their evening tasks, the task of children being to play and of their older sisters to go in and help their mothers to make dinner.

"Everything is acceptance," said O.Z. "People get used to what they have. They figure it's the way it's supposed to be and they don't think it's going to change. All those court decisions are so far away. And Alamo Heights seems far away, so people don't compare. And that's important. If you don't know what you're missing, you're not going to get angry. How can you desire what you cannot dream of?" But this may not really be the case; for many of the women in this neighborhood do get to see the richer neighborhoods because they work in wealthy people's homes.

According to the principal of Cooper Middle School, crack addiction isn't a real problem yet for younger children. "Here it's mainly chemical inhalants. It can blind you, I've been told. They get it mainly out of spray-paint cans and liquid paper," he says wearily.

But a social worker tells me there's a crack house right on Guadalupe. "There is a lot of prostitution here

as well," she says. "Many of these teen-age girls help-
ing their mothers to make supper will be pregnant soon.
They will have children and leave school. Many will then
begin the daily trip to Alamo Heights. They'll do domes-
tic work and bring up other people's kids. By the time
they know what they were missing, it's too late."

It is now the spring of 1991. A year and a half has
passed since these events took place. The Texas legislature has at last, and with much rhetoric about what many
legislators call "a Robin Hood approach," enacted a new
equalizing formula but left a number of loop-holes that
perpetuate the fiscal edge enjoyed by very wealthy districts. Plaintiffs' attorneys are guarded in their expectations. If the experience of other states holds true in
Texas, there will be a series of delays and challenges and,
doubtless, further litigation. The implementation of the
newest plan, in any case, will not be immediate. Twenty-
three years after Demetrio Rodriguez went to court, the
children of the poorest people in the state of Texas still
are waiting for an equal chance at education.

I stopped in Cincinnati on the way home so that I
could visit in a school to which I'd been invited by some
friends. It was, I thought, a truly dreadful school and,
although I met a number of good teachers there, the
place left me disheartened. The children were poor, but
with a kind of poverty I'd never seen before. Most were
not minority children but the children of poor Appalachian whites who'd settled in this part of Cincinnati years
before and led their lives in virtual isolation from the city
that surrounded them.

The neighborhood in which they lived is known as
Lower Price Hill. Farther up the hill, there is a middle-
income neighborhood and, at the top, an upper-income

area—the three communities being located at successive levels of the same steep rise. The bottom of the hill, which stands beside the banks of the Ohio River, is the poorest area. The middle of the hill is occupied by working families that are somewhat better off. At the top of the hill there is a luxury development, which has a splendid view of Cincinnati, and a gourmet restaurant. The division of neighborhoods along this hill, with an apportionment of different scales of economics, domicile and social station to each level, reminded me of a painting by Giotto: a medieval setting in which peasants, burghers, lords and ladies lead their separate lives within a single frame.

To get to the neighborhood you have to drive from the center of the city through the West Side, which is mainly black, and then along a stretch of railroad tracks, until you come to the Ohio River. Lower Price Hill is on the north side of the river.

Some indication of the poverty within the neighborhood may be derived from demographics. Only 27 percent of adults in the area have finished high school. Welfare dependence is common, but, because the people here identify the welfare system with black people, many will not turn to welfare and rely on menial jobs; better-paying jobs are quite beyond their reach because of their low education levels.

The neighborhood is industrial, although some of the plants are boarded up. Most of the factories (metal-treatment plants and paint and chemical manufacturers) are still in operation and the smoke and chemical pollutants from these installations cloud the air close to the river. Prostitutes stand in a ragged line along the street as I approach the school. Many of the wood-frame houses are in disrepair. Graffiti (FUCK YOU, painted in neat letters) decorates the wall of an abandoned building near the corner of Hatmaker Street and State.

The wilted-looking kids who live here, says Bob Moore, an organizer who has worked with parents in the neighborhood for several years, have "by far the lowest skills in math and reading in the city." There is some concern, he says, about "developmental retardation" as a consequence perhaps of their continual exposure to the chemical pollutants, but this, he says, is only speculation. "That these kids are damaged is quite clear. We don't know exactly why."

Oyler Elementary School, unlike so many of the schools I've seen in poor black neighborhoods, is not so much intense and crowded as it is depleted, bleak and bare. The eyes of the children, many of whom have white-blond hair and almost all of whom seem rather pale and gaunt, appear depleted too. During several hours in the school I rarely saw a child with a good big smile.

Bleakness was the order of the day in fifth grade science. The children were studying plant biology when I came in, but not with lab equipment. There was none. There was a single sink that may have worked but was not being used, a couple of test tubes locked up in a cupboard, and a skeleton also locked behind glass windows. The nearly total blankness of the walls was interrupted only by a fire safety poster. The window shades were badly torn. The only textbook I could find (*Mathematics in Our World*) had been published by Addison-Wesley in 1973. A chart of "The Elements" on the wall behind the teacher listed no elements discovered in the past four decades.

"A lot of these kids have behavior problems," the science teacher said. He spoke of kids with little initiative whose "study habits," he said, "are poor." Much of what they learn, he said, "is gotten from the streets." Asked if more supplies, a cheerier classroom or a better lab would make a difference, he replied that he was "not sure money is the answer."

The class was studying a worksheet. He asked a question: "What is photosynthesis?"

After a long wait, someone answered: "Light."

"This is the least academic group I have," he told me after they were gone.

Children who attend this school, according to a school official, have the second-highest dropout rate in Cincinnati. Of young people age 16 to 21 in this community, 59.6 percent are high school dropouts. Some 85 percent of Oyler's students are below the national median in reading. The school spends $3,180 for each pupil.

The remedial reading program, funded by a federal grant, has only one instructor. "I see 45 children in a day," she says. "Only first and second graders—and, if I can fit them in, a few third graders. I have a waiting list of third grade children. We don't have sufficient funds to help the older kids at all."

There are four computers in the school, which holds almost 600 children.

The younger children seem to have a bit more fire than those in the science class. In a second grade class, I meet a boy with deep brown eyes and long blond hair who talks very fast and has some strong opinions: "I hate this school. I hate my teacher. I like the principal but she does not like me." In the morning, he says, he likes to watch his father shave his beard.

"My mother and father sleep in the bedroom," he goes on. "I sleep in the living room. I have a dog named Joe. I have a bird who takes her bath with me. I can count to 140. My mother says that I do numbers in my sleep."

Three girls in the class tell me their names: Brandy, Jessica, Miranda. They are dressed poorly and are much too thin, but they are friendly and seem glad to have a visitor in class and even act a little silly for my benefit.

Before I leave, I spend part of an hour in a class

of industrial arts. The teacher is superb, a painter and an artisan, who obviously likes children. But the class is reserved for upper-level kids and, by the time they get here, many are worn down and seem to lack the spark of merriment that Jessica and Brandy and their classmates had. It does seem a pity that the best instruction in the school should be essentially vocational, not academic.

Next year, I'm told, the children of this school will enter a cross-busing program that will mix them with the children of the black schools on the West Side. Middle-class white neighborhoods, like Rose Lawn for example, will not be included in the busing plan. Nor will very wealthy neighborhoods, like Hyde Park, be included.

I ask a teacher why Hyde Park, where friends of mine reside, won't be included in desegregation.

"That," he tells me, "is a question you don't want to ask in Cincinnati."

Cincinnati, like Chicago, has a two-tier system. Among the city's magnet and selective schools are some remarkable institutions—such as Walnut Hills, a famous high school that my hosts compared to "a *de facto* private school" within the public system. It is not known if a child from Lower Price Hill has ever been admitted there. Few of these children, in any case, would have the preparation to compete effectively on the exams that they would have to take in order to get in. Long before they leave this school, most of their academic options are foreclosed.

From the top of the hill, which I returned to visit the next day, you can see across the city, which looks beautiful from here. You also have a good view of the river. The horizon is so wide and open, and so different from the narrow view of life to be surmised from the mean streets around the school—one wonders what might happen to the spirits of these children if they had the chance to breathe this air and stretch their arms and see so far. Might they feel the power or the longing to become inheritors of some of this remarkable vast nation?

Standing here by the Ohio River, watching it drift west into the edge of the horizon, picturing it as it flows onward to the place three hundred miles from here where it will pour into the Mississippi, one is struck by the sheer beauty of this country, of its goodness and unrealized goodness, of the limitless potential that it holds to render life rewarding and the spirit clean. Surely there is enough for everyone within this country. It is a tragedy that these good things are not more widely shared. All our children ought to be allowed a stake in the enormous richness of America. Whether they were born to poor white Appalachians or to wealthy Texans, to poor black people in the Bronx or to rich people in Manhasset or Winnetka, they are all quite wonderful and innocent when they are small. We soil them needlessly.

Readers who would like to help inner-city children, and the families of those children, to cope with the challenges and crises that confront them to the present day are invited to make contributions to the Education Action Fund, a tax-exempt foundation based in Cambridge, Massachusetts. For more information, readers should feel free to contact the author at jonathankozol@gmail.com or to write to 16 Lowell Street, Cambridge, Massachusetts 02138.

APPENDIX

Comparisons of School Funding in Three Geographical Regions

TABLE I

School Funding in the Chicago Area
(Figures for the 1988–1989 School Year)

School or District	Spending Per Pupil
Niles Township High School	$9,371
New Trier High School	$8,823
Glencoe (elementary and junior high schools)	$7,363
Winnetka (elementary and junior high schools)	$7,059
Wilmette (elementary and junior high schools)	$6,009
Chicago (average of all grade levels)	$5,265

SOURCE: Chicago Panel on School Policy and Finance.

TABLE II

School Funding in New Jersey
(Figures for the 1988–1989 School Year)

District	Spending Per Pupil
Princeton	$7,725
Summit	$7,275
West Orange	$6,505
Cherry Hill	$5,981
Jersey City	$4,566
East Orange	$4,457
Paterson	$4,422
Camden	$3,538

SOURCE: Educational Law Center, Newark, New Jersey.

TABLE III

School Funding in the New York City Area
(Figures for the 1986–1987 School Year)

District	Spending Per Pupil
Manhasset	$11,372
Jericho	$11,325
Great Neck	$11,265
Bronxville	$10,113
Rye	$9,092
Yonkers	$7,399
Levittown	$6,899
Mount Vernon	$6,433
Roosevelt	$6,339
New York City	$5,585

SOURCE: "Statistical Profiles of School Districts" (New York State Board of Education).

TABLE IV

The Widening Gap
(School Funding in Six Districts in the New York City Area:
Changes in a Three-Year Period)

District	1986–1987 School Year	1989–1990 School Year
Manhasset	$11,372	$15,084
Jericho	$11,325	$14,355
Great Neck	$11,265	$15,594
Mount Vernon	$6,433	$9,112
Roosevelt	$6,339	$8,349
New York City	$5,585	$7,299

SOURCE: "Statistical Profiles of School Districts" (New York State Board of Education) and *New York Times.*

NOTES

     1. LIFE ON THE MISSISSIPPI

9   "EAST OF ANYWHERE": *St. Louis Post-Dispatch,* May 22, 1988.

98 PERCENT BLACK: James D. Nowlan, "Report on the Potential for Civic Reform in East St. Louis, Illinois," a memorandum to Thomas Berkshire, assistant to Illinois Governor James Thompson, June 30, 1989.

NO OBSTETRIC SERVICES: *St. Louis Post-Dispatch,* May 14, 1989.

NEARLY A THIRD OF FAMILIES LIVE ON LESS THAN $7,500: *St. Louis Post-Dispatch,* May 14, 1989.

75 PERCENT ON WELFARE: *New York Times,* April 4, 1991. Also see *St. Louis Post-Dispatch,* May 22–28, 1988 (series on East St. Louis); *Belleville* (Illinois) *News-Democrat,* February 20–27, 1988 (series on East St. Louis); *Illinois Times,* February 2–8, 1989.

"MOST DISTRESSED SMALL CITY IN AMERICA": Memo of Thomas Berkshire (assistant to Illinois Governor James Thompson) to the Municipal Bankruptcy Task Force, November 30, 1988. only three of 13 buildings, etc.: *St. Louis Post-Dispatch,* May 22, 1988.

10   RATE OF CHILD ASTHMA: According to the *St. Louis Post-Dispatch* (May 14, 1989), the frequency of asthma in East St. Louis is not only higher than in white communities of Illinois but 53 percent higher than among black populations elsewhere in the state.

"AMERICA'S SOWETO": *St. Louis Post-Dispatch,* April 23, 1989; *Illinois Times,* February 2, 1989; conversation with *St. Louis Post-Dispatch* reporter Patrick Gauen.

1,170 EMPLOYEES LAID OFF: *St. Louis Post-Dispatch,* May 22, 1988.

HEATING FUEL, TOILET PAPER: *St. Louis Post-Dispatch,* March 22, 1989.

ALL BUT 10 PERCENT OF EMPLOYEES MAY BE LAID OFF: *St. Louis Post-Dispatch,* April 24, 1989.

CITY HALL AND FIRE STATION MAY BE SOLD: *St. Louis Post-Dispatch,* April 25, 1989.

CITY HALL IS LOST IN COURT JUDGMENT: *Boston Globe,* September 29, 1990.

HIGHEST PROPERTY-TAX RATE IN THE STATE: *St. Louis Post-Dispatch,* May 22, 1988.

GARBAGE, THREAT OF CHEMICAL SPILLS, ETC.: *St. Louis Post-Dispatch,* May 22, 1988.

11 CHEMICAL SPILL AT MONSANTO: *St. Louis Post-Dispatch,* July 31, 1988.

GOVERNOR JAMES THOMPSON AND REPUBLICAN STATE LEGISLATOR: *St. Louis Post-Dispatch,* March 22, 1989.

ILLINOIS POWER COMPANY SUPERVISOR: *St. Louis Post-Dispatch,* May 22, 1988.

11, 12 BLUFFS AND BOTTOMS, SEWAGE, FLOODING: James Nowlan cited above.

12 TUNICA, MISSISSIPPI: *Wall Street Journal,* October 13, 1989.

12, 13 VILLA GRIFFIN, SEWAGE, AND HEALTH DANGERS: *St. Louis Post-Dispatch,* March 16 and 19, 1989. Also see *St. Louis Post-Dispatch,* February 17 and March 15, 1989.

12 to 14 SEWAGE PROBLEMS, CHEMICALS, LEAD POISONING, CONTAMINATION: *St. Louis Post-Dispatch,* April 2, 1989.

15 to 24 INTERVIEWS WITH CHILDREN AND POST-DISPATCH REPORTER: March 1990.

19, 20 CHEMICAL PLANTS PAY NO TAXES TO EAST ST. LOUIS: *St. Louis Post-Dispatch,* May 23, 1988.

POPULATION OF SAUGET: *Newsweek,* April 16, 1990; James Nowlan, cited above; *St. Louis Post-Dispatch* reporter Safir Ahmed.

20, 21 FLOODGATE BROKE, BOND AVENUE, ETC.: *St. Louis Post-Dispatch* reporter Patrick Gauen.

GREENPEACE STUDY: "We All Live Downstream: The Mississippi River and the National Toxics Crisis," Greenpeace, December 1989.

DEAD CREEK: James Nowlan cited above; also, *St. Louis Post-Dispatch* reporters Safir Ahmed and Patrick Gauen.

23 TELEPHONE DIRECTORY: The "Metro East" directory for the area east of St. Louis, printed by Heritage Publishing Co., does not list East St. Louis numbers. "I surmise," says *St. Louis Post-Dispatch* reporter Patrick Gauen, "that the company finds it easier to sell advertising if East St. Louis is omitted." Also see James Nowlan, cited above.

LIFE MAGAZINE: Special issue on race, Spring 1988.

25, 26 HEALTH AND HOSPITAL STATISTICS, FOOD EXPENDITURES, UNDER-IMMUNIZATION, HOMICIDE RATE: *St. Louis Post-Dispatch,* May 14, 1989.

"THE HEAT CAN BRING OUT THE BEAST": *St. Louis Post-Dispatch,* May 22, 1988.

"EVACUATION PLAN": James Nowlan cited above.

27 to 29 HISTORY OF EAST ST. LOUIS: *St. Louis Post-Dispatch,* May 23, 1989.

FLOODING OF SCHOOLS: *St. Louis Post-Dispatch,* March 15, 21, and 29 and April 28, 1989.

29, 30 TEACHER LAYOFFS AND SUBSTITUTE TEACHERS: *St. Louis Post-Dispatch,* March 15, 21, and 24, 1989.

GOVERNOR THOMPSON'S COMMENTS: *St. Louis Post-Dispatch,* March 21, 1989.

GOVERNOR ANNOUNCES GRANT FOR SEWER IMPROVEMENT: *St. Louis Post-Dispatch, March* 21, 1989.

TEACHERS' PAYCHECKS DELAYED, ETC.: *St. Louis Post-Dispatch,* March 16 and April 2, 1989.

ILLINOIS BOARD OF EDUCATION ASSUMES FINANCIAL SUPERVISION: *Belleville News-Democrat,* December 20, 1988.

30, 31 STATE SUPERINTENDENT AND CHAIRMAN OF STATE BOARD CITED: *St. Louis Post-Dispatch,* April 28, 1989.

31 SPORTS FACILITIES: *St. Louis Post-Dispatch,* April 23, 25, 26, and 28, 1989. A new football stadium is under construction in 1991, according to teachers at the school.

31 to 33 FOOTBALL COACH, TEACHERS, STUDENTS, PRINCIPAL, SUPERINTENDENT QUOTED: Author's interviews, March 1990.

35 to 37 SOLOMON'S ESTIMATES FOR GRADUATION RATES AND ACADEMIC PROGRAMS: According to a "School Report Card" issued by the Illinois Department of Education, 32 percent of students at East St. Louis High are in college preparatory courses and the graduation rate is 65 percent. Discrepancies between official figures and

the estimates of teachers are familiar in most urban systems.

45, 46   LANDSDOWNE AND KING JUNIOR HIGH SCHOOLS, EAST ST. LOUIS HIGH SCHOOL, ETC.: *St. Louis Sun,* November 3 and 5, 1989.

ONE FULL-COLOR WORKBOOK: *St. Louis Post-Dispatch,* February 26, 1989.

SPENDING IN EAST ST. LOUIS SCHOOLS COMPARED TO SPENDING IN NEARBY DISTRICTS AND TO STATE'S TOP-SPENDING DISTRICTS.: Illinois State Board of Education, "Illinois Public Schools Financial Statistics, 1986–1987 School Year" (Springfield: 1988). Also see per-pupil spending figures for Chicago suburbs on pages 66 and 89 to 90 and notes for page 69.

46, 47   CUTS IN SCHOOL PERSONNEL DEMANDED BY STATE BOARD OF EDUCATION: *St. Louis Post-Dispatch,* March 15, 1989.

2. OTHER PEOPLE'S CHILDREN

51   DESCRIPTION OF NORTH LAWNDALE: *The American Millstone: An Examination of the Nation's Permanent Underclass,* by the staff of the *Chicago Tribune,* a collection of articles that ran originally in the *Tribune* (Chicago: Contemporary Books, Inc., 1986).

REVEREND JIM WOLFF CITED: *The American Millstone;* author's interview, March 1990.

53   "NEARLY 1,000 INFANTS . . .": *Chicago Reporter,* May 1990.

53ff.   BETHUNE ELEMENTARY SCHOOL: Author's interviews, October 1990.

55   MANLEY HIGH SCHOOL GRADUATION RATE: Report of the Chicago Panel on School Policy and Finance, April 24, 1985; author's interview with G. Alfred Hess, executive director of Chicago Panel, March 1991.

COLLEGE AND PRISON STATISTICS: "Chicago Schools: Worst in America," a seven-month series by Bonita Brodt and other reporters of the *Chicago Tribune* (Chicago: Contemporary Books, Inc., 1988), identified hereafter as *"Tribune* series." Also see *The American Millstone.*

57   PRINCIPALS HAVE NO CHOICE ABOUT ACCEPTING TENURED TEACHERS: Under Chicago's recent school re-

forms, this policy has changed somewhat and teachers may more easily be removed from classrooms.

63 NUMBER OF TEACHERS OVER 60 YEARS OF AGE: *Tribune* series.

SUBSTITUTES REPRESENT MORE THAN ONE QUARTER OF CHICAGO FACULTY: Of 28,675 teachers in the system in 1988, 7,294 were substitutes, of whom 4,350 taught on a permanent basis. (*Tribune* series.)

5,700 CHILDREN IN 190 CLASSROOMS: *Tribune* series.

NEARLY TWICE THE STUDENT POPULATION OF NEW TRIER HIGH SCHOOL: New Trier enrollment was 2,913 students in the 1988–1989 school year. ("Information for College Admissions Counselors 1988–1989," New Trier High School, Winnetka, 1989).

DU SABLE HIGH SCHOOL: *Tribune* series.

64 SOUTH SHORE HIGH SCHOOL: *Chicago Reporter,* September 1984. Three years later, despite considerable adverse publicity, there had been only slight improvement. Of 770 entering freshmen, only 204 graduated with their class. (*Chicago Reporter,* January 1987.)

64, 65 CALUMET AND BOWEN HIGH SCHOOL: *Tribune* series.

LATHROP ELEMENTARY SCHOOL: *The American Millstone.* A library has been constructed since this series was published.

SCHOOL BOARD PRESIDENT AND CHICAGO MAYORS DID NOT SEND THEIR CHILDREN TO PUBLIC SCHOOL, AND COMMENTS OF FORMER GOVERNOR JAMES THOMPSON: *Tribune* series.

65, 66 SCARCITY OF SUBSTITUTES GROWS MORE ACUTE IN MAY: *Tribune* series.

DROPOUT RATE OF NEARLY 50 PERCENT: In the past five years, the *Chicago Tribune* has on various occasions placed the high school dropout rate at 55 percent *(The American Millstone),* 48 percent and "nearly 50 percent" (both in *Tribune* series), and at 43 percent (column by Clarence Page, November 15, 1987). The *Chicago Sun-Times* (November 1, 1988) and *USA Today* (September 29, 1989) placed the number at 50 percent.

PER-PUPIL SPENDING IN CHICAGO AND NEW TRIER DISTRICTS: In 1989, according to G. Alfred Hess of the Chicago Panel on School Policy and Finance, Chicago spent $5,265 for each student; because more money is spent, in high school than in elementary school, the figure is adjusted here to $5,500. In the same year, according to Hess, New Trier High School spent above $8,500 and Niles High School spent above $9,000 (author's interview, April 1991). Also see "Illinois Public Schools Financial Statistics," published annually by the Illinois State Board of Education.

66ff. DISCUSSION OF SCHOOL FUNDING: See notes for pages 251 to 254. For matters specific to Illinois, I have relied upon discussions with George Alan Hickrod and Larry Frank of the Center for the Study of Educational Finance, Illinois State University, Normal, Illinois, and with G. Alfred Hess of the Chicago Panel on Public School Policy and Finance, 1990 and 1991.

67 POOR COMMUNITIES TEND TO TAX HIGH, SPEND LOW: "Chicago schools are poor because the city itself is poor. . . . Overall, suburban tax rates have to be only half as large as Chicago's to raise the same amount of money." (*Tribune* series.)

FEDERAL PROPERTY-TAX AND MORTGAGE-INTEREST DEDUCTIONS AND FEDERAL GRANTS TO LOCAL PUBLIC SCHOOLS: Office of Management and Budget, the White House, 1986; Congressional Budget Office, 1986.

68 JONATHAN WILSON, COUNCIL OF URBAN BOARDS OF EDUCATION: Conversations with author, March 1991.

ADDED BURDEN FACED BY CITIES: "The total property tax rate in Chicago," according to the *Chicago Tribune* (1988), "is just over $10.35 per $100 assessed value, one of the highest in Cook County, but only 36 percent of that goes to schools." In the suburbs, by comparison, "school taxes make up an average of about 60 percent" of the total property tax rate. "We pay a fantastic amount for police and fire protection in Chicago . . . ," says G. Alfred Hess of the Chicago panel on School Policy and Finance. "This city is in the cruel box of having to decide which services to provide to poor families." (*Tribune* series.)

69 FEDERAL AND STATE CONTRIBUTIONS: Author's interviews with Harold Howe II, former U.S. Commissioner of Education, and G. Alan Hickrod, February and March 1991.

STATES PAY ROUGHLY HALF OF SCHOOL EXPENDITURES: The extreme exceptions are New Hampshire, where the state provides almost no aid, and Hawaii, where the state pays 92 percent of school expenditures. (*Boston Globe,* February 9, 1991.)

EXTREMES OF HIGH AND LOW SPENDING IN ILLINOIS: Education Equity Coalition (Chicago Urban League, Chicago Panel on School Policy and Finance, and League of Women Voters of Illinois), "The Inequity in Illinois School Finance" (Chicago: January 1991); also *Illinois School Law Quarterly,* January 1991. According to the *New York Times* (December 19, 1990), "Overall spending per student among districts in Illinois ranges from $2,100 to nearly $10,000, and this gap is growing."

"THE APPEARANCE OF CALCULATED UNFAIRNESS": John E. Coons, William H. Clune III, and Stephen D. Sugarman, *Private Wealth and Public Education* (Cambridge: Harvard University Press, 1970). Coons is the senior author of this work.

"VICTIM-THINKING": See for example, Shelby Steele, *The Content of Our Character* (New York: St. Martin's Press, 1990).

70   "THESE KIDS ARE AWARE OF THEIR FAILURES": *Tribune* series.

70, 71   CHILDREN'S ABSENCES, REVEREND CHARLES KYLE, AND TRIBUNE'S ESTIMATE OF "ACTUAL" DROPOUT RATE: *Tribune* series. G. Alfred Hess, of the Chicago Panel on School Policy and Finance, believe that the *Chicago Tribune* estimate ("close to 60 percent") is high and would place the actual figure at 47 to 50 percent. Dropout figures for students who go from nonselective elementary schools to nonselective high schools often far exceed these estimates, however. At several nonselective high schools, dropout rates are in the area of 75 percent.

71   ANDERSEN, MCKINLEY, WOODSON, BETHUNE ELEMENTARY SCHOOLS: *Chicago Tribune,* July 31, 1987; also G. Alfred Hess, interview with author, March 1991.

71, 72   READING LEVELS CITYWIDE AND AT 18 HIGH SCHOOLS WITH HIGHEST RATES OF POVERTY: Don Moore, Executive Director, Designs for Change, interviews with author, 1990 and 1991; "The Bottom Line" (Chicago: Designs for Change, 1985).

72   COMMUNITY COLLEGE STATISTICS: Jack Wuest of the Alternative Schools Network, interview with author, March 1990.

72 to 74   CHICAGO'S MAGNET AND SELECTIVE SCHOOLS: *Tribune* series.

74ff.   DISPUTE SURROUNDING SOUTH LOOP ELEMENTARY SCHOOL: *New York Times,* April 2, 1989; *Chicago Tribune,* May 3, 1989. Since the events described here, I am told that South Loop Elementary School has canceled the restrictions placed on children from the projects. As a result, most of the families from the new development have removed their children.

76, 77   "CHOICE" PLAN IN EAST HARLEM: Deborah Meier, "Choice Can Save Public Education," *The Nation,* March 4, 1991.

77 to 79   GOUDY ELEMENTARY SCHOOL: The portrait of the school in 1988 and the dialogue with Keisha are based upon an article by *Chicago Tribune* reporter Bonita Brodt, *Tribune* series. For significant changes at Goudy two years later, see my visit to the school on pages 83 to 84.

79ff.   NEW TRIER HIGH SCHOOL: Gene I. Maeroff, "Let's Hear It for New Trier," *Town and Country,* June 1986; *Chicago Tribune,* July 7, 1989; "Program of Studies, 1989–1990" and other documents provided by New Trier High School; author's conversations with New Trier High School graduates, 1989 and 1990. Earlier background material on New Trier High School: *Washington Post,* October 12, 1980.

81   GOUDY ELEMENTARY SCHOOL CLASS SIZE: *Tribune* series.

WORTH OF TAXABLE PROPERTY PER PUPIL: G. Alfred Hess, author's interview, April 1991.

81, 82   SUBURBAN RESIDENTS OPPOSE REDISTRIBUTION OF SCHOOL FUNDING: "By a nine-to-one ratio," according to the *Chicago Tribune,* "suburban residents oppose any effort to get them to pay more for city schools, and only a third of the suburbanites think a lack of funds is a major city school problem." According to G. Alfred Hess of the Chicago Panel on School Policy and Finance, legislative representatives of the suburban districts "are the worst of the no-more-money-for-the-schools people." (*Tribune* series.)

83   CHICAGO SCHOOL REFORM: Author's conversations with G. Alfred Hess, John McDermott, Don Moore, Jack Wuest, William Ayers, *Chicago Tribune* reporters

Bonita Brodt and Karen Thomas, and Chicago teachers Robin Cohen and Quinn Brisben, 1989 to 1991.

83, 84   IMPROVEMENTS AT GOUDY ELEMENTARY SCHOOL: Interviews at the school, March 1990.

84ff.   DU SABLE HIGH SCHOOL: Interviews at the school, March 1990; Du Sable High School yearbook and "School Report Card," 1989; "Where's Room 185?" (a publication of the Chicago Panel on Public School Policy and Finance, December 1986); *Tribune* series; *Chicago Tribune,* May 12, 1989 and March 14, 1990.

85   TOP SALARIES, DU SABLE AND SUBURBS: According to the *Chicago Tribune* (May 12, 1989), maximum salary for teachers in the Chicago public schools was $40,579; at New Trier High School, $59,400; at Niles Township High School, $62,834; at Glenbard High School, $57,600; at Downers Grove High School, $58,887.

88   JAMES D. SQUIRES CITED: *Tribune* series.

"ABOUT $2,000": "Black in White America," ABC News, August 29, 1989.

89   SOCIOLOGIST CITED: Author's interview, March 1990.

89, 90   SCHOOLS IN MAYWOOD, EAST AURORA, NILES: Illinois State Board of Education, "Illinois Public Schools Financial Statistics, 1986–1987 School Year," (Springfield: 1988). Also see *Chicago Tribune,* June 17, 1987, and *Chicago Sun-Times,* November 1, 1988.

92   "THIS SCHOOL IS RIGHT FOR THIS COMMUNITY": *Washington Post,* October 12, 1980.

93   OFFICE EDUCATION COURSE CANCELED AT NEW TRIER HIGH SCHOOL: *Washington Post,* October 12, 1980.

94   STUDENT-COUNSELOR RATIOS, SCHOOL LIBRARY STATISTICS, ETC.: *Chicago Sun-Times,* April 14, 1985.

94, 95   JOHN COONS CITED: See notes for page 69.

95, 96   PROPOSAL TO CUT CLASS SIZE: The proposal of Chicago's 54-member Education Summit is discussed in a *Chicago Tribune* editorial, April 1, 1988.

95   RESPONSE OF ASSISTANT EDUCATION SECRETARY CHESTER FINN: *Chicago Tribune* editorial, April 1, 1988.

RESPONSE OF EDUCATION SECRETARY WILLIAM BENNETT: *Chicago Tribune,* March 24, 1988.

95, 96   CITATION FROM NEW YORK TIMES: March 22, 1987.

96   CHICAGO TRIBUNE EDITORIAL: April 1, 1988.

A SIMILAR PLAN VETOED BY GOVERNOR: *Chicago Tribune,* February 2, 1987.

97   "A CASTE SOCIETY": Francis Keppel, *The Necessary Revolution in American Education* (New York: Harper & Row, 1966).

98   BUSINESS OPPOSITION TO TAX INCREMENTS TO HELP CHICAGO SCHOOLS: "City and state business associations have consistently lobbied against tax increases for education. . . . Some business lobbies continue their long opposition. . . ." (*Tribune* series.) According to the *Tribune* (February 8, 1988), the presidents of both the Illinois State Chamber of Commerce and the Illinois Manufacturers Association "have announced that once again they will fight any increase in state taxes to give more money to education." According to Hess, of the Chicago Panel on School Policy and Finance, "One has to keep in mind that the corporations are not monolithic. Individual corporate leaders have begun to speak more openly of the financial needs of the Chicago schools. But an executive may speak in favor of more taxes while other representatives of the same firm may continue to oppose such taxes." On the public level, he says, "business leaders are not yet in favor of more money for Chicago's schools." (Conversation with author, March 1991.)

"DECK CHAIRS ON THE TITANIC": *Tribune* series.

99ff.   MOTHER IN CHICAGO: Conversations with author, 1990.

3. INEQUALITIES OF PUBLIC EDUCATION
IN NEW YORK

101   LORD ACTON CITED: George Alan Hickrod, "Reply to the 'Forbs' Article," *Journal of School Finance,* vol. 12 (1987).

101, 102   PER-PUPIL SPENDING, NEW YORK CITY AND SUBURBS: Office for Policy Analysis and Program Accountability, New York State Board of Education, "Statistical Profiles of School Districts," (Albany: January 1, 1989). Numbers cited are for 1986–1987 school year.

102   QUESTION ASKED BY NEW YORK CITY BOARD OF EDUCATION AND RESPONSE OF COMMUNITY SERVICE SOCIETY: Community Service Society of New York, "Promoting Poverty: The Shift of Resources Away from Low-Income New York City School Districts," (New York: 1987).

102, 103   CONTRAST BETWEEN SCHOOLS IN DISTRICT 10, STATE-
           MENTS OF PRINCIPALS AND SUPERINTENDENT: *New
           York Times,* January 2, 1987. District 10 Superintendent
           Fred Goldberg resigned under pressure in 1991. A
           highly respected veteran of the New York City public
           schools, he struck me, in the course of an April 1990
           interview, as an enlightened educator caught up in a
           compromising situation that was not of his own mak-
           ing. Educators in New York believe that he was made
           to pay an unfair price for the profound racism rooted in
           the city's public schools.

103 to 119 AUTHOR'S VISITS IN DISTRICT 10: February and May
           1990.

119 to 121 INEQUITIES IN NEW YORK CITY SCHOOLS: *New York
           Times,* July 2, 1987; *New York Post,* July 2, 1987; *The
           (New York) City Sun,* July 15–21, 1987; "Promoting
           Poverty" (Community Service Society of New York),
           cited above.

121, 122   OVERVIEW OF MORRIS HIGH SCHOOL: *New York Times,*
           December 10, 1988.

122 to 130 INTERVIEWS AT MORRIS HIGH SCHOOL: February 1990.

124 to 126 RACIAL BREAKDOWN AT MORRIS HIGH SCHOOL: New
           York City Board of Education, Division of High
           Schools, "School Profiles" (New York: 1988).

128   DROPOUT AND SAT STATISTICS, MORRIS HIGH: Inter-
           views with school personnel; New York City Board of
           Education, Office of Research, Evaluation, and Assess-
           ment, "The Annual Dropout Report 1987–88" (New
           York: April 1989).

130   INEQUITIES BETWEEN SELECTIVE AND NONSELECTIVE
           SCHOOLS IN NEW YORK CITY: Editorial by Diane
           Camper, *New York Times,* July 9, 1986.

130 to 132 JACKSON HIGH SCHOOL, WORDS OF PRINCIPAL AND
           NEIGHBORHOOD RESIDENT: Advocates for Children of
           New York, "The Report of the New York Hearing on
           Our Children at Risk" (New York, 1984).

132   NATHAN GLAZER CITED: *Harvard Educational Review,*
           vol. 57, No. 2 (1987).

136   "A STUDENT MAY BE IN THE WRONG CLASS": "The Re-
           port of the New York Hearing on Our Children at
           Risk," cited above.

           PUPIL-COUNSELOR RATIO IN NEW YORK CITY HIGH
           SCHOOLS: According to *Time* magazine (September 17,

1990), "An impossible caseload of 1,000 high school students for every guidance counselor makes a mockery of the profession." New York financier Felix Rohatyn (*New York Times,* September 2, 1989) says, "There is now one counselor for every 700 children in the system."

"AS MANY AS THREE OUT OF FOUR BLACKS," ETC.: "School Strategies for Promoting the Education Success of At-Risk Children," report of Commissioner's Task Force on the Education of Youth At-Risk, New York State Board of Education (Albany: October 13, 1988).

DROPOUT RATES IN NEW YORK CITY: According to the New York City Board of Education ("Annual Dropout Report," April 1989), the graduation rate for students in the class of 1987 five years after entering ninth grade was 54 percent, indicating that 46 percent had failed to graduate. This is the figure that appeared in Sara Rimer's story in the *New York Times,* March 12, 1989. By using another method of calculation, however, the Board of Education said the dropout rate was "hovering around 30 percent." According to the *New York Times* (May 2, 1989), "New figures confirm that one in every four New York City public school students drops out of school." There is no evidence that anyone in the press or school department ever tries to reconcile these numbers.

JUNIOR HIGH SCHOOL DROPOUTS NOT INCLUDED IN OFFICIAL DROPOUT FIGURES: Peter Flanders, Office of Research Evaluation and Assessment, New York City Board of Education, author's interview, March 1991. According to a RAND Corporation study ("High Schools with Character," 1990) "nearly 10 percent" of New York City students "disappear" before they enter high school—most of them after their eighth grade year.

136, 137   NUMBER-JUGGLING BY SCHOOL BOARDS: *New York Times,* April 11, 1989; *New Jersey Reporter,* May 1988.

137   "I HATED THE SCHOOL": National Coalition of Advocates for Children, "Barriers to Excellence," (Boston: 1985).

OFFICIAL OF RHEEDLEN FOUNDATION CITED: "Barriers to Excellence," cited above.

"CHILDREN WHO JUST DISAPPEAR FROM THE FACE OF THE EARTH": *New York Times,* February 3, 1987.

138, 139   PHYSICAL CONDITIONS OF SCHOOLS: *New York Times,* March 12 and June 19, 1990.

139   DISCUSSION OF P.S. 94: *New York Times,* March 12 and 17, May 23, and June 8, 1990.

140   INFANT MORTALITY IN CENTRAL HARLEM AND EAST HARLEM: *New York Times,* September 30 and October 1, 1990.

SENATOR BILL BRADLEY CITED: *Boston Globe,* September 29, 1990.

UNITED HOSPITAL FUND CITED: *New York Observer,* March 6, 1989.

PROFESSOR ELI GINZBERG CITED: *New York Times,* October 11, 1986. See also "Sick at Their Heart, Cities Become Medical Disaster Area for the Poor," *New York Times,* December 24, 1990.

LOWER QUALITY OF EDUCATION "ACCEPTED AS A FACT": *New York Times,* July 2, 1987.

141   SHORTAGES OF EQUIPMENT AND SUPPLIES IN NEW YORK CITY HOSPITALS: *New York Times,* October 7 and 10, 1986 and March 10, 1989.

DAVID DINKINS CITED: *New York Times,* December 14, 1987.

JOURNAL OF THE AMERICAN MEDICAL ASSOCIATION CITED: Article by Dr. Mark Epstein and Dr. Mark Wenneker appeared in the issue of January 13, 1989.

141   JOURNAL OF THE AMERICAN MEDICAL ASSOCIATION CITED: Issue of January 13, 1989.

141, 142   "A DIFFERENT SUBJECTIVE RESPONSE" TO BLACK PATIENTS: The physician cited is Dr. Richard Cooper, a cardiologist at Chicago's Cook County Hospital. (*Boston Globe,* January 13, 1989.)

142   PHYSICIAN IN SOUTH BRONX CITED: Unnamed by request.

143, 144   HANDCUFFS PURCHASED FOR NEW YORK CITY SCHOOLS: *New York Observer,* April 24, 1989.

144   90 PERCENT OF NEW YORK CITY PRISON INMATES ARE HIGH SCHOOL DROPOUTS: Advertisement placed by the United Federation of Teachers in the *New York Times,* May 22, 1990. See also "Where We Stand," column by Albert Shanker, American Federation of Teachers, *New York Times,* October 21, 1990.

DISPROPORTIONATE TRACKING OF BLACK AND HISPANIC CHILDREN IN SPECIAL CLASSES: "Barriers to Excellence," cited above.

145 to 147   PER-PUPIL SPENDING IN LONG ISLAND AND WESTCHESTER COUNTY: New York State Department of Education, "Statistical Profiles of School Districts," cited above. Also see *Newsday,* May 18, 1986. According to Sandra Feldman, President of the United Federation of Teachers in New York City, "the average per-pupil expenditure is nearly $2,500 higher" in the suburbs "right outside the city." (*The School Administrator,* March 1991.) According to the *New York Times* (May 4, 1991), New York City now spends $7,000 for each pupil. The wealthiest suburbs spend approximately $15,000.

147   NEW YORK STATE COMMISSIONER OF EDUCATION CITED: *Newsday,* February 1, 1989.

148   NEW TRIER HIGH SCHOOL OFFICIAL CITED: See notes for page 92.

150   $200,000 MORE EACH YEAR: In the school year ending in June of 1987, per-pupil funding was $5,585 in New York City, about $11,300 in Jericho and Manhasset. For 36 children, the difference was over $200,000.

151 to 158   DATA ON RYE HIGH SCHOOL: Author's visit, May 1990; Rye High School Guidance Department, "The Rye High School Profile," 1990.

152   PER-PUPIL FUNDING AT RYE HIGH SCHOOL: According to "The Rye High School Profile," cited above, the figure for 1989–1990 was $12,076.

159, 160   MISSISSIPPI DATA: *Time,* November 14, 1988; *Newsweek,* December 13, 1982; *Governing Magazine,* January 1990.

4. CHILDREN OF THE CITY INVINCIBLE

161 to 165   WALL STREET JOURNAL CITATIONS: Editorial, June 27, 1989; Education Supplement, March 31, 1989; also February 9, 1990.

161   SCHOOLS THAT SPEND LESS THAN THE AVERAGE OF TEN YEARS AGO: The average expenditure for public schools in the United States in 1980–1981 was $2,502. (National Center for Education Statistics, "Digest of Education Statistics," 1990.)

165, 166   CAMDEN STATISTICS: *Abbott* v. *Burke,* decision of Administrative Law Judge Stephen L. Lefelt, OAL DKT.

NO. EDU 5581–88, August 24, 1985 (identified here-
after as "Lefelt"); *Abbott* v. *Burke,* Plaintiffs Brief before
Supreme Court of New Jersey, June 16, 1989; *New
York Times,* June 12, 1988, January 2 and September 7,
1989, and February 7, 1990; U.S. Bureau of the Census,
"Ranking of Places by 1987 Per Capita Income," series
P-26, no. 88, Washington, D.C., 1990.

165 to 189 INTERVIEWS AT PYNE POINT JUNIOR HIGH SCHOOL,
CAMDEN HIGH SCHOOL, WOODROW WILSON HIGH
SCHOOL: March 1990.

167, 168 PYNE POINT JUNIOR HIGH SCHOOL, 98 PERCENT BLACK
AND LATINO: Lefelt.

171 STUDENTS LEAVE CAMDEN HIGH SCHOOL FOR LUNCH:
Lefelt.

174 "WORK-A-TEXT STUDY PROGRAM FOR WRITING":
Instructivision, Inc., Livingston, New Jersey, 1987.

176 to 178 INTERVIEW WITH CAMDEN HIGH SCHOOL TEACHERS:
March 1990.

177, 178 CAMPBELL'S AND RCA SHUTTING DOWN OR CUTTING
BACK ON OPERATIONS: Interview with Reverend Michael Doyle of Sacred Heart Church, Camden, March
1990; *New York Times,* February 7, 1990; (South New
Jersey) *Courier-Post,* March 7, 1990.

PLANS FOR RIVERFRONT CURTAILED: According to
Reverend Michael Doyle, an aquarium was finally
completed. The riverfront hotel and other plans are in
abeyance.

178 to 180 REVEREND MICHAEL DOYLE AND LOU ESOLA CITED:
Interviews in November 1990.

179 HOUSES SOLD FOR AS LITTLE AS $1,000: *New York
Times,* September 7, 1989.

180 DROPOUT RATE AT WOODROW WILSON HIGH SCHOOL:
Lefelt.

180, 181 PER-PUPIL SPENDING, CAMDEN VS. WEALTHY SUBURBS:
According to the *New York Times* (May 14, 1990),
Princeton was spending $8,344 per pupil, and Camden
was spending $4,184, in the 1988–1989 school year.

189 to 191 EAST ORANGE, MONTCLAIR, MILLBURN: Lefelt; *New
York Times,* March 5, 1990; WWOR TV, February 23,
1989.

190, 191 JERSEY CITY DATA: Lefelt; U.S. Bureau of the Census,
"Rankings of Places by 1987 Per Capita Income," cited
above.

191, 192   DROPOUT AND FAILURE RATES, JERSEY CITY AND PRINCETON: Lefelt; also superintendent's office, Princeton Public Schools, author's interview, March 1991.

192   IRVINGTON DATA: Lefelt; also "Schools for Tomorrow," a videotape produced by the Irvington Public Schools and narrated by Superintendent Anthony Scardaville, 1985. See also *Abbott* v. *Burke,* Plaintiffs' Brief before Supreme Court of New Jersey, June 16, 1989.

193   "IT HARDLY SEEMS FAIR": Kathy Lally (a parent and journalist), *Baltimore Sun,* February 19, 1989.

193 to 197   PATERSON DATA AND DISCUSSION OF FORMER PRINCIPAL JOE CLARK: Lefelt; author's interviews at East Side High School and with school official, March 1990; *Boston Globe,* January 13, 1991.

197, 198   CHERRY HILL AND PRINCETON: *New Jersey Monthly,* September 1988.

199, 200   KINDERGARTENS COMPARED IN PATERSON AND WAYNE, AND QUESTION OF NEW JERSEY JUDGE: Lefelt.

200   ATTEMPTS OF URBAN DISTRICTS TO RENT SPACE IN SUBURBS: Lefelt.

201 to 205   DECISION OF NEW JERSEY JUDGE: Lefelt.

205, 206   RULING OF SUPREME COURT OF NEW JERSEY: *Abbott* v. *Burke,* 119 N.J. 287 (1990).

206   REACTIONS OF LETTER-WRITERS AND WEST ORANGE SUPERINTENDENT: *Bergen Record,* June 5 and 6 and July 27, 1990; *New York Times,* July 16, 1990.

206, 207   WALL STREET JOURNAL APPLAUDS TAX REVOLT: July 3, 1990.

   DEFENDANTS SAY COMPARISONS TO PRINCETON ARE UNFAIR: Lefelt.

207, 208   PHILADELPHIA INQUIRER CITED: August 28, 1988.

210   ATTORNEY MARILYN MORHEUSER CITED: Author's interview, March 1990.

5. THE EQUALITY OF INNOCENCE

212, 213   MARYLAND SCHOOL EQUITY DISCUSSION: "A Growing Inequality," The Abell Foundation, Inc., Baltimore, January 1989; interview with Robert Embry, president of The Abell Foundation, April 1991.

213, 214   JOHN COONS CITED: *Private Wealth and Public Education* (Cambridge: Harvard University Press, 1970).

217   INTENTIONAL ISOLATION OF BLACK COMMUNITIES IN
      CHICAGO: "The Wall," series in the *Chicago Tribune*,
      November 30 through December 12, 1986.

218   "TWO WORLDS OF WASHINGTON": *Wall Street Journal*,
      April 14, 1989.

218 to 225 INTERVIEWS WITH CHILDREN IN ANACOSTIA SCHOOL
      AND WITH DELABIAN RICE-THURSTON: April 1989.
      (Mrs. Rice-Thurston is executive director of Parents
      United for the District of Columbia Public Schools.)
      Also see "Business and Civic Leader Study of the Fis-
      cal Needs of the District of Columbia Public Schools,"
      published by Parents United (December 1985: Wash-
      ington, D.C.).

225, 226 "LIKE SOLDIERS WHO HAVE SEEN TOO MUCH COMBAT":
      New York Times, May 15, 1989.

225   PROSTITUTES ROUNDED UP: *Boston Globe*, July 27, 1989
      and *New York Times*, July 27, 1989.

226 to 230 INTERVIEW WITH CHILDREN IN HOUSING PROJECT:
      August 1989.

231   PUBLIC REACTIONS TO BLACK INFANT DEATH RATE: *Bos-
      ton Globe* editorial, September 21, 1990.

231, 232 PSYCHIATRIST IN BOSTON: Unnamed by request.

233   SOUTH AFRICAN WOMAN CITED: Social scientist Mam-
      phela Aletta Ramphele, in *Boston Globe*, March 6, 1989.

237   BOSTON GLOBE COLUMNIST CITED: Mike Barnicle, *Bos-
      ton Globe*, August 24, 1989.

238   DISCUSSION OF RICHARD GREEN: Joe Klein, "Race,"
      New York Magazine, May 29, 1989.

      HIGH CASUALTY RATE AMONG URBAN SUPERINTEN-
      DENTS: *Boston Globe*, December 16, 1990 and March
      14, 1991; *Boston Herald*, February 19, 1990; author's
      interviews with Gary Marx (American Association
      of School Administrators), Jonathan Wilson (Council
      of Urban Boards of Education), and Mike Casserly
      (Council of Great City Schools), March 1991.

239, 240 DETROIT SCHOOL DATA: *Detroit Free Press*, March 6,
      1988; *New York Times*, December 18, 1988; author's
      interview with *Detroit Free Press* reporter Cassandra
      Spratling, April 1991.

      SCHOOL FUNDING IN DETROIT AND SUBURBS AND REAC-
      TION TO SCHOOL EQUALIZING PLANS: *Detroit Free Press*,
      March 6, 1988.

240, 242   CHRISTOPHER JENCKS AND CHARLES BENSON CITED:
           Arthur Wise, *Rich Schools, Poor Schools* (Chicago: University of Chicago Press, 1967).

242 to 244 DISCUSSION OF MILLIKEN CASE: Richard Kluger, *Simple Justice* (New York: Vintage Books, 1977).

      244   MINIMUM OF $2,800 IN 1988: *Detroit Free Press,* March 6, 1988.

      245   MICHIGAN DISTRICTS THREATENED WITH SHUTDOWN: *Detroit Free Press,* March 6, 1988.

            PROBLEMS FACING SCHOOL DISTRICTS IN MASSACHUSETTS: *Boston Globe,* April 23, 1989 and September 12 and 30, 1990.

246, 247   MIDYEAR CUTS IN DETROIT, MICHIGAN FUNDING STATISTICS, COMMENTS OF SUPERINTENDENTS: *Detroit Free Press,* March 6, 1988.

      247   PRESIDENT GEORGE BUSH CITED: Press release, The White House, April 13, 1989.

6. THE DREAM DEFERRED, AGAIN,
IN SAN ANTONIO

249, 250   JOHN COONS CITED: *Private Wealth and Public Education* (Cambridge: Harvard University Press, 1970).

251 to 254 HISTORY AND WORKINGS OF SCHOOL FINANCE SYSTEM: Arthur E. Wise, *Rich Schools, Poor Schools* (Chicago: University of Chicago Press, 1967); Arthur E. Wise and Tamar Gendler in *The College Board Review,* Spring 1989; G. Alan Hickrod, Illinois State University, Normal, Illinois (conversations with author, 1991); John Coons, cited above; James Gordon Ward, "An Inquiry Into the Normative Foundations of American Public School Finance," *Journal of Education Finance,* Spring 1987.

255, 257   A VIRTUALLY NATIONAL SCHOOL SYSTEM: "A National Curriculum," Quality Education for Minorities Network, Background, Issues, and Action Paper Note, vol. 1, no. 3 (March 7, 1991); *Boston Globe,* April 17, 1989.

      258   JUDGE STEPHEN LEFELT CITED: See notes for page 137.

258, 259   CLASS ACTION SUIT IN TEXAS: Thomas J. Flygare, "School Finance a Decade After *Rodriguez,*" *Phi Delta Kappan,* March 1983.

259 to 265 U.S. SUPREME COURT DECISION: *San Antonio Independent School District* v. *Rodriguez,* March 21, 1973, in "Cases Adjudged in the Supreme Court at October Term,

1972," United States Reports, vol. 411 (Washington, D.C.: U.S. Government Printing Office, 1974). The opinion of Justice Lewis Powell begins on page 5. The opinion of Justice Thurgood Marshall begins on page 86. Also see Richard Kluger, *Simple Justice* (New York: Vintage Books, 1977).

266, 267 SCHOOL INEQUITIES IN CALIFORNIA AND FINDINGS OF CALIFORNIA COURTS: James W. Guthrie, "United States School Finance Policy, 1955–1980," *Educational Evaluation and Policy Analysis* vol. 5, no. 2 (Summer 1983).

SIGNIFICANCE OF PROPOSITION 13: James W. Guthrie, cited above; Donald Wicket, "School Finance Issues Related to the Implementation of *Serrano* and Proposition 13," *Journal of Education Finance,* Spring 1985; William L. Taylor and Dianne M. Piché, "A Report on Shortchanging Children: The Impact of Fiscal Inequity on the Education of Students at Risk," report to the Committee on Education and Labor, U.S. House of Representatives, December 1990.

267 SOUTHERN VOTERS' RESPONSE TO DESEGREGATION: Francis Keppel, *The Necessary Revolution in American Education* (New York: Harper & Row, 1966).

ALL BUT 5 PERCENT OF CALIFORNIA DISTRICTS ARE WITHIN $300 OF EACH OTHER: Author's interview with Raymond M. Reinhard, Legislative Budget Committee, Office of Legislative Analyst, Sacramento, California, March 1991.

CALIFORNIA'S SPENDING FOR EDUCATION, ETC., COMPARED TO OTHER STATES: Taylor and Piché, cited above.

268 BEVERLY HILLS, BALDWIN PARK: U.S. Bureau of the Census, "Ranking of Places by 1987 Per Capita Income," series P-28, no. 88, Washington, D.C., 1990; *Wall Street Journal,* October 13, 1989; Charles S. Benson and Kevin O'Halloran, "The Economic History of School Finance in the United States" *Journal of Education Finance,* Spring 1987; Toni Cook, former assistant to California assemblyman Elihu Harris, author's interview, March 1991.

267, 268 RANGE OF FUNDING IN CALIFORNIA: In Kern County, California the McKittrick Elementary District spent $7,518 per pupil in 1990, while Bakersfield, California ("a problem-ridden, inner-city district," according to the *Bakersfield Californian*) spent $2,756. (*Bakersfield Californian,* July 3, 1990.)

270   RANGE OF FUNDING IN TEXAS: *West's Education Law Reporter,* December 7, 1989.

STATE GUARANTEES AN AVERAGE MINIMUM OF $1,477: *San Antonio Express-News,* October 8, 1989.

270ff.   O. Z. WHITE CITED: Author's interviews with Professor White, of Trinity University, 1989 and 1990.

VISIT TO COOPER MIDDLE SCHOOL: April 1989.

271, 272   DATA ON COOPER MIDDLE SCHOOL, SAN ANTONIO INDEPENDENT SCHOOL DISTRICT, EDGEWOOD DISTRICT AND ALAMO HEIGHTS: Texas Education Agency, "1987–1988 PEIMS Fall Collection of Financial Budgeted Data" (Austin: 1988); additional data provided by principal of Cooper Middle School, school departments of Alamo Heights and San Antonio Independent School Districts, Terry Hitchcock of the Texas Education Agency, O. Z. White, and social workers in Cassiano neighborhood, author's interviews, 1989 and 1991.

272, 273   RULING OF TEXAS SUPREME COURT: *"Edgewood v. Kirby,"* *West's Education Law Reporter,* December 7, 1989; *New York Times,* October 3, 1989.

273   REACTION OF DEMETRIO RODRIGUEZ AND OTHERS IN SAN ANTONIO: *San Antonio Express-News,* October 3, 8 and 9, 1989.

274, 275   REACTION OF TEXAS POLITICIANS AND COMMENTS OF U.S. EDUCATION SECRETARY: *New York Times,* October 3, 1989 and March 11, 1990; *San Antonio Express-News,* October 3, 1989.

277   NEW FORMULA, FURTHER DELAY: *San Antonio Express-News,* October 2, 1990, February 8 and 9 and March 1, 1991; *Dallas Morning News,* April 12, 1991.

277, 278   LOWER PRICE HILL, INDUSTRIAL POLLUTION, SCHOOL COMPLETION DATA: Bob Moore, interview, May 1989; *Cincinnati Enquirer,* April 1, 1989; "Report on Health, Education and Pollution in Lower Price Hill," Executive Summary, Lower Price Hill Task Force (Cincinnati Federation of Teachers, Ohio Citizens Action, Appalachian Council), June 1990; author's visit, May 1989.

279, 280   READING LEVELS, OTHER DATA ON OYLER ELEMENTARY SCHOOL: Materials provided by school system.

ACKNOWLEDGMENTS

In researching this book, I have relied upon the help of several writers and attorneys who have had a long involvement with school equity litigation. Most helpful have been Marilyn Morheuser, Albert Kauffman, Stephen Spitz, Roderick Boggs and Arthur Wise.

I am also indebted to Bonita Brodt and Karen Thomas of the *Chicago Tribune,* Safir Ahmed and Patrick Gauen of the *St. Louis Post-Dispatch,* Sara Rimer of the *New York Times,* and Cassandra Spratling of the *Detroit Free Press.* In Illinois I was given help by Don Moore, John McDermott, Jack and Maria Wuest, Quinn Brisben, Robin Cohen, William Ayers and Larry Frank, and especially by Alfred Hess and George Alan Hickrod, who also read this book in progress and was generous with his time. In Washington I was helped by Delabian Rice-Thurston and Ella McCall. In Camden Reverend Michael Doyle was of great assistance, and Bob Moore made possible my interviews in Cincinnati. In Texas I relied upon the help of O. Z. White.

Among those who read and criticized early versions of this book are Harold Howe II, Mary Frances Berry, Jonathan Wilson, Meyer Weinberg, Benjamin DeMott, Charles Schultz, Alvin Poussaint, Carol Chomsky, Peter Edelman and Colin Greer. I am, as always, indebted to Tisha Graham, who has advised me on everything that I have written for ten years. Special thanks are also due to James Wade and Bruce Harris. The book was typed in many successive versions by Marilyn Weller, who also offered good advice throughout and has my gratitude for her amazing patience.

My deepest debt is to Cassie Schwerner, who began this book with me in 1988, did all of the research, served as my initial editor, provided constant criticism and encouragement, and helped to push the equity and segregation issues to a more complete and open exposition than I had originally intended. She has been the best friend and the wisest counselor a writer could have hoped for.

INDEX

New from Jonathan Kozol

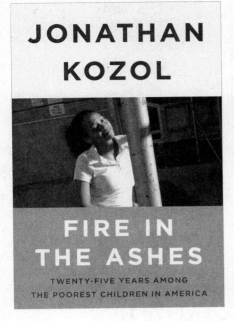

FIRE IN THE ASHES
Twenty-Five Years
Among the Poorest
Children in America

In this powerful and culminating work about a group of inner-city children he has known for many years, Jonathan Kozol returns to the scene of his prize-winning books *Rachel and Her Children* and *Amazing Grace,* and to the children he has vividly portrayed, to share with us their fascinating journeys and unexpected victories as they grow into adulthood.

B\D\W\Y

Available wherever books are sold.

Also by Jonathan Kozol

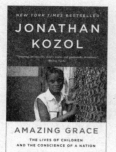

AMAZING GRACE
The Lives of Children
and the Conscience
of a Nation

**ORDINARY
RESURRECTIONS**
Children in the
Years of Hope

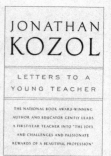

**LETTERS TO A
YOUNG TEACHER**

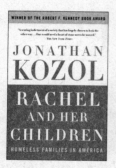

**RACHEL AND HER
CHILDREN**
Homeless Families in
America

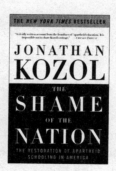

**THE SHAME OF THE
NATION**
The Restoration of
Apartheid Schooling
in America

B\D\W\Y *Available wherever books are sold.*